Meditation
the only way

THE GOLDEN FUTURE
(VOLUME 1)

FULL CIRCLE

FULL CIRCLE books
by Osho

- The True Name
- The Secret
- Truth Simply Is
- In Search of Celebration
- From Sex to Superconsciousness
- Never Born, Never Died
- Walking in Zen Sitting in Zen
- So Lost So at Home
- Walk without Feet, Fly without Wings, Think without Mind
- Ah, This!
- Try It My Way
- Won't You Join the Dance?
- Priests and Politicians — The Mafia of the Soul
- My Diamond Days with Osho
- Tantra
- The Goose Is Out
- Sex, Money and Power
- The Rebel
- A New Vision of Women's Liberation
- I Teach Religiousness Not Religion
- Words From a Man of No Words

OSHO

Meditation
the only way

THE GOLDEN FUTURE
(VOLUME 1)

FULL
CIRCLE

MEDITATION : THE ONLY WAY (The Golden Future (Vol-I))
© 1980, 2009 OSHO International Foundation
First Paperback Edition, March 2009
ISBN 978-81-7621-183-3

 Published by **FULL CIRCLE** PUBLISHING
J-40, Jorbagh Lane, New Delhi-110003
Tel: 24620063, 24621011 • Fax: 24645795
or Post Box No. 3005, Lodhi Road Post Office, New Delhi-110003
E-mail: fullcircle@vsnl.com • *website:* www.atfullcircle.com

For more information: www.osho.com
The material in this book is a transcript of a series of original OSHO Talks, *The Golden Future,* given to a live audience. All of Osho's talks have been published in full as books, and are also available as original audio recordings. Audio recordings and the complete text archive can be found via the online OSHO Library at www.osho.com

Typesetting: SCANSET
J-40, Jorbagh Lane, New Delhi-110003

Printed at Rakesh Press, New Delhi-110028

PRINTED IN INDIA
09/09/01/03/21/SCANSET/RP/RP/RP

$\mathscr{C}$ontents

PREFACE

It is true that science and technology have taken a wrong turn. Descartes was wrong when he said that man and nature are enemies; Bertrand Russell was wrong when he said that we have to conquer nature. These people gave a wrong direction to science. Nature and man have to be friends. There is no question of conquering. We are part of nature, and the part cannot conquer the whole. The part can only dissolve into the whole, rejoice in being one with the whole.

Science has to be given a new turn so that it becomes a bridge between man and nature. And the same science that has created atom bombs and nuclear weapons can also create a far greater consciousness for man, far healthier human beings, more beautiful trees, bigger flowers. This planet, although it is very small, contains the potentiality of being the richest planet in this vast universe where millions and millions of stars are surrounded by more and more planets.

Right now the count is three million stars, but they don't say that is the end. That is as far as our scientific instruments can see. There is beyond, unlimited, with no boundaries. But in this whole expanse, only this small earth has evolved to the point of consciousness, of love, of beauty, of music, of poetry, of sensitivity, of meditativeness.

It should be a determination in every intelligent being that we are not going to allow any vested interest to destroy this planet. This planet has to remain. And there is a golden future just ahead on the horizon – but we must cut the roots, whatever the cost. This is the only revolt I teach.

All revolutions have failed because they were cutting leaves and branches. I teach a total revolt against the past, against all vested interests.

The question is of tremendous importance: to save man is to save the greatest creation of the universe. It has taken four million years for this earth to create man. It is so precious...and the future is much more valuable, because inside you the possibility of a Gautam Buddha, the possibility of a Zarathustra, the possibility of a Lao Tzu is there.

You can also blossom in the same silence, in the same peace, in the same beauty, in the same ecstasy.

Osho
Om Mani Padme Hum
Chapter #23

CHAPTER 1

The Language of the Golden Future

The body knows its own silence —
that is its own well-being,
its own overflowing health, its own joy.
The mind also knows its silence,
when all thoughts disappear
and the sky is without any clouds,
just a pure space.
But the silence I am talking about
is far deeper.

Osho,

A while ago you said something about silence which startled me. In my sleepiness, I'd simply thought of it as just an absence – an absence of noises. But you were saying it had positive qualities, a positive sound. And in my meditations, I've noticed the distinction between a silence in my body and a silence in my mind. I can have the first, without the second. Beloved master, please talk to me about silence.

Silence usually is understood to be something negative, something empty, an absence of sound, of noises. This misunderstanding is prevalent because very few people have ever experienced silence. All that they have experienced in the name of silence is noiselessness. But silence is a totally different phenomenon. It is utterly positive. It is existential, it is not empty. It is overflowing with a music that you have never heard before, with a fragrance that is unfamiliar to you, with a light that can only be seen by the inner eyes. It is not something fictitious; it is a reality, and a reality which is already present in everyone – just we never look in. All our senses are extrovert. Our eyes open outside, our ears open outside, our hands move outside, our legs...all our senses are meant to explore the outside world.

But there is a sixth sense also, which is asleep because we have never used it. And no society, no culture, no educational system helps people to make the sixth sense active. That sixth sense, in the East, is called "the third eye." It looks inwards. And just as there is a way of looking in, so there is a way of hearing in, so there is a way of smelling in. Just as there are five senses moving outward, there are five counter-senses moving inward. In all, man has ten senses, but the first sense that starts the inner journey is the third eye, and then other senses start opening up.

Your inner world has its own taste, has its own fragrance, has its own light. And it is utterly silent, immensely silent, eternally silent. There has never been any noise, and there will never be any noise. No word can reach there, but *you* can reach. The mind cannot reach there, but you can reach because you are not the mind. The function of the mind is again to be a bridge between you and the objective world, and the function of the heart is to be a bridge between you and yourself.

The silence that I have been talking about is the silence of the heart. It is a song in itself, without words and without sounds. It is only out of this silence that the flowers of love grow. It is this silence that becomes the garden of Eden. Meditation, and only meditation, is the key to open the doors of your own being.

You are asking, "A while ago you said something about silence which startled me in my sleepiness. I had simply thought of it as just an absence – an absence of noises. But you were saying it had positive qualities, a positive sound. And in my meditations, I have noticed a distinction between a silence in my body and a silence in my mind."

Your experiences are true. The body knows its own silence – that is its own well-being, its own overflowing health, its own joy. The mind also knows its silence, when all thoughts disappear and the sky is without any clouds, just a pure space. But the silence I am talking about is far deeper.

I am talking about the silence of your being.

These silences that you are talking about can be disturbed. Sickness can disturb the silence of your body, and death is certainly going to disturb it. A single thought can disturb the silence of your mind, the way a small pebble thrown into the silent lake is enough to create thousands of ripples, and the lake is no longer silent. The silence of the body and the mind are very fragile and very superficial, but in themselves they are good. To experience them is helpful, because it indicates that there may be even deeper silences of the heart.

And the day you experience the silence of the heart, it will be again an arrow of longing, moving you even deeper.

Your very center of being is the center of a cyclone. Whatever happens around it does not affect it; it is eternal silence. Days come and go, years come and go, ages come and pass, lives come and go, but the eternal silence of your being remains exactly the same – the same soundless music, the same fragrance of godliness, the same transcendence from all that is mortal, from all that is momentary.

It is not *your* silence.

You *are* it.

It is not something in your possession; you are possessed by it, and that's the greatness of it. Even you are not there, because even your presence will be a disturbance.

The silence is so profound that there is nobody, not even you. And this silence brings truth, and love, and thousands of other blessings to you. This is the search, this is the longing of all the hearts, of all those who have a little intelligence.

But remember, don't get lost in the silence of the body, or the silence of the mind, or even the silence of the heart. Beyond these three is the fourth. We, in the East, have called it simply "the fourth," *turiya*. We have not given it any name. Instead of a name we have given it a number, because it comes after three silences – of the body, of the mind, of the heart – and beyond it, there is nothing else to be found.

So, don't misunderstand. Most of the people...for example, there are people who are practicing yoga exercises. Yoga exercises give a silence of the body, and they are stuck there. Their whole life, they practice, but they know only the most superficial silence.

Then there are people who are doing concentrations like transcendental meditation, of Maharishi Mahesh Yogi. It can give you a silence which will be only of the mind. Just by repeating a name or a mantra...the very repetition creates in its wake, a silence in the mind. But it is not meditation, and it is not transcendental.

And there are Sufis who know the third, which is the deepest of the three. But still it is not the goal, the target; your arrow is still falling short. It is very deep because Sufis know the heart more than anybody else. For centuries they have been working on the heart, just as yogis have been working on the body, and people of concentration and contemplation have been working on the mind.

The Sufis know the immense beauty of love. They radiate love, but still the home has not been reached. You have to remember the fourth. Unless you reach the fourth, continue the journey.

People misunderstand very easily. Just a little bit of experience and they think they have arrived. And mind is very clever to rationalize.

There is a Sufi story about Mulla Nasruddin. The Mulla hears a commotion in the street outside his house in the middle of the night. His wife tells him to go down, and after many arguments he puts a blanket on his shoulders and goes down to the street. There were many people in the street and a lot of noise, and in the crowd somebody steals his blanket.

The Mulla goes home naked, and his wife asks him, "What was that all about?" The Mulla says, "It seems to be about my blanket, because as they got the blanket they all disappeared. They were just waiting for the blanket. And I was telling you 'Don't force me to go there.' Now I have lost my blanket and I have come naked. It was none of our business."

He has found a rationalization, and it looks logical, that as they got his blanket they all disappeared. And the poor Mulla thinking that perhaps that was the whole problem.... "Their argument and their noise just in front of my house in the middle of the night, and my foolish wife persuaded me finally to lose my blanket!"

Mind is continuously rationalizing, and sometimes it may appear that what it is saying is right, because it gives arguments for it. But one has to beware of one's own mind, because in this world nobody can cheat you more than your own mind. Your greatest enemy is within you, just as your greatest friend is also within you.

The greatest enemy is just your first encounter, and your greatest friend is going to be your last encounter – so don't be prevented by any experience of the body or the mind or the heart. Remember always one of the famous statements of Gautam Buddha. He used to conclude his sermons every day with the same two words, "*Charaiveti, charaiveti*." Those two simple words – just one word repeated twice – means "Don't stop; go on, go on."

Never stop until the road ends, until there is nowhere else to go – *charaiveti, charaiveti*.

Osho,

Is it really worth putting any energy into improving my personality?

*H*ave you ever heard me? I have been constantly telling you that the personality has to be dropped so that your individuality can be discovered. I have been insisting that the personality is not you; it is a mask people have put over you. It is not your authentic reality, it is not your original face. And you are asking me, "Is it really worth putting any energy into improving my personality?"

Put your energy into destroying your personality. Put your energy into discovering your individuality. And make the distinction very clear: individuality is that which you have brought from your very birth. Individuality is your essential being, and personality is what the society has made of you, what they wanted to make of you.

No society up to now has been able to give freedom to their children to be themselves. It seems risky. They may prove rebellious. They may not follow the religion of their forefathers; they may not think the great politicians are really great; they may not trust in your moral values. They will find their own morality, and they will find their own lifestyle. They will not be replicas, they will not repeat the past; they will be beings of the future.

This has created fear that they may go astray. Before they go astray, every society tries to give them a certain direction how to live, a certain ideology of what is good and what is evil, a certain religion, a certain holy scripture. These are ways to create the personality, and the personality functions like an imprisonment. You are asking me, that you want to improve this personality. Are you your own enemy?

But this is not only you. Millions of people in the world know only their personality; they don't know that there is anything more than personality. They have completely forgotten themselves, and they have forgotten even the way to reach themselves. They have all become actors, hypocrites. They have become puppets in the hands of the priests, of the politicians, of the parents; they are doing things which they never want to do and they are not doing things which they are hankering to do.

Their life is split in such a diametrically opposite way that they can never be at peace. Their nature will assert itself again and again, will not leave them at peace. And their so-called personality will go on repressing it, forcing it deeper into the unconscious. This conflict divides you and your energy – and a house divided cannot stand long. This is the whole misery of human beings – why there is not much dance, much song, much joyfulness.

People are so much engaged in warfare with themselves. They don't have energy, and they don't have time to do anything else except fight with themselves. Their sensuality they have to fight, their sexuality they have to fight, their individuality they have to fight, their originality they have to fight. And they have to fight for something which they don't want to be, which is not part of their nature, which is not their destiny. So they can pretend to be false for a time – again the real asserts.

Their whole life goes on, up and down, and they cannot figure out who really they are: the repressor or the repressed? the oppressor or the oppressed? And whatever they do, they cannot destroy their nature. They can certainly poison it; they can certainly destroy its joy, they can destroy its dance, they can destroy its love. They can make their life a mess, but they cannot destroy their nature completely. And they cannot throw away their personality, because their personality carries their forefathers, their parents, their teachers, their priests, their whole past. It is their heritage; they cling to it.

My whole teaching is, don't cling to personality. It is not yours, and it is never going to be yours. Allow your nature full freedom. And respect yourself, be proud of being yourself, whatever you are. Have some dignity! Don't be destroyed by the dead.

People who have been dead for thousands of years are sitting on your head. They are your personality – and you want to improve on them? So call a few more dead! Graves have to be searched for... bring out more skeletons, surround yourself with all kinds of skeletons. You will be respected by the society. You will be honored, rewarded; you will have great prestige, you will be thought to be a saint. But living with the dead, surrounded by the dead, you will not be able to laugh – it will be so out of place – you will not be able to dance, you will not be able to sing, you will not be able to love.

Personality is a dead thing. Drop it! – in a single blow, not in fragments, not slowly, today a little bit and then tomorrow a little bit, because life is short and tomorrow is not certain.

The false is false. Discard it totally!

Every real human being has to be a rebel...rebel against whom? – against his own personality.

The Japanese-American was a long-time customer at this Greek restaurant, because he had discovered that they made specially tasty fried rice. Each evening he would come in the restaurant, and he would order "flied lice." This always caused the Greek restaurant owner to nearly roll on the floor with laughter. Sometimes he would have two or three friends stand nearby just to hear the Japanese customer order his "flied lice."

Eventually the customer's pride was so hurt that he took a special diction lesson just to be able to say "fried rice" correctly. The next time he went to the restaurant he said very plainly, "Fried rice, please."

Unable to believe his ears, the Greek restaurant owner said, "Sir, would you repeat that?"

The Japanese-American replied, "You heard what I said, you flucking Gleek!"

How long can you go on pretending? The reality is going to come up some day or other, and it is better that it comes sooner.

There is no need to improve your diction! Just drop that whole personality thing. Just be yourself. Howsoever raw and howsoever wild it appears to be in the beginning, soon it starts having its own grace, its own beauty.

And the personality...you can go on polishing it, but it is just polishing a dead thing which is going to destroy not only your time, your energy, your life, but also the people who are around you.

We are all affecting each other. When everybody is doing something, you also start doing it. Life is very contagious; everybody is improving his personality – that's why the idea has arisen in your mind.

But my people are not doing that. My people are not a herd, not a mob. They are respectful of themselves, and they are respectful of others. They are proud of their freedom and they want everybody else to be free, because their freedom has given them so much love and so much grace. They would like everybody else in the world to be free, loving and graceful.

This is possible only if you are original – not something put together, not something false, but something that grows within you, which has roots in your being, which brings flowers in its time. And to have one's own flowers is the only destiny, is the only significant way of life.

But the personality has no roots; it is plastic, it is phony. Dropping it is not difficult; it needs just a little courage. And my feeling of thousands of people is that everybody has that much courage, just people are not using it. Once you start using your courage, sources which are dormant become active, and you become capable of having more courage, of more rebelliousness.

You become a revolution in yourself.

A man who is a revolution unto himself is a joy to see, because he has fulfilled his destiny. He has transcended the ordinary mob, the sleeping crowd.

Osho,

In these days I feel a little plant growing inside of me, which is still very delicate and fragile. I feel like I have to take immense care of this little flower just starting to open, not to water it too much, nor too little, nor to expose it too much to the wind. My beloved Osho, please tell me how to take care of this little plant, since in this moment it would still be very easy for me to destroy it.

*J*t is good news that you are feeling a little plant growing inside you. Naturally it will be, in the beginning, very delicate and very fragile. And your feeling is right, that you "have to take immense care of this little flower just starting to open, not to water it too much, nor too little, nor to expose it too much to the wind."

All that is needed are three things.

When your consciousness starts growing, you need more meditation. And there is no limit to meditation, so you need not be worried that meditation can be too much and can kill the flower. Meditation is always too little, because there is always too much ahead of you, and meditation will make the fragile and delicate flower more and more strong.

You need a silent being.

Caring too much can be dangerous, it can become an anxiety.

Being worried too much that you should water less or you should water more, that you may expose it to the winds, to the sun, to the rain too much or too little...caring can become a tremendous turmoil in your being, and your very caring can destroy the flower. Instead of caring, you need a more silent, more conscious, more peaceful being, which will give a strength to something new that is growing in you.

Secondly, care is not enough; love is needed. Care is more a technical word; love is totally different. Care needs a certain education. Care is just like a nurse who knows what has to be done, what is right to be done – but there is no love in her heart, she functions technically.

Love is more like a mother, who may not know the art of nursing, but she need not know. Love is enough unto itself. Love is a mysterious phenomenon; it knows what is needed. It simply knows without any education.

So what you need is meditation, love, and the third thing – which you may not have thought of at all – a joyous life, because all that is great in you only grows when joy is showering on it. It grows only when you are in a space of blissfulness, when there is laughter, there is song and there is dance.

And I know perfectly your fear. You say, "Please tell me how to take care of this little plant." I will not say how to take care, because I don't want you to become a nurse. I want you to become a mother. I want you to be love, not technical knowledge, because these flowers don't need technical knowledge.

You are afraid, "...since in this moment, it would still be very easy for me to destroy it." That danger is very real. When something inside you grows it brings new responsibilities, because now you need more meditation, you need more love, you need more joy.

This flower inside you can become a burden to you if you don't understand the language of meditation, the language of love, the language of blissfulness. You can destroy the flower by your own hands, just to get rid of the responsibility. But this flower is not only responsibility: it is also your growth, your maturity.

This flower is not something separate from you.

It is your own being.

To destroy it means to commit suicide.

But your question is more concerned about the technicalities of care, and I would like you to change the focus.

Inner growth does not need any technical knowledge, any technical expertise. All that it needs is very simple and very joyful, and it is not a burden. Meditation will make you lighter, less loaded with all kinds of rubbish. Love will also give you new skies, new freedoms. Blissfulness will give you wings to move into those new skies and new spaces.

But the question carries the implication that for centuries in the West the mind has become technically oriented. It has created great technology, great science, but it has destroyed man completely. The house is full of all kinds of gadgets, just the master of the house has disappeared, is lost in the gadgets.

The East has never been technically oriented; it is more concerned with values than with techniques. For example, in the East if somebody is sick, then the wife will not be ready for her husband or her lover to be taken care of by a nurse. It simply will not come to her mind. This is the time when she is needed, and if love cannot heal, then no other technique is going to heal. It is not a question of expertise.

In the West the same situation will have a totally different response. The wife or the husband would like to call a nurse to take care. And he seems, or she seems, to be more logical because the nurse is trained in taking care; she knows the know-how.

But in the East it is almost inconceivable that love can be replaced by expertise of any kind. Expertise can be called in only when there is no love, when the wife feels it is a burden and it is a good chance to get rid of this fellow...call a nurse. And she has good reason; every logic is in her support. The doctor will support her, that this is a very loving decision. But the reality is just the opposite; it is not a loving decision.

So don't ask me about how to take care. Ask me how to be more meditative, how to be more loving, how to be more joyful, because that which is growing within you needs nourishment – and your meditation will give it nourishment, your joy will give it warmth, your love will give it dignity.

A man, narrowly reared by a widowed mother, got married. He telephoned back to his mother from the honeymoon hotel to say that he knew there was something he had to do in bed, but he did not know what it was.

"Why," said his mother, "you put your…eh, that is, you put the hardest part of yourself in the place where your wife wee-wees."

At midnight the hotel rang the fire brigade for help. "We have got a young man with his head jammed in a chamber pot."

Avoid technical knowledge!

Osho,

How come I have always felt, ever since childhood, that I am more than two people? Could you say something please?

*E*verybody is born as one single individual, but by the time he is mature enough to participate in life he has become a crowd. It is not anything special that you are feeling; it is almost the case with everybody. The only difference is that you are becoming aware of it, which is good. People are not aware of it.

If you just sit silently and listen to your mind, you will find so many voices. You will be surprised, you can recognize those voices very well. Some voice is from your grandfather, some voice is from your grandmother, some voice is from your father, some voice is from your mother, some voice is from the priest, from the teacher, from the neighbors, from your friends, from your enemies. All these voices are jumbled up in a crowd within you, and if you want to find your own voice, it is almost impossible; the crowd is too thick.

In fact, you have forgotten your own voice long before. You were never given freedom enough to voice your opinions. You were always taught obedience. You were taught to say yes to everything that your elders were saying to you. You were taught that you have to follow whatever your teachers or your priests are doing. Nobody ever told you to search for your own voice – "Have you got any voice of your own or not?"

So your voice has remained very subdued and other voices are very loud, very commanding, because they were orders and you had followed them – in spite of yourself. You had no intention to follow, you could see that this is not right. But one has to be obedient to be respected, to be acceptable, to be loved.

Naturally only one voice is missing in you, only one person is missing in you, and that is you; otherwise there is a whole crowd. And that crowd is constantly driving you mad, because one voice says, "Do this," another voice says, "Never do that! Don't listen to that voice!" And you are torn apart.

This whole crowd has to be withdrawn. This whole crowd has to be told, "Now please leave me alone!" The people who have gone to the mountains or to the secluded forests were really not going away from the society; they were trying to find a place where they can disperse their crowd inside. And those people who have made a place within you are obviously reluctant to leave.

But if you want to become an individual in your own right, if you want to get rid of this continuous conflict and this mess within you, then you have to say good-bye to them – even when they belong to your respected father, your mother, your grandfather. It does not matter to whom they belong. One thing is certain: they are not *your* voices. They are the voices of people who have lived in their time, and they had no idea what the future was going to be. They have loaded their children with their own experience; their experience is not going to match with the unknown future.

They are thinking they are helping their children to be knowledgeable, to be wise, so their life can be easier and more comfortable, but they are doing just the wrong thing. With all the good intentions in the world, they are destroying the child's spontaneity, his own consciousness, his own ability to stand on his feet, and to respond to the new future which their old ancestors had no idea of.

He is going to face new storms, he is going to face new situations, and he needs a totally new consciousness to respond. Only then is his response is going to be fruitful; only then can he can have a victorious life, a life that is not just a long, long-drawn-out despair, but a dance from moment to moment, which goes on becoming more and more deep to the last breath. He enters into death dancing, and joyously.

It is good that you are becoming aware that it seems you are more than one person. Everybody is! And by becoming aware, it is possible to get rid of this crowd.

Be silent, and find your own self.

Unless you find your own self, it is very difficult to disperse the crowd, because all those in the crowd are pretending, "I am your self." And you have no way to agree, or disagree.

So don't create any fight with the crowd. Let them fight amongst themselves – they are quite efficient in fighting amongst themselves. You, meanwhile, try to find yourself. And once you know who you are, you can just order them to get out of the house – it is actually that simple! But first you have to find yourself.

Once you are there, the master is there, the owner of the house is there. And all these people, who have been pretending to be masters themselves, start dispersing. A man who is not a crowd is truly the "superman" of which we have been talking as Zarathustra's great hope.

The man who is himself, unburdened of the past, discontinuous with the past, original, strong as a lion and innocent as a child... he can reach to the stars, or even beyond the stars; his future is golden.

Up to now people have always been talking about the golden past. My people have to learn the language of the golden future.

There is no need for you to change the whole world; just change yourself and you have started changing the whole world, because you are part of the world. If even a single human being changes, his change will radiate in thousands and thousands of others. He will become a triggering point for a revolution which can give birth to the superman.

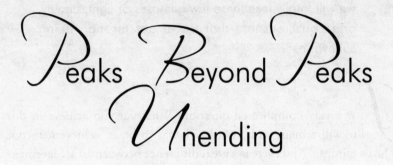

CHAPTER 2

Peaks Beyond Peaks Unending

You have to wake up.
And waking up is such a simple thing —
just the way you wake up in the morning.
Have you ever observed...do you do some gymnastics,
some exercises, some chanting? You simply wake up!
The night is over and you open your eyes
and jump out of the bed.
Spiritual awakening is not different from that.

Osho,

When you said that if we don't achieve total consciousness in this life, we will have to start from the very beginning again, and go through the whole evolution of mankind one more time, I was very touched. Is it possible that we will totally lose these few glimpses of light, beauty, and consciousness that we've got through being sannyasins?

*I*t is a very complicated question. Whatever you achieve in this life will remain with you, but it has to be an achievement not just a glimpse. And there is a great difference between an achievement and a glimpse. You can see the Himalayan peaks from thousands of miles away – it is a glimpse; but to reach those peaks will be an achievement.

A glimpse helps you to move onward, towards achievement; but unless something becomes a crystallized experience in your life, it is going to be lost – you will have to start from the very beginning.

There will be a little difference, and that will be that in your unconscious a shadow of your past life, a faraway echo – as if you have seen something – will remain. And when you again get the glimpse you may feel that this is not new, I have known it before. But otherwise, only crystallized achievements go with you, consciously, into the other life…knowingly, not just a dark shadow, a faraway echo in the unconscious, but consciously knowing that these Himalayan peaks exist, and you have been on those peaks. There will be no doubt about it, no wavering about it, no question about it.

You are asking, "Is it possible that we will totally lose these few glimpses of light, beauty, and consciousness that we have got through being sannyasins?" Such glimpses you have got in many lives before too, and you have lost them. They never became part of your being; they remained only beautiful memories. But the memories are not achievements. It is as if you have seen something in a dream – perhaps it may be true, perhaps it may not be true.

So if you feel that there is something happening now, make every effort that it does not remain only a glimpse but becomes an actual experience, becomes part of your being. Only then can it go with you into another life.

It is possible to take all your experiences with you into another life, and never to begin from scratch but always to begin where you had left off in the past life. But be clear that just a glimpse is very fragile, just a glimpse is very superficial. Howsoever touching it may be in the moment, even tomorrow you may start doubting whether it really happened or you imagined it. And the life after this life is a faraway journey.

Glimpses are simply incentives to move towards crystallization. Make it an experience so deep that it becomes part of you, and there is no way to forget it or to lose it. Don't remain satisfied with glimpses. Enjoy them, but use them only as an indicator towards greater things to happen.

To see something from far away is one thing, and to become that thing is totally another. A glimpse of love is just like a breeze that passes within seconds; a glimpse of silence is just like the fragrance of a rose flower that you felt for a moment, and now you don't know where it has gone.

When I say, "Crystallize your experience," I mean it is not enough to have beautiful glimpses. It is good, but not good enough. You should become the fragrance of the rose itself; the glimpse was only an arrow pointing towards the possibility – it did its work, but you remain there. In the past life also, many times you have come across many beautiful experiences and right now you don't know even that there have been past lives.

Only once in a while you see somebody, and you have a very strange feeling, almost weird, as if you have seen this man before – and certainly not in this life. You come to a place, and suddenly you are startled, as if you had come to this place before too – although certainly not in this life. Everything seems to be known, but has been dormant in your unconscious.

Life has a mechanism that whenever a person dies, unless he is enlightened, he becomes almost unconscious; he goes into a coma before death, actual death, happens. So he knows nothing about the death, and he remains in a state of coma till he is born again. All those nine months in the mother's womb are a state of coma; the child is fast asleep twenty-four hours a day for nine months.

It rarely happens that somebody dies consciously. It happens only to great meditators, who know well the path death will be coming on because in their meditations they have traveled on the path again and again – it is the same path. As they go deep in their meditation the body is left far away, mind is left far away, the heart is left far away; only a beautiful silence – fully alert and conscious – remains.

The same happens when you die. If you have been meditating, then death is not a new experience. You will be surprised that in your meditation you have been dying every day, and you have been coming back to life every day. Such a person dies very consciously, so he knows what death is – and such a person remains conscious in the mother's womb. He is also born consciously. From his very first moment on the earth, he knows all that has passed before in the past life, and he remembers it.

I have come across many children.... And this happens most particularly in India, because outside India – where Christianity is prominent or Judaism is prominent or Mohammedanism is prominent – they have conditioned the mind that there is only one life. They don't know anything about meditation. They have substituted meditation with prayer, and prayer is praising a fictitious god; it is very childish.

Meditation needs no god – you are enough. You are a reality, and you explore your reality to the deepest core.

In India all the religions are agreed on one point; they differ in their philosophies, they differ on every other thing, but on one thing they are all agreed – that life is a continuity; death comes millions of times. Death is only a change of the body, a change of the house, and this process goes on – unless you become totally enlightened. Then there is no need to enter another womb, because life was just a school, a training; you have completed it. Your enlightenment is the culmination of your education about existence. Now you need not enter into another body. You can enter into the womb of the universe itself – you are prepared for it.

So whenever you are having glimpses, don't be satisfied with them. Your glimpses should create great discontent in you, not content. They should create a longing that what is seen far away you would like to come closer, and closer, and closer. You don't want just to see it, even from closeness; you want to *become* it.

You can become love, you can become silence, you can become joy, you can become all these experiences: beauty, light, consciousness. These are not things that you cannot become; they are your potentials. So take every glimpse to its ultimate end. That's what I call crystallization.

Once it is crystallized, once you have known yourself to be love, yourself to be light, yourself to be consciousness, then there is no problem of forgetting it. Then these experiences will go with you. And in your future life you will be growing further ahead, from consciousness to super-consciousness; you will be going beyond these experiences. But if you remain satisfied with your glimpses, there is every danger they will be erased. Death is such a shock and such a surgery and such a long coma that when you wake up, you will have forgotten all those glimpses.

"Someone stole my bike," complained a priest to his minister friend.

"Bring up the Ten Commandments in your sermon tomorrow, and as soon as you mention, 'Thou shalt not steal,' look around in your congregation; you will find the guilty party. Invite him to come forward. Tell him that this is the way to confess, and this is the way to get the forgiveness of God," the minister said confidently.

The next day the priest visited the minister and happily reported that he had found his bike. "Yes," he went on, "when I came to 'Thou shalt not commit adultery', I remembered where I had left it."

Osho,

Is it possible that I always transform my feelings and
experiences into words and images only to get rid
of them? Is it possible that I come to your feet with
tremendous thirst, and when I am filled with energy, I am
overwhelmed with this absolute need of sharing – only to
get rid of it? Is it possible that this urge for sharing is only
my illusion, or just my way to escape? Somebody told
me that I should be more generous with myself. What
can I do if I know not any other way to be generous with
myself than sharing? Is it time for me to learn another
way? Please help me with your guidance.

*W*hat you are experiencing and what you are doing is
perfectly right. Sharing your experiences, your energy,
your love, your blissfulness, is not an escape from them, neither is
it a way to get rid of them. On the contrary, the more you share,
the more you will have.

It is not the ordinary economics. In the ordinary economics
you share and you lose; in the spiritual economics you share
and you get more. In ordinary economics you have to be a miser,
then only you can become rich...accumulate, never share. In the
spiritual economics, if you are a miser whatever you have will be
lost. It can live only if you share; it is a living experience. By sharing
it continues a dynamic movement.

I have heard about a young man who had just received a great
lottery prize, and he was immensely pleased. He stopped his car
because a beggar was standing there. He used to stand there every
day, but he had never stopped his car. But today was different. He
gave him a note of one hundred rupees. The beggar laughed.

The man said, "I don't understand. Why are you laughing?"

He said, "It reminds me...once I used to have my own car and I used to be just as generous as you are. I am laughing because soon you will be standing by my side. Don't be so generous! Learn something from my experience."

In the ordinary economics, the moment you give something, that much is less. But have you felt that by giving love you have less love? Or by sharing your joy, have you felt that your joy is a little bit less?

If you have watched, you will be surprised: by sharing, your joy is a little bit more; by loving, your sources of love are flowing more – you are juicier. By dancing...just to share yourself with your friends you will not find yourself losing something, but gaining something.

Don't listen to other people. They know only about the ordinary economics. They don't know anything about a higher economics, where giving is sharing and where not giving is very destructive.

The more you give, the more you will have, the less you give, the less you will have. And if you don't give at all, you will not have anything at all.

But the people who are suggesting to you that this is not right are creating a problem in your mind about whether you are doing right or wrong. You are doing absolutely right. Do it with more totality, without any hesitation, and without holding anything back. Don't listen to others. Listen to your own experience; watch your own experience – when you give, do you lose something or do you gain something? That should be the decisive thing, not people's advice. The advice of others is dangerous....

When the Eisenbergs moved to Rome, little Hymie came home from his school in tears. He explained to his mother that the nuns were always asking these Catholic questions and how was he, a nice Jewish boy, supposed to know the answers?

Mrs. Eisenberg's heart swelled with maternal sympathy. "Hymie," she said, "I'm going to embroider the answers on the inside of your shirt, and you just look down and read them the next time those nuns pick on you."

"Thanks Mum," said Hymie, and he didn't bat an eye when Sister Michele asked him who was the world's most famous virgin. "Mary," he answered.

"Very good," said the nun. "And who was her husband?"

"Joseph," answered the boy.

"I see you have been studying. Now, can you tell me the name of their son?"

"Sure," said Hymie, "Calvin Klein."

Osho,

To me, your fantastic variation of dynamic meditation you do with us at the end of every evening discourse is one of the most energy-laden experiences I've ever had. All your lovers are radiating, everything is vibrating. I feel we are broadcasting energy waves like a huge radio antenna. The glow must even be visible from outer space. Osho, if we don't wake up this time, then what? Or are you keeping even louder alarms up your sleeve?

*I*t is almost impossible for you not to wake up this time. I am going to do everything to wake you up. I have ice cold water prepared; I am preparing people to pull you out of your bed and give you a good beating.

But anyway, you have to wake up, because for me this is the last time. I will not be here again, so I have to do everything that I can do. And if you miss it will be really unfortunate, because one never knows when you will come across a man who loves you so much that he can be so hard and so cruel as to hit on your head, not bothering what happens to your skull – but somehow you should get up and open your eyes.

The masters in the past have done strange things to wake up their disciples. One Zen master, Fui Hai, had a big monastery. It had two wings, right and left, and in the middle was his cottage. He had a beautiful cat, and all the monks of the monastery loved it. There were almost one thousand monks, five hundred on one side and five hundred on the other side. And they all used to fight, particularly when the master was not at home. The problem was the cat – who should have it?

The right wingers said, "It belongs to us, we are older than you." It was true; the right wing was made first and the left wing was added later on. But the left wingers said, "It is true that your wing was made first, but then there was no cat. The cat came when the left wing was being made. We own it."

It was a constant fight, and the cat was being taken from this wing to that wing, and the master got fed up with this whole thing – every day complaints.

One day he gathered all the monks, except one monk who was not present; he had gone to the city to purchase a few things for the monastery.

The master said, "Today I am going to decide this constant quarrel amongst the two wings." He took a knife and said, "Either you say that this cat belongs to one wing, then it's life can be saved; otherwise I'm going to cut it in two and give to both wings half of the cat. There seems to be no other way; it has to be divided."

They all loved the cat, they all wanted it to be in their wing… they were all silent.

·The master said, "If somebody can do something which shows his understanding and his deep meditation, to whichever wing he belongs, he will be the owner of the cat and that wing will have the cat. Come out! You can save the life of the cat; otherwise the cat is finished."

But people knew that you cannot deceive the master. He had such a clarity of vision that you cannot pretend that you are great meditators; so nobody came out. He cut the cat in two and gave half of the cat to each wing. Everybody was sad – because what can you do with half the cat? And the master was also sad that out of one thousand monks not a single man could do something to save the cat.

At that very time, when he was sitting sadly and the whole monastery was sad, the man who had not been in the monastery came back from the city. He heard the whole story of what had happened. There was blood, the cat had died, and both the wings had half of the cat.

They said, "We had never expected that our master will be so cruel, so hard; he is such a loving and compassionate person. But we cannot blame him; he had given us chances."

But the man came in front of the master and gave him a good slap on the face.

The master laughed and said, "If you had been here, the poor cat would have been saved. You show your meditativeness. Without your meditations you cannot hit your master; to hit your master you have to know that the body is not you, so the master's body is also not the master. You are not hitting the master but just the body, and that's what I have done. I have cut only the body, not the cat. The cat is still alive, must be born somewhere else. But you have come a little late."

There is another story about Lin Chi, a Japanese Zen master. He had a disciple to whom he had given the traditional Zen koan to meditate – "Meditate on the sound of one hand clapping." Now this is absurd. One hand cannot clap, and one hand cannot make any sound. Without clapping there is no possibility of any sound. "Meditate on it and when you have found the sound of one hand clapping, come and report."

The young monk went out into the garden, sat under a tree, tried in many ways to think what could be the sound of one hand clapping. Suddenly, he heard a cuckoo in the bamboo grove and he said, "This must be it!" He rushed and told the master, "I have found it. It is the cuckoo in the bamboo grove."

The master hit him hard on the face and said, "Don't be foolish; next time be a little more intelligent. Go and meditate again!"

Every day he would come, and by and by it became such a situation; sometimes he would come...the wind passing through the pine trees creates a certain sound, perhaps that is the.... Or sometimes the water running down creating sounds, perhaps that is it.... Or sometimes the lightning in the clouds. Slowly, slowly it became a routine thing. The master would not even ask; as he entered he would slap him, and tell him, "Go back and meditate."

But the monk said, "I have not even told you...."

The master said, "I know what it will be. You just go. Meditate more!"

He said to many other monks, "This seems to be too much. First he used to at least hear my answer; now he assumes that the answer is going to be wrong!"

But one day he did not come. Two days passed, and seven days passed.... The master went to the tree where he used to sit and meditate, and the monk was sitting there, utterly silent.

His master shook him and told him, "So at last you have heard it. This is the sound of one hand clapping, this silence.... But why did you not come to report?"

He said, "I forgot everything; the silence was so sweet, so blissful. I am grateful to you that you never listened to my answers, and you went on giving me hard hits. Your compassion is beyond the grasp of ordinary people."

So don't be bothered and don't be concerned about others. You have to wake up. And waking up is such a simple thing – just the way you wake up in the morning. Have you ever observed...do you do some gymnastics, some exercises, some chanting? You simply wake up! The night is over and you open your eyes and jump out of the bed.

Spiritual awakening is not different from that. Once you understand that you are spiritually asleep.... and that is the problem. People don't think they are spiritually asleep, that's why they go on sleeping. Once you understand you are spiritually asleep, then waking is a very simple matter.

The hardest thing is to accept that deep in your being there is a sleep, an unconsciousness. Whatever meditations are being done here are just to shake you, to bring you to a point where the sleeping consciousness cannot sleep anymore; it has to wake up. It is only a question of simple understanding: You can wake up right now! This silence is enough.

Brigitte lay in bed on the first night of their honeymoon while Pat sat fully clothed on an armchair in the bedroom. "Why don't you come to bed?" Brigitte asked him.

"My mother told me that this would be the most exciting night of my life," said Pat, "and I don't want to miss any of it by going to sleep!"

It is very easy to misunderstand.

It is also very easy to understand.

It all depends on you.

Are you ready to wake up? Then nothing can prevent you, and no technique is needed. But if you are not ready to wake up, then no technique can help you. You have to see your life as the life of a somnambulist who is sleep-walking, doing things asleep... fighting, saying the same things which he has said before and have always brought anger, irritation, in other people.

It is a question of watching your life. Is it a life of a man who is awake? Can a man who is awake behave the way the world is behaving?

You have been angry, you have been sorry for it thousands of times, and it has still not become clear to you that again you will be angry and again you will be sorry. What you are doing, it cannot be said that you are doing it fully awake. Your whole life is more like a robot; you are just going through mechanical actions. You suffer, and you decide to change, but when the time to change comes, you forget it completely.

I have heard about a Christian monk who used to give sermons in different places, and his basic sermon was based on Jesus' teaching of the Sermon on the Mount. He would say again and again that if somebody slaps you on one cheek, give him the other cheek too.

One man had been listening to this so many times, he got bored. One day he stood up when the monk was saying this, and went ahead and slapped him. There was great anger in the Christian monk's eyes, but seeing the crowd – and remembering what he has been telling them for so many years – he gave the other cheek, hoping that this idiot will not hit it. But that man was also a unique individual – he hit even harder!

And that very moment, chaos broke; the Christian monk jumped on the man and started hitting him. The man said, "What are you doing? It is against your preachings! I have been listening to your sermons."

The monk said, "Forget all my sermons. Jesus only said 'Give the other cheek.' There is no third cheek. Now I am free, and I will show you...."

But the man said, "Giving the other cheek means you should not be revengeful."

The monk said, "Forget all that nonsense! Giving the other cheek simply means giving the other cheek, and there is no third cheek. You have made me completely free, and now I will teach you the real lesson!"

And he has been teaching his whole life...but perhaps that was also talking in his sleep, never penetrating to the meaning of the words he is saying and what he is doing.

Gurdjieff remembers his father. His father died when Gurdjieff was only nine years old, and must have been a very unique man. He called Gurdjieff close to him and told him, "I'm dying, and I don't have anything as a heritage for you. I'm leaving you poor and orphaned. Just one advice I want to give to you – that is the advice given to me by my father. I have found that that advice has proved to me the richest thing that any father can give to his son. You are so young; perhaps you may not be able to understand it. Just remember it; soon you will be able to understand it also, and whether you understand it or not, start behaving accordingly. Listen very closely and then repeat to me what I'm saying."

It was simple advice. The advice was that If somebody insults you, humiliates you, hurts you, you are not to react immediately. You have to say to that person, "You will have to wait twenty-four hours, and then I will come to answer you. This is something sacred to me; I have given a promise to my dying father. So wait twenty-four hours and then go to the person. In those twenty-four hours you will see that he was right, or you may see that he was not right, but it is absolutely stupid to get into a quarrel. Those twenty-four hours will have given you a chance to be more alert. People react immediately – there is not time enough to be aware. They react just like machines. So if you find that he was right, go and thank him. If you find he was wrong, there is no need to go; or if you want to go, you can go and say 'You seem to be in a misunderstanding.'

And Gurdjieff used to say, later in his life, "That simple advice of my dying father has transformed my whole life because it gave me a certain awareness, a certain awakening. I could not do anything immediately, instantly. I had to wait for twenty-four hours. And you cannot remain angry for twenty-four hours."

A man who is awake behaves in a totally different way from the whole humanity, which is fast asleep.

One of my friends, he was a colleague in the same university where I was a teacher, said to me "I have been trying to drop my smoking, for almost twenty years."

I said, "That is too long a time to drop a cigarette; just give me a cigarette and I can drop it right now."

He said, "Don't make a laughing stock of me. I have worked hard to drop it, and sometimes for a few hours, or sometimes even for few days, I manage not to smoke. But finally I have to give way. And now I have even dropped fighting; it is meaningless – twenty years fighting."

I said, "You don't understand simple laws of life. You are a man fast asleep, and in sleep you cannot make any decisions, any commitments. My suggestion is that you do one thing: you smoke more consciously."

He said, "What – smoke? I want to drop it."

I said, "Just listen to what I am saying, you smoke *more* consciously. Take the packet from your pocket very slowly and consciously. Pull the cigarette out very slowly – there is no hurry. Look at the cigarette from all sides, put it in your mouth, wait. There is no hurry. Go very slow-motion, just as if a film is going in slow motion."

He said, "What is that going to do?"

I said, "That we will see later on...then take your lighter, look at it."

He said, "You are making me a fool – what is that going to do?"

I said, "You just.... Twenty years you have done it your way; twenty days you do it my way. Look at the lighter, then light the cigarette, then smoke as slowly as possible. And be watchful that the smoke is going in, then the smoke is going out." That is the oldest meditation, *Vipassana*. Gautam Buddha may never have thought that it will be used with a cigarette and a cigarette lighter – but I have to manage for him.

He would not do *Vipassana*, but this.... He said, "Okay, I will try it, twenty days it is not much."

But the second day he came to me and said, "This is strange. Doing things so slowly makes me so alert; smoking, and watching the smoke going in and the smoke going out makes me so silent that already, in two days, I am smoking almost fifty percent less."

I said, "Just wait twenty days."

He said, "I don't think it will last twenty days; at the most five days and it will be finished."

I said, "Don't be in a hurry to finish it, because if anything remains clinging it will enforce you again. So go very slowly; there is no hurry, and there is no harm. It does not matter – at the most you may die two years earlier. But anyway, what were you going to do in those two years – just smoke...more! So there is no harm anyway; the world is too populated, and if people go on disappearing a little earlier, making space for other people, it is very compassionate of them."

He said, "You are a strange fellow." And after the fourth day he told me, "Now, as my hand moves towards the pocket, suddenly a stop comes – from where, I don't know. I have not been smoking for one whole day because each time I try to take a cigarette, I cannot take the packet out. What is the secret of it?"

I said, "There is no secret; you have just learned to smoke consciously, with awareness. And nobody can smoke with awareness, because smoking is not a sin – smoking is simply a stupidity. If you are alert and awake, you cannot be so stupid. There is fresh air available; you can go and have good breathing, deep breaths, fresh air, perfumed with flowers. You must be an idiot if you have to pay money to make your breathing dirty, dirty with nicotine, harming your lungs, harming your life; and there is no point in it."

People are really fast asleep; it is a wonder they don't snore with open eyes.

King Arthur, going on a two-year dragon hunting expedition, ordered Merlin the Wise to make a chastity belt for Guinevere to wear whilst he was away. Merlin came up with a very unorthodox design – one that had a large gaping aperture in the area that would normally be most strongly fortified.

"That's absurd," said Arthur. "This belt is not functional."

"Yes, it is," said Merlin. Picking up a spare magic wand, he passed it through the opening – instantly a guillotine-like blade came down and chopped the wand in two.

"Ingenious!" cried Arthur.

After outfitting Guinevere with the belt, he rode off to slay dragons, his mind at peace.

Two years later, when Arthur came back, his first official act was to assemble all of the Knights of the Round Table and send them to the court physician for a special inspection. His frown grew severe as he learned that every member of the Round Table was nicked, cut, or scratched – all but one. Sir Lancelot was impeccable.

Arthur called for him immediately, and smiled at his best knight. "Sir Lancelot," he declared, "you are the only one of my knights who did not assail the chastity of my lady while I was off slaying dragons. You have upheld the honor of the Round Table and I am proud of you. You shall be rewarded. You may have anything in the kingdom you desire, you have but to name it. State your wish Sir Lancelot."

But Sir Lancelot was speechless....

CHAPTER 3

Untry and Untry Again

When you are not trying,
and you are relaxed —
you are not even bothered about meditation
and things like that —
you suddenly find the footsteps of the unknown,
something from nowhere, approaching you.
Look at it with wonder, not with desire.
Look at it with gratitude, but not with greed.

Osho,

Many years ago, it seems, I used to be able to meditate
– I think. A beautiful, silent, transparent state would
arrive from somewhere; I presumed this was meditation.
Now, nothing comes except a racing mind. What
happened?

*P*rema Veena, it always almost happens this way. The days when
you were feeling a kind of meditation happening to you were
the days you were not looking for it – it was happening to you. Now
you are trying to make it happen, and that makes all the difference.
All the things that are really valuable in life only happen; you cannot
make them happen, you cannot do them. It may be meditation, it
may be love, it may be blissfulness, it may be silence.

Anything that goes beyond your mind is beyond your capacity
to do it; you can only do things which come in the territory of
the mind.

The mind is the doer, but your being is not a doer. Your being
is just an opening, and a deep acceptance of whatever happens,
with no complaint, with no grudge – just a pure gratefulness. And
that, too, is not done by you; that is also part of the happening.
We have to make this distinction very clear; almost everybody gets
confused. Something happens to you – it is so beautiful, so blissful
– the mind starts immediately desiring that it should happen more,
that it should happen more often, that it should go deeper. The
moment mind comes in, it disturbs everything. Mind is the devil,
the destroyer.

So one has to be very aware that mind should not be allowed
to interfere in things of the beyond. Mind is perfectly good as a
mechanic, a technician. Give your mind what it can do, but don't let
it interfere in things which are beyond its capacity. But one of the
problems is that mind is nothing but desiring – desiring for more. As
far as the world of doing is concerned, you can have a bigger house,

you can have a better house, you can have better furniture – you can do everything better; it is within the capacity of the mind.

But beyond the mind…mind can only desire, and each desire is going to be frustrated. Instead of bringing more meditation, it will bring you more frustration. Instead of bringing you more love, it will bring to you more anger. Instead of silence and peace, it will bring more traffic of thoughts – and that happens to almost everybody. So it is something natural that one has to grow out of.

You are saying, "Many years ago, it seems, I used to be able to meditate. A beautiful, silent, transparent state would arrive from somewhere; I presumed this was meditation." Neither were you expecting it, nor were you desiring it; it was just a guest, like a breeze that comes to you. But you cannot keep it, and you cannot order it to come. It comes when it comes. And once you understand this, you stop trying.

You have heard the expression, "Try and try again. I would like to say to you: Untry and untry again. Whenever the idea of trying arises, immediately drop it. It is going to lead you into failure, into frustration, and if you can drop it…and everybody can drop it, because it never brings anything. What is the problem in dropping the failure, frustration, despair and hopelessness? Just drop them and forget all about meditation.

One day, suddenly, you will find a window opens, and a fresh breeze with new rays has filled your heart. Again, don't commit the same mistake! Be thankful for what is happening, but don't ask for more – and more will be coming. Don't ask, "Come again" – your asking will become the barrier.

It will come again, it will come more often. Slowly, slowly it becomes your heartbeat; waking, sleeping, it is always there, it never goes. But it is not your doing. You cannot brag that "I have done it." You can only say, "I have allowed the unknown to do it to me." It is always from the unknown that great experiences enter into our small hearts, and when we are trying hard to get them, we become so tense that the very tension prevents them.

When you are not trying, and you are relaxed – you are not

even bothered about meditation and things like that – you suddenly find the footsteps of the unknown, something from nowhere, approaching you. Look at it with wonder, not with desire. Look at it with gratitude, but not with greed.

You are saying, "Now, nothing comes except a racing mind. What happened?" You became aware of the unknown. A little taste of meditation, and you became greedy, desirous. Your desire, your greed spoilt the whole game. Still, everything can be put right. You see the mind continuously racing; let it race – you simply watch, just be a bystander, an observer.

Just watching the mind is one of the greatest secrets of life, because it does not show that it works – but it works! Just as you watch, indifferent, uninterested, as if it has nothing to do with you, those thoughts start getting thinner; there is less traffic on the track of the mind.

Slowly, slowly there are small gaps, and in those gaps you will have a glimpse of what you used to have. But don't jump upon it, don't be greedy. Enjoy it, it will also pass; don't try to cling to it. Thoughts will start coming again; again a gap will come, a bigger gap. Slowly, slowly bigger gaps will be happening when the mind will be empty.

In that empty mind the beyond can enter into you, but the basic condition is that you should not cling to it. If it comes – good; if it does not – good. Perhaps you are not ripe, perhaps it is not the time – still, be grateful. One has to learn watchfulness and gratefulness. Even when nothing is happening that you deep down want to happen, still be grateful. Perhaps it is not the right time for you, perhaps it will not help your growth.

I have often told you the story of a Sufi mystic, Junnaid. He was the master of Al Hillaj Mansoor and because of Mansoor he became very famous. Mansoor was killed by the orthodox, traditionalist fanatics, and because of Mansoor, Junnaid's name also became famous – Mansoor was Junnaid's disciple.

Junnaid used to go for a pilgrimage every year to the Mohammedan holy place, Kaaba. It was not very far from his place, and Mohammedans are expected by their tradition at least once in a life to go to Kaaba; otherwise they are not complete Mohammedans. But Kaaba was so close to his place that every year he used to go with his disciples. He was the revolutionary kind of saint. In fact, any kind other than the revolutionary are not saints – just facades, actors, pretenders, and hypocrites.

The people in the villages where Junnaid had to pass were very angry with him. A few villages were so angry that they would not give him anything to eat, or even water to drink and would not allow him to stay in the village.

It was Junnaid's usual prayer – Mohammedans pray five times a day – and after each prayer he would raise his hands to God and he would say, "I am so grateful to You. How should I express my gratefulness? You take care of me in every possible way; Your compassion is infinite, your love knows no bounds."

The disciples were tired because five times every day, and in situations where they could see there is no care taken by God – they have not received food, they have not received water, they have not received shelter from the hot sun in the desert.... Once it happened that for three days continually they were thrown out, stoned, given no food, no water, no shelter; but Junnaid continued his prayer the same way.

On the third day, the disciples freaked out. They said, "Enough is enough. Why are you saying, 'You are compassionate,' 'Your love is great,' 'You take care of us in every possible detail?' For three days we have not eaten a single thing, we are thirsty, we have not slept under shelter, we have been sleeping in the desert, shivering in the cold night. For what are you being grateful?"

The answer that Junnaid gave to his disciples is worthy of being remembered. He said, "For these three days, do you think I cannot see that food has not been given to us, that we have been thrown out, that we have been stoned, that we are thirsty, that for three days we had to remain in the open desert...? Don't you see that I am also aware of it? But this does not mean that he is not taking care of us. Perhaps this is the way he is taking care of us; perhaps this is what we need at this time.

"It is very easy, when life is going comfortably, to thank God. That thankfulness means nothing. These three days I have been watching. Slowly, slowly, all of you have stopped thanking Him after the prayer; you failed the test. It was a beautiful test. Even if death comes to me, I will die with gratefulness. He gave me life; He took it away. It was His, it is His, it will be His. Who am I to interfere in His affairs?"

So there will be times when you will not find any moment of peace, silence, meditation, love, blissfulness. But do not lose hope. Perhaps those moments are needed to crystallize you, to make you strong. Be grateful not only when things are going good, but be grateful when everything is going wrong. A man who can be grateful when everything is going wrong is really grateful; he knows the beauty of gratefulness. For him, things can go wrong forever, but his gratefulness is such a transforming force, it is going to change everything.

So don't be worried about the racing mind; let it race. Allow it to race as fully as possible; don't prevent it, don't try to stop it – you just be a watcher. You get out of the mind and let the mind race, and soon, without fail, as a natural law, gaps will start happening. And when gaps happen, don't get too happy that, "I have got it." Remain relaxed. Enjoy those gaps also, but without greed and without desire, because they will disappear; and they will disappear soon if you become greedy. If you are ungreedy, undesirous, they may stay longer.

This is the whole training of meditation. Soon, the day comes when the mind is completely silent, filled with great joy, silence. But remember, it is not your doing. If even for a single moment you think it is your doing, it may disappear. Always remember that you are the doing of existence. All that is great is going to happen to you not by your effort, but by your relaxed openness, availability.

Just keep your doors open.

The guest will come – it has never been otherwise.

The guest always comes.

Pat's son became an actor, and one evening rushed home to his father in a state of great excitement, "Guess what Dad," he announced, "I have just been given my first part. I play a man who has been married for twenty-five years."

"Keep it up my son," said Pat, "someday you may get a speaking part, too."

In the case of Veena, it is just the opposite. Right now you are in the speaking part; just keep on, someday you will certainly get the silent part too. But there is nothing to be worried about. Life has to be taken very playfully, with a great sense of humor. In good times and bad times, when things are happening and when things are not happening, when the spring comes and when, sometimes, the spring does not come to you....

Remember, we are not the doers as far as things beyond mind are concerned; we are only receivers. And to become a receiver, you have just to become a watcher of your mind because through watching those gaps appear. In those gaps your door is open. And through that door stars can enter into you, flowers can enter into you. Even when stars and flowers enter into you, don't be greedy, don't try to keep them in. They come out of freedom and you should remember, they will remain with you only in freedom. If you destroy their freedom, they are destroyed too. Their freedom is their very spirit.

It is my continual experience of thousands of people that when they come for the first time to meditate, meditation happens so easily because they don't have any idea what it is. Once it has happened, then the real problem arises – then they want it, they know what it is, they desire it. They are greedy for it; it is happening to others and it is not happening to them. Then jealousy, envy, all kinds of wrong things surround them.

Always remain innocent as far as things beyond mind are concerned. Always remain amateur, never become an expert. That is the worst thing that can happen to anybody.

Osho,

A few days ago, I heard you say that the voice speaking inside of us is always the mind, so I wonder who in me is hearing this voice. When I try to find the answer, I only find silence.

*C*hidvilas, the moment you look into your self you only find silence. But are you not aware that you are also there? Who finds the silence? Silence itself can not find itself; there is somebody as a witness who is finding the silence. Just your focus is wrong; you are still focusing on the object. It is just an old habit, perhaps cultivated for many, many lives, that you always focus yourself on the object, and you always forget yourself.

An ancient Eastern story is that ten blind men crossed a stream. The current was very strong, so they took hold of each other's hands because they were afraid somebody may be taken away by the current. They reached the other shore, and somebody amongst them suggested, "It is better we should count because the current and the stream were really dangerous. Somebody may have slipped, and we may not even be aware."

So they started counting. It was a great shock, and they were all crying and weeping; everybody tried, but the count was always nine – because nobody was counting himself. Naturally, he would start counting, "One, two, three, four, five, six, seven, eight, nine.... My God, one has gone!" So they all were crying.

A woodcutter was watching all this drama and he said...he had never seen ten blind men together, in the first place. Second, what a stupid idea these people had. What was the need to cross the stream when it was so strong and flooded? And, above all, now they were counting, and crying and weeping for someone – they did not know who, but certainly someone had been taken away by the current. Watching them counting, he was simply amazed how was it possible that they were ten persons, but the count always came to nine?

Some help was needed, so he came down from his tree and he said, "What is the matter?"

They all said, "We have lost one of our friends. We were ten, and now we are only nine."

The man said, "I can find your tenth man. You are right, you used to be ten, but there is a condition."

They said, "We will accept any condition, but our friend...."

He said, "It is not a very big condition, it is a simple condition. I will hit on the first man's head; he has to say "one." Then I will hit on the second person's head two times; he has to say "two." Then I will hit on the third person's three times; he has to say "three." As many times as I hit, the person has to speak the number."

They said, "If this is the way to find the lost friend, we are ready."

So he enjoyed hitting very much, and he hit them in turn. When he had hit the tenth man ten times he said "ten." All the nine said, "You idiot, where have you been? Unnecessarily we have all been beaten! Where you have been hiding up to now?"

He said, "I was standing here, I was myself counting, and it always came to nine. This man seems to be a miracle man; he managed to find the tenth man."

The story is significant for the simple reason that it has become our habit not to count ourselves. So when you are watching your thoughts, inside, you are not aware that there is a watcher too. When you are watching silence, you are not aware that you cannot watch silence if you are not there.

Chidvilas, you are asking, "A few days ago I heard you say that the voice speaking inside of us is always the mind, so I wonder who in me is hearing this voice?" Certainly I am not hearing it, and as far as I know nobody else is hearing it. You must be the guy who is hearing this voice. Everybody else has his own problem!

"When I try to find the answer I only find silence." But then too the question arises: Who finds the silence? It is the same guy who was hearing the voice. His name is Chidvilas.

You have to become more subjective, more alert to yourself; we are always alert to everything around us.

Pat followed his friend Mike's example and left Ireland to work in England. Though they had since lost contact, Mike had mentioned how easy it was to get a job at Whipsnade Open Zoo, so Pat applied. Unfortunately they had no keeper's jobs available; there was not even the position of a sweeper vacant.

"But I tell you what, Pat," the manager said, "the gorilla died a couple of days ago, and what is a zoo without a gorilla? But we have kept his pelt entire; now if you crawl into that skin and take over his enclosure, we will feed and house you, and pay you handsomely as well."

Pat had a look over the lovely field that was the gorilla enclosure; he surveyed the comfortable gorilla house, and tested the bed provided. He agreed to take the job. Very soon Pat had become a great favorite with visitors to the zoo. Being a bit of an extrovert, he would always put on a good act – tumbling, chest-thumping, and growling. But the climax of his performance was most popular. Whenever there was a good crowd, Pat would scale a large oak tree at the side of his enclosure where it adjoined the lion's pen and pelt the lioness with acorns. The big-maned lion, in particular, would roar with rage and stamp about, and the crowd would roar with delight.

One public holiday a particularly large crowd had gathered, and Pat was aloft and reaching the peak of his performance. He had just finished off the acorn pelting with a bit of chest-thumping when the branch he was balanced on broke; he fell to the ground at the lion's feet. Pat jumped up, shouting for help, and was about to scarper when the lioness whispered, "Hold your tongue Pat, sure do you want to lose us the best jobs we have ever had?"

Here, everybody has different skins only; inside is the same consciousness. Whether you are hearing a voice, or you are hearing silence, remember more about yourself – who is the watcher? who is the witness?

In every experience, when you are angry, when you are in love, when you are in greed, when you are in despair, it is the same key: just watch – are you really in danger, or are you only a witness. Here we are, just sitting. Deep down, who are you? Always a witness.

Whatever happens on the outside – you may be young, you may be old, you may be alive, you may be dead – whatever happens on the outside, inside is the same witness. This witness is our truth. This witness is our ultimate reality, our eternal reality.

So all your work is concerned with shifting your focus from the object to the subject. Don't be bothered about anger, or silence, or love. Be concerned about whom all this is happening to, and remain centered there. This centering will bring you the greatest experience of your life. It will make you a superman.

Osho,

Eleven years ago, when I first sat in front of you, I was so overwhelmed by your energy, by your love, by you, that I could do nothing but cry and bow down to your feet in silent expression; and yet I felt very much understood by you. At that time you told me to keep my energy inside and bring it to my *hara*. Since then this suggestion stays with me, and my belly has become my best friend, and the place below my navel a mirror of my feelings. In all this time tears and laughter of joy and gratitude for being able to spend this life with you have kept back most of my words. My beloved master, I feel that behind this small suggestion of yours lies more than I can imagine. Would you please say something more about the hara, and guide me further?

*D*eva Radhika, *Hara* is the center from where a life leaves the body. It is the center of death. The word *hara* is Japanese; that's why in Japan, suicide is called *hara-kiri*. The center is just two inches below the navel. It is very important, and almost everybody in the world has felt it. But only in Japan have they gone deeper into its implications.

Even the people in India, who had worked tremendously hard on centers, had not considered the hara. The reason for their missing it was because they had never considered death to be of any significance. Your soul never dies, so why bother about a center that functions only as a door for energies to get out, and to enter into another body? They worked from sex, which is the life center. They have worked on seven centers, but the hara is not even mentioned in any Indian scriptures.

The people who worked hardest on the centers for thousands of years have not mentioned the hara, and this cannot be just a coincidence. The reason was that they never took death seriously. These seven centers are life centers, and each center is of a higher life. The seventh is the highest center of life, when you are almost a god.

The hara is very close to the sex center. If you don't rise towards higher centers, towards the seventh center which is in your head, and if you remain for your whole life at the sex center, then just by the side of the sex center is the hara, and when then life will end, the hara will be the center from where your life will move out of the body.

Why have I told Radhika this? She was very energetic, but not aware of any higher centers; her whole energy was at the sex center, and she was overflowing. Energy overflowing at the sex center is dangerous, because it can start releasing from the hara. And if it starts releasing from the hara, then to take it upwards becomes more difficult. So I had told her to keep her energy in, and not to be so expressive: Hold it in! I simply wanted the hara center, which was opening and which could have been very dangerous, to be completely closed.

She followed it, and she has become a totally different person. Now when I see her, I cannot believe the expressiveness that I had seen at first. Now she is more centered, and her energy is moving in the right direction of the higher centers. It is almost at the fourth center, which is the center of love and which is a very balancing center. There are three centers below it, and three centers above it.

Once a person is at the center of love, there is very rarely a possibility for him to fall back down, because he has tasted something of the heights. Now valleys will be very dark, ugly; he has seen sunlit peaks, not very high, but still high; now his whole desire will be....

And that is the trouble with all lovers: they want more love, because they don't understand that the real desire is not for more love, but for something more than love. Their language ends with love; they don't know any way that is higher than love, and love does not satisfy. On the contrary, the more you love the more thirsty you become.

At the fourth center of love, one feels a tremendous satisfaction only when energy starts moving to the fifth center. The fifth center is in your throat, and the sixth center is your third eye. The seventh center, the *sahasrar*, is on the top of your head. All these centers have different expressions and different experiences.

When love moves to the fifth center then whatever talents you have, any creative dimension, is possible for you. This is the center of creativity. It is not only for songs, not only for music; it is for all creativity.

Hindu mythology has a beautiful story. It is a myth, but the story is beautiful, and particularly for explaining to you the fifth center. Indian mythology says that there is a constant struggle between evil forces and good forces. They both discovered that if they made a certain search in the ocean they could find nectar, and that whoever drank it would become immortal. So they all tried to find it.

But as life balances everywhere, there too.... Before they found the nectar they found poison which was hiding the nectar underneath it. Nobody was ready to test it; even the very sight of it created sickness. One of them thought that the first hippie of the world, perhaps might be willing – he was the god Shiva. So they asked Shiva, "You test it." He said, "Okay."

He not only tested it, he drank it all, and it was pure poison. He kept it just in his neck, at the fifth center. The fifth center is the creative center. It became completely poisoned, and Shiva became the god of destruction. So Hindus have three gods: Brahma who creates the world, Vishnu who sustains the world, and Shiva who destroys the world. His destructiveness came from his creative center being poisoned. And the poison was so great that it cannot be a small destruction; he can only destroy the whole of existence.

When Vishnu is tired of maintaining it, Shiva destroys it. By that time Brahma has forgotten – millions of years have passed since he created the world; he again starts creating it – just an old routine! Brahma is the creator god, but in the whole of India there is only one temple devoted to Brahma, because who cares about him? He has done his work; it is futile to say anything to him. Vishnu has millions of temples, because he is the sustainer god. Krishna and Rama are all incarnations of Vishnu.

But nobody can compete with Shiva. Shiva has more shrines to him than anybody else. He is a hippie, so he does not need very great temples or anything – just anywhere, under any tree. Just put a round stone, oval shape, and he does not ask much – a few leaves, not even flowers. A few leaves you can drop there, a few drops of water on his head, just to keep him cool...so people have created devices; they just hang a small pot on top of his head with a small drip, drip, drip. It keeps him cool, so he does not get annoyed with anybody and destroy the world.

Everybody is afraid of him, so naturally he has many more worshipers, many more temples, and many more shrines. In every small village you will find at least a dozen Shiva shrines, because they cost nothing; any poor man can afford it. And he has to be concerned about it because Shiva can destroy. Keep him satisfied! And he does not ask much; just keep his head cool. Flowers are costly, but any two leaves and his worship is finished.

Shiva became the destroyer of the world because his fifth center had accumulated the whole poison of existence in it. It is our creative center, that's why lovers have a certain tendency to creativity. When you fall in love, you suddenly feel like creating something – it is very close. If you are guided rightly, your love can become your great creative act. It can make you a poet, it can make you a painter, it can make you a dancer, it can make you reach to the stars in any dimension.

The sixth center which we call the third eye is between the two eyes. This gives you a clarity, a vision of all your past lives, and of all the future possibilities. Once your energy has reached your third eye, then you are so close to enlightenment that something of enlightenment starts showing. It radiates from the man of the third eye, and he starts feeling a pull towards the seventh center.

Because of these seven centers, India never bothered about hara. Hara is not in the line; it is just by the side of the sex center. The sex center is the life center, and hara is the death center. Too much excitement, too much uncenteredness, too much throwing your energy all over the place is dangerous, because it takes your energy towards the hara. And once the route is created, it becomes more difficult to move it upwards. Hara is equally parallel to the sex center, so the energy can move very easily.

It was a great discovery by the Japanese: they found that there was no need to cut your head off, or shoot your brains out to kill – they are all unnecessarily painful; just a small knife forced exactly at the hara center, and without any pain, life disappears. Just make the center open and life disappears, as if the flower opens and the fragrance disappears.

The hara should be kept closed. That's why, Radhika, I had told you to be more centered, to keep your feelings inside, and to bring it to your hara. "Since then this suggestion stays with me, and my belly has become my best friend, and the place below my navel a mirror of my feelings."

If you can keep your hara consciously controlling your energies, it does not allow them to go out. You start feeling a tremendous gravity, a stability, a centeredness, which is a basic necessity for the energy to move upwards.

You are asking, "I feel that behind this small suggestion of yours lies more than I can imagine." Certainly, there is much more...

A Pole is walking down the street, and passes a hardware store advertising the sale of a chain saw that is capable of cutting seven hundred trees in seven hours. The Pole thinks that it is a great deal and decides to buy one.

The next day he comes back with the saw, and complains to the salesman, "The thing did not come close to chopping down the seven hundred trees that the ad said it would."

"Well," said the salesman, "let us test it out back." Finding a log, the salesman pulls the starter cord, and the saw makes a great roaring sound.

"What is that noise?" asked the Pole.

So he must have been cutting by hand and it was an electric saw!

Radhika, your hara center has so much energy that, if it is rightly directed, enlightenment is not a faraway place.

So these two are my suggestions: keep yourself as much centered as possible. Don't get moved by small things – somebody is angry, somebody insults you, and you think about it for hours. Your whole night is disturbed because somebody said something.... If the hara can hold more energy, then naturally that much more energy starts rising upwards. There is only a certain capacity in the hara, and every energy that moves upwards moves through the hara; but the hara should just be closed.

So one thing is that the hara should be closed. The second thing is that you should always work for higher centers. For example, if you feel angry too often you should meditate more on anger, so that anger disappears and its energy becomes compassion. If you are a man who hates everything, then you should concentrate on hate; meditate on hate, and the same energy becomes love.

Go on moving upwards, think always of higher ladders, so that you can reach to the highest point of your being. And there should be no leakage from the hara center.

India has been too concerned about sex for the same reason:

sex can also take your energy outside. It takes...but at least sex is the center of life. Even if it takes energy out, it will bring energy somewhere else, life will go on flowing.

But hara is a death center. Energy should not be allowed through the hara. A person whose energy starts through hara you can very easily detect. For example, there are people with whom you will feel suffocated, with whom you will feel as if they are sucking your energy. You will find that, after they are gone, you feel at ease and relaxed, although they were not doing anything wrong to you.

You will find just the opposite kind of people also, whose meeting you makes you joyful, healthier. If you were sad, your sadness disappears; if you were angry, your anger disappears. These are the people whose energy is moving to higher centers. Their energy affects your energy. We are affecting each other continually. And the man who is conscious, chooses friends and company which raises his energy higher.

One point is very clear. There are people who suck you, avoid them! It is better to be clear about it, say good-bye to them. There is no need to suffer, because they are dangerous; they can open your hara too. Their hara is open, that's why they create such a sucking feeling in you.

Psychology has not taken note of it yet, but it is of great importance that psychologically sick people should not be put together. And that is what is being done all over the world. Psychologically sick people are put into psychiatric institutes together. They are already psychologically sick, and you are putting them in a company which will drag their energy even lower.

Even the doctors who work with psychologically sick people have given enough indication of it. More psychoanalysts commit suicide than any other profession, more psychoanalysts go mad than any other profession. And every psychoanalyst once in a while needs to be treated by some other psychoanalyst. What happens to these poor people? Surrounded by psychologically sick people, they are continually sucked, and they don't have any idea how to close their haras.

There are methods, techniques to close the hara, just as there are methods for meditation, to move the energy upwards. The best and simplest method is: try to remain as centered in your life as possible. People cannot even sit silently, they will be changing their position. They cannot lie down silently, the whole night they will be turning and tossing. This is just unrest, a deep restlessness in their souls.

One should learn restfulness. And in these small things, the hara stays closed. Particularly psychologists should be trained. Also, psychologically sick people should not be put together.

In the East, particularly in Japan in Zen monasteries, where they have become aware of the hara center, there are no psychologists as such. But in Zen monasteries there are small cottages, far away from the main campus where Zen people live, but in the same forest or in the same mountain area. And if somebody who is psychologically sick is brought to them, he is given a cabin there and he is told to relax, rest, enjoy, move around in the forest – but not to talk. Anyway there is nobody to talk to! Only once a day a man comes to give food; he is not allowed to talk to that man either, and even if he talks, the man will not answer. So his whole energy is completely controlled. He cannot even talk; he cannot meet anybody.

You will be surprised to know that what psychoanalysis cannot do in years, is done in three weeks. In three weeks time the person is as healthy as normal people are. And nothing has been done – no technique, nothing. He has just been left alone so he cannot talk. He has been left alone so he can rest and be himself. He is not expected to fulfill somebody else's expectations.

Radhika, you have done well. Just continue whatever you are doing, accumulating your energy in yourself. The accumulation of energy automatically makes it go higher. And as it reaches higher you will feel more peaceful, more loving, more joyful, more sharing, more compassionate, more creative.

The day is not faraway when you will feel full of light, and the feeling of coming back home.

CHAPTER 4

Patience is the Way of Existence

The inner growth is very still and very silent.
You cannot hear your own footsteps.
You only become aware when you
reach a certain stage. And it is a surprise
because all the time you were thinking
nothing is happening...
suddenly, the flowers have come.
This is what I mean by patience

Osho,

I keep going where you are and can't move away. Still, something is missing. At the junction of two paths, the inner one and the outer one, with tears in his eyes, the stubborn donkey is starving. The outer path does not attract him much anymore, and when it does the hope is quickly smashed. Seeing your finger pointing to the moon, still he is not going very much on the inner path. I do not know quite how to speak to him. Disgusted with tunafish sandwiches, he became accustomed to starvation. Is this just fear, laziness, impatience? Does he just need a juicy joke? Beloved Osho, give him a little push.

*I*t is one of the significant things to understand that unless you attain the ultimate, the feeling of something missing is going to remain with you. And this feeling is not against you; this feeling is a kind of reminding you that you have not reached yet, that you have to go on and on.

Don't take the feeling of missing as negative; it is healthy and positive. It shows that you are aware of where you are and you are also sensitive to where you should be, and between the two, the gap is the feeling of missing.

I would like to read your question: "I keep going where you are and can't move away."

I have been aware of it. For the whole year I have been moving from one place to another place and you have remained constantly moving with me. It is not just attachment with me – it is something more. It is not a question of being with me: it is a question of being in the same state of being as I am.

You don't want to miss any opportunity, any single moment. And one never knows – your time may come and you may be far away from me.

Still something is missing. It will go on missing for a little time more. You are growing, but to reach to the flowers, to reach to the fruits, it takes a long time to grow. And spiritual growth is not like seasonal flowers; they come within weeks and they are gone. The spiritual growth is of the eternal: once it comes, it remains – remains forever.

Naturally, compared to eternity our time scale is very small. A few days pass, or a few months or a few years; we start feeling, is there something wrong? Am I doing right? And these are natural feelings. But I have been watching you. Nothing is wrong, everything is as it should be. You are silently growing. All growth is silent, it makes no noise. And suddenly one day...the flowers appear.

Just by the side of Chuang Tzu hall there were no flowers three days ago. Then one day the storm came and the rains came, and in the morning suddenly there were beautiful sunflowers – just in one night. I had seen the place; in the evening there were no flowers, in the morning there were flowers.

It takes time for the growth, but when the right moment comes it is an explosion. Suddenly, all over, is the spring. And it is good that until it happens you go on feeling that something is missing. You should not forget for a single moment that something is missing. That will be dangerous.

Millions of people have forgotten it completely. They are absolutely content and feeling that all that they need they have – nothing is missing. They are the poorest people in the world. They don't have a longing for higher reaches, they don't want to climb mountains, they don't want to go to the stars – in their dark caves they are perfectly comfortable. One should have compassion for them. Their contentment is their spiritual death.

You need a spiritual discontentment which constantly moves you, like an arrow, towards faraway goals.

"At the junction of two paths, the inner one and the outer one, with tears in his eyes, the stubborn donkey is starving. The outer path does not attract him much anymore, and when it does the hope is quickly smashed. Seeing your finger pointing to the moon, still he is not going very much on the inner path."

The inner growth is very still and very silent.

You cannot hear your own footsteps.

You only become aware when you reach a certain stage. And it is a surprise because all the time you were thinking nothing is happening...suddenly, the flowers have come. This is what I mean by patience.

To grow cedars of Lebanon one needs great patience. They are not seasonal flowers and you cannot see the growth. It is happening every moment, all these trees are growing every moment. But existence functions very silently.

You are growing, and even you cannot be aware of it unless something totally new happens and makes you aware that you have reached some space that was unknown to you. And that can happen any moment.

On your part great patience is needed, and a trust that the whole existence is in support of all those who are trying to grow spiritually. It is not you who are trying to grow spiritually; it is existence who, through you, is trying to reach to its utmost heights.

"I do not quite know how to speak to him. Disgusted with tunafish sandwiches, he became accustomed to starvation. Is this just fear, laziness, impatience? Does he just need a juicy joke?"

It is a combination of many things. Fear is always there, and will remain until you come to know that there is no death. Fear is the shadow of death. When death disappears the shadow disappears.

There is impatience, but you have to use your impatience not against your growth, but in favor of it. Be impatiently very patient. Your impatience should only show your longing. It should not be against your patience; it should be simply a tremendous desire of your being to crystallize, to reach somewhere where life becomes meaningful, blissful, where fear disappears, death disappears, where one becomes acquainted with one's own immortality.

And it is not laziness. It appears so, because you don't see every day new spaces; it almost seems as if you are standing, not moving. In the inner journey this has been felt by many many people, by almost everybody. And the reason is the nature of movement.

You are sitting in a train and the train is moving; h[ow do you] know that the train is moving? Because you cannot see t[he....] the only idea that the train is moving is given to you by [the trees] and the houses and the stations that are passing by on bo[th sides.] They are going in the opposite direction; the faster they ar[e going,] the faster you feel your train is moving.

Just for a moment imagine that your train is moving in a place where there is nothing on either side, you cannot see anything that is moving backwards. Will you feel that your train is moving? For example if the train is moving in the sky – no trees, no houses, no stations – you will not be able to feel the movement of the train. This is the reason why we cannot feel the movement of the earth. It is moving faster than any train, but there is nothing against which you can feel its movement.

In the inner journey this is the problem. You are alone. There are no trees, no stations, no houses; it is just like the sky. How can you feel if there is any movement happening or not? One becomes aware of the movement only when one comes to certain definite spaces which are different from those with which he is acquainted. Then suddenly one realizes that one has moved very fast. In fact, even if in many lives you can achieve enlightenment, it is too early. But I am saying you can achieve it now; all that is needed is that you don't look at things negatively.

Our mind is a very negative phenomenon. Relaxation it will call laziness, deep longing it will call impatience. Always remember mind is negative. It does not know how to say yes. And that is the meaning of trust: saying yes.

You are in a perfectly good situation. Say yes to it, and say yes as deeply and as totally as possible. And any negative thing that mind brings, change it into the positive. It says it is laziness. Tell it, it is not; it is relaxation, it is restfulness. It says it is impatience. Tell it, it is not; it is a great longing, a great passion to realize oneself, to realize one's treasures – not to die without realizing oneself.

And you are asking, "Does he just need a juicy joke?"

That I can do! Whenever it needs any juicy joke, you bring your donkey to me.

Patrick's wife lived way out in the country and was taken ill one day, shortly before her child was due. It was quite dark when the doctor arrived and he asked, "Where is the little lady?"

Patrick: "She is over there in the barn where she collapsed." With Patrick holding the lamp the doctor set about his job.

"Patrick, you are the proud father of a little boy."

Patrick said, "Doctor, we will have a drink."

"Just a minute, hold the light a little closer. You are the father of two!"

"We will open a bottle," said Patrick.

"Wait!" said the doctor. "Hold the light a little closer. You are the father of three."

"And sure it is going to be a celebration and all," said Patrick.

"Just a minute," said the doctor, "hold the light a little closer."

"I don't want to be difficult, doctor," said Patrick, "but do you think this bloody light is attracting them?"

Children go on coming as the light is coming closer....

Remain joyous, wait with great love. Everything takes its own time, impatience makes no sense. Patience is the way of existence. Remain relaxed, because the more excited you become the farther away is the goal. The experience is going to happen only when you are utterly silent, just a pool of silence...your whole energy so relaxed, as if it is absent.

When you have become just a zero you become a womb. And out of this nothingness is born your original, your authentic reality.

Osho,

I feel that I don't love you enough, don't appreciate you enough, am not open enough. I feel like I am trundling along in a creaky old bullock cart, while you are flying by in all your beauty and grace and vastness. Beloved Osho, I am exasperated by my state of retardation. Why is it that I don't respond?

Prem Veena, it is something intrinsic to love that it always feels it is not enough. Only a small love feels enough. The greater the love, the more you are aware of the feeling that "I don't love enough." That is one of the signs of a great love.

If somebody comes and says to me, "I love you very much – I love you totally," then his love is certainly going to be very small. Otherwise to love totally is a tremendous phenomenon; it will change you entirely.

So there is no need to be worried that your love is not enough. You want to love more, and if your love is great it will never be enough; it will always be something less than you wanted it to be.

And the same is true about appreciation. You say, "I don't appreciate you enough, am not open enough." Just a little appreciation and just a little opening is enough for my purposes. I can sneak in from any small opening! One thing is certain – you are not a China wall.

I can understand. You have been long enough with me and it is natural to expect.... But you don't know how much you have changed. I remember exactly, photographically, the day you came to me. You had not come for yourself, you had come for a totally different reason. You had brought a young man; you had come for him.

He was a complete crackpot; he wanted to live only on water. And because in one of my lectures I had mentioned that I know a man who has lived for many years only on water, you brought that young man – because he was moving from place to place, inquiring for somebody who can teach him the art of how to live on water.

You had not said a single word about yourself. You were only concerned that somehow either he drops this idea or he finds some way – it had become a torture. There are ways people can live… but they need years of training, and they lead nowhere. What is the point? Even if you can live only on water that does not make you spiritual; that does not bring liberation to your being. And it takes fifteen to twenty years' long training to come to the point where you can drop all food, and just air and water are enough for you.

So I told the man, "It is possible and I can give you the address. But if you want my advice I would say don't go there because that man is cracked. You are only half cracked right now; there is still time to come back. What are you going to gain? Why are you obsessed with the idea?" The obsession was that if you live only on pure water and air, you become physically immortal.

I said, "That is nonsense! Many people have lived on water and air and none of them are alive; not a single one has become immortal. If you really want to become immortal, I can show you the way; because it is not a question of becoming immortal, it is a question of discovering. You are immortal already – you are just not aware. Awareness has to be brought…" and just as I was talking to the man about awareness and meditation – he was not interested; he disappeared, he never came again.

But Veena was caught. That was accidental! Since then she has been doing meditation, sometimes successfully, and whenever you succeed in meditation there are moments of failure; there are days and there are nights.

Naturally, after so many years, fifteen or sixteen years, she feels like "I'm trundling along in a creaky old bullock cart, while you are flying by in all your beauty and grace and vastness."

You should be happy, at least you have a creaky old bullock cart! There are millions who don't have even that. And if it is too creaky just ask some Italian sannyasin to make it a little greasy. Sarjano can do it. And to make a flying bullock cart will be a great joy and a miracle – just take a little care with the bullock cart. Anyway it is moving. Or perhaps you would like it to go on being creaky because that gives you the idea that you are moving. But there is no hurry. You need not fly. Sometimes it is dangerous.

Just the other day I received a letter from Canada. A young woman wants to come here, but the problem is she is very much afraid of flying. Now from Canada to here, coming in a creaky old cart will really take so long. So she has asked me, "First help me to get rid of this paranoia. I cannot enter an airplane."

I have all kinds of crackpots all over the world! But they are very nice people. Just a day before another woman from Germany asked – her problem is even more difficult – her problem is that she is afraid to leave her house. "Help me, I want to come to Pune!"

Now this woman who is afraid of flying can have other means suggested to her: trains, cars, buses, a horse; but the woman who is afraid to leave the house.... But I have to suggest something to them – and just because the suggestion is coming from me, it works. It has nothing in it; I just have to invent suggestions: "Just keep an onion in your mouth, and leave the house and no danger will ever happen to you! And when I am suggesting there must be some great secret in onions...soon the woman will be here, because these fears are all just mind-made, mind-manufactured.

There is no fear in flying, there is no fear of coming out of the house; millions of people are coming out of the house every day, and thousands are flying. And the rate of accidents is not much more than the rate of death which naturally happens, so whether you are sleeping on your bed or flying in an airplane does not make any difference. The rate of death is the same.

In fact, on the bed it is more, because 99% of people die on the bed. If somebody wants to be really afraid of any place, it is your bed. Avoid it! Keep it for show but never sleep on it! In the night close the doors and sleep on the floor, because I have never heard of anybody dying on the floor. And there are people who are trying....

My legal secretary Anando sleeps in her bath, just to avoid death! – because nobody has ever died in the bath. She keeps her bed ready; that is just for show. Whenever I ask Shunyo to find her I have to tell her, "Look in her bathroom." And she is sleeping with her blanket and with her clothes in the bathtub. A great device to avoid death!

Veena, don't be exasperated by your state. You are growing. Everybody has his own pace of growth. Some people grow fast, some people grow slowly – whatever is natural to them – and there is no question of superiority or inferiority. But if you ask me I will say you are going perfectly right. You are responding to me as deeply as your nature allows in this moment.

Forcing anything is going against nature. Accepting, relaxing, contented, allowing the flow of nature to take you, is what Lao Tzu used to call 'the watercourse way.' Sometimes the river flows fast. Sometimes it flows very slowly. Sometimes it falls with great speed in waterfalls from the mountains to the plains. But one thing is certain: whether slow, fast or very fast, every river reaches to the ocean.

And it does not matter that somebody reaches a little earlier and somebody reaches a little later. What matters is that one reaches.

Just think of the moment – your joy, your peace, your centeredness. The more you enjoy them, the more they grow, and faster. But don't think in terms of becoming rich very fast. Even if the richness is of the inner world, to become rich fast one has to use wrong means – and in the inner world you cannot use wrong means. That will not be profitable; that will be a loss. In the outside world, if you want to become rich faster then you have to use wrong means.

But to be with me, at least one thing has always to be remembered: we are not looking for any profit, we are not looking for any reward. Our reward is in this moment. Our profit is our joy in this moment.

Farelli came from Italy, opened a restaurant and became very successful. He still practiced the simplest form of bookkeeping. He kept the accounts payable in a cigar box, accounts due on a spindle, and cash in the register. One day his youngest son, who had just graduated as an economics major, said to him, "Pa, I don't see how you run your business this way. How do you know what your profits are?"

"Well, sonny boy," replied Farelli, "when I got off-a the boat I no have nothing but-a the pants I was-a wearing. Just-a the pants.

Today your brother is a doctor, your sister is-a the teacher and you just-a graduate."

"I know, papa, but...."

"Your mama and me have a nice-a car, a nice-a house, a good-a business and everything is-a paid for. So you add all-a that together, you subtract-a the pants and that's-a the profit."

Why get into so much unnecessary detail? That poor Italian was doing very well! Now to count all these things and then to subtract the pants-a...and the remaining is all the profit.

On the path there is no need to keep any accounts. Each moment live totally, joyously, and move on. Don't carry even the memory of that moment: that too becomes a burden, that too prevents you from responding to reality spontaneously. If you want to be spontaneous and responsive then you need a very clean, mirror-like mind. No dust should gather on it.

And Veena, as far as I see you are doing perfectly well. But these are human desires that again and again arise in people – perhaps things can be done better; perhaps rather than going by a bullock cart I can go by an airplane. These ideas simply create anxiety in you and disturb your natural growth.

Live each moment and don't let it gather in your memory. Keep your memory clean.

And everything that you have never imagined, never dreamt of, is going to happen to you.

CHAPTER 5

Just a Little Knack of Losing Yourself

Don't be a tourist, don't be in a hurry.
Sit down and relax.
Gaze into the silence, into the depth,
and allow that depth to enter into your eyes,
so that it can reach to your very being.
A moment comes when the gazer and the gazed become one,
the observer and the observed become one.
That is the moment of meditation.

Osho,

Nietzsche wrote: "He who fights with monsters should look to it that he himself does not become a monster, and when you gaze long into an abyss the abyss also gazes into you." The last phrase seems such a beautiful description of the art of meditation. Would you comment?

*F*riedrich Nietzsche is a strange philosopher, poet and mystic. His strangeness is that his philosophy is not the ordinary rational approach to life; his strangeness is also that he writes poetry in prose. He is also a strange mystic, because he has never traveled the ordinary paths of mysticism. It seems as if mysticism happened to him.

Perhaps being a philosopher and a poet together, he became available to the experiences of the mystic also. The philosopher is pure logic, and the poet is pure irrationality. The mystic is beyond both. He cannot be categorized as rational, and he cannot be categorized as irrational. He is both, and he is neither.

It very rarely happens that a philosopher is a poet also, because they are diametrically opposite dimensions. They create a tremendous inner tension in the person. And Nietzsche lived that tension to its very extreme. It finally led him into madness, because on the one hand he is one of the most intelligent products of Western philosophy, without parallel, and on the other hand so full of poetic vision that certainly his heart and his head would have been constantly fighting. The poet and the philosopher cannot be good bedfellows. It is easy to be a poet, it is easy to be a philosopher, but it is a tremendous strain to be both.

Nietzsche is not in any way mediocre – his philosopher is as great a genius as his poet. And the problem becomes more complicated because of this tension between the heart and the mind. He starts becoming available to something more – more than philosophy, more than poetry. That's what I am calling mysticism.

His statement is of tremendous importance: "He who fights with monsters should look to it that he himself does not become a monster."

I have always been telling you that you can choose a friend without being too cautious, but you cannot afford an enemy without being very alert – because the friend is not going to change you, but the enemy *is* going to change you. With the friend there is no fight, with the friend there is no quarrel; the friend accepts you as you are, you accept the friend as he is. But with the enemy the situation is totally different. You are trying to destroy the enemy and the enemy is trying to destroy you. And naturally you will affect each other, you will start taking methods, means, techniques from each other.

After a while it becomes almost impossible to find who is who. They both have to behave in the same way, they both have to use the same language, they both have to be on the same level. You cannot remain on your heights and fight an enemy who lives in the dark valleys down below; you will have to come down. You will have to be as mean, as cunning as your enemy is – perhaps you will have to be more, if you want to win.

Nietzsche is right. "He who fights with monsters should look to it that he himself does not become a monster. And when you gaze long into an abyss, the abyss also gazes into you."

The second part of the statement is actually the very essence of meditation: it is gazing into emptiness, nothingness, into an abyss. And when you gaze into an abyss it is not one-sided; the abyss is also gazing into your eyes.

When I am looking at you, it is not only that I am looking at you; you are also looking at me. The abyss has its own ways of gazing into you. The empty sky also gazes into you, the faraway star also looks into you. And if the abyss is allowed to gaze into you, soon you will find a great harmony between yourself and the silence of the abyss, you will also become part of the abyss. The abyss will be outside you and also inside you.

What he is saying is immensely beautiful and truthful. The

meditator has to learn to gaze into things which he wants to become himself. Look into the silent sky, unclouded. Look long enough, and you will come to a point when small clouds of thoughts within you disappear, and the two skies become one. There is no outer, there is no inner: there is simply one expanse.

For thousands of years meditators have been gazing at the early sun in the morning, because later it becomes too difficult to gaze into it. But the early sun, just rising above the horizon, can be looked into without any danger to the eyes. And if you allow, then the light and the color that is spread all over the horizon starts spreading within you – you become part of the horizon. You are no longer just a gazer; you have become part of the scenery.

An ancient parable in China is that an emperor who was very interested in paintings, and had a great collection of paintings, announced a great prize for the best painting. All the great painters of the country arrived in the capital and started working.

One painter said, "It will take at least three years for me."

The emperor said, "But I'm too old."

The painter said, "You need not be worried. You can give me the award right now. If you are not certain of your life, I am certain about my painting. But I'm not asking either. I am just saying that I am going to do a job that has never been done. I want to show you what a painting should really be; so forget about your death and forget about the award. You allow me three years and a separate place in the palace. Nobody can come while I'm working; for three years I have to be left alone."

Each day was such an excitement for the emperor. The man was a well-known painter, and not only a painter – he was a Zen master too. Finally those three years passed, and the painter invited the emperor...he took him into the room. On the whole wall he had painted a beautiful forest with mountains, with waterfalls, and a small footpath going round about and then getting lost into the trees behind the mountains.

The painting was so alive, so three-dimensional, that the emperor forgot completely that it was a painting and asked the painter, "Where does this footpath lead to?"

The painter said, "I have never gone on it, but we can go and have a look at where it goes."

The story is that the painter and the emperor both walked on the path, entered the forest, and have not returned since then. The painting is still preserved; it shows the footprints of two persons on the footpath. It seems to be absolutely unbelievable, but the meaning is of tremendous importance.

The painter is saying that unless you can be lost in a painting, it is not a painting. Unless you can become part of the scene, something is dividing you; you are not allowing yourself, totally, to be one with it, whether it is a sunrise or a sunset....

A meditator has to learn in different ways, from different sides of life, to be lost. Those are the moments when you are no more, but just a pure silence, an abyss, a sky, a silent lake without any ripples on it. You have become one with it. And all that is needed is – don't be just a passer-by, don't be a tourist, don't be in a hurry. Sit down and relax. Gaze into the silence, into the depth, and allow that depth to enter into your eyes, so that it can reach to your very being.

A moment comes when the gazer and the gazed become one, the observer and the observed become one. That is the moment of meditation – and there are no more golden experiences in existence. These golden moments can be yours...just a little art, or rather a little knack, of losing yourself into something vast, something so big that you cannot contain it. But it can contain *you*! And you can experience it only if you allow it to contain you.

Friedrich Nietzsche is right; he must have said what he had experienced himself. It was unfortunate that he was born in the West. In the East he would have been in the same category as Gautam Buddha or Mahavira or Bodhidharma or Lao Tzu. In the West he had to be forced into a madhouse.

He himself could not figure it out. It was too much: on the one hand his great philosophical rationality, on the other hand his insights into poetry, and those sudden glimpses of mystic experiences...it was too much. He could not manage and started falling apart. They were all so different from each other, so diametrically opposite...he tried hard somehow to keep them together, but the very effort of trying to keep them together became a nervous breakdown.

The same experience in the East would have been a totally different phenomenon. Instead of being a nervous breakdown, it would have been a breakthrough. The East has been working for thousands of years; its whole genius has been devoted to only one thing, and that is meditation. It has looked into all possible nooks and corners of meditation, and it has become capable to allow poetry, to allow philosophy, without any problem, without any opposition and tension. On the contrary they all become, under meditation, a kind of orchestra – different musical instruments, but playing the same tune.

There have been many misfortunes in the world, but I feel the most sorry for Friedrich Nietzsche because I can see what great potential he had. But being in a wrong atmosphere, having no precedent and having no way to work it out by himself, alone.... It was certainly too much for an individual, for *any* individual, to work it out alone.

Thousands of people have worked from different corners, and now, in the East, we have a whole atmosphere in which any kind of genius can be absorbed. And meditation will not be disturbed by genius; meditation will be enhanced, and his own particular dimension – poetry, literature, science – will also be enhanced.

Nietzsche was just in a wrong place, surrounded by wrong people who could only think of him as mad. And to them, he *appeared* mad.

Two kids were playing on the sea beach. One of them asked the other, "What do you want to be when you grow up?"

He said, "When I grow up I want to be a great prophet. I'm going to speak of profound truths."

The first boy said, "But they say nobody listens to the prophets, so why become a prophet?"

"Ah," he said, "us prophets are very obstinate."

This very obstinacy became a problem, because the whole society was against him, a single man single-handedly fighting for truths which people cannot even understand, but are absolutely ready to misunderstand. If a man is sincere and if he cannot understand a thing he should say, "I do not understand it." But people are not so sincere. When they don't understand a thing they immediately start misunderstanding it. Misunderstanding is their way of hiding their ignorance.

The people who have come to know some truth are certainly obstinate. You can crucify them, but you cannot change their minds. You can throw them into madhouses, but they will go on repeating their insights. Their insights become more valuable than their lives themselves.

The East, at least in the past, has been the best soil for prophets, for philosophers, for poets, for mystics. It is no longer the case, but still something of the past goes on echoing in the atmosphere. The West has corrupted the East too. The West knows the tradition of Socrates being poisoned, it knows Jesus Christ's crucifixion; the East was absolutely innocent. It was an accepted fact that everybody had the right to say his truth. If you don't agree with him, that does not mean that you have to kill him. Don't agree – that is your right; at least we can agree to disagree with each other, but there is no need to bring swords when you don't have arguments. Swords cannot become arguments.

But the atmosphere has been changing for almost two thousand years, since this country became invaded again and again by barbarous, uncivilized, uncultured people who had no idea what philosophy was. And finally, for three hundred years the West has tried in every possible way to corrupt the mind of the East through its educational system – through schools, through colleges, through universities.

Now even in the East crucifixion is possible. Just the other day one of the great Hindu religious leaders, equivalent to the pope of the Catholics, Shankaracharya Swarupananda, was here for a few days. I told Neelam, when she informed me of this, that he would say something against me certainly. But he spoke against me only on the last day, before leaving, so when the information came to me, he had already gone.

What he had spoken against me is so poor that one feels great pity. What has happened to the great philosophical traditions of the East? – and these people represent those traditions. He said about me: "He is the most dangerous man, unparallelled in the history of mankind." He has not given any reason why. To me this is a compliment. But at least I have the right to ask what is the reason for giving me such a great compliment – "unparallelled in the whole history of mankind." And what danger am I?

This was not the way of the East. When I was listening to his statement I remembered about the original *shankaracharya*, Adi Shankaracharya. He is a predecessor of nearly fourteen hundred years ago. He died a young man, he died when he was thirty-three. He created a new tradition of sannyasins, he created four temples in all the four directions, and he appointed four shankaracharyas, one for each direction. I remembered about him that he traveled all over the country defeating great, well-known philosophers – that was in a totally different atmosphere.

One great philosopher was Mandan Mishra; he had a great following. Still in his memory a town exists. I have been there many times. It is on a beautiful bank of the Narmada, one of the most beautiful rivers. That is the place where the river descends from the mountains, so it has tremendous beauty. The city is called Mandala, in memory of Mandan Mishra.

Shankara must have been at the age of thirty when he reached Mandala. Just on the outskirts of the town, by a well, a few women were drawing water. He asked them, "I want to know where the great philosopher Mandan Mishra lives."

Those women started giggling and they said, "Don't be worried, you just go inside. You will find it."

Shankara said, "How will I find it?"

They said, "You will find it, because even the parrots around his house – he has a big garden and there are so many parrots in the garden – they repeat poetries from the *Upanishads*, from the *Vedas*. If you hear parrots repeating, singing beautiful poetries from the Upanishads, you can be certain that this is the house of Mandan Mishra."

He could not believe it, but when he went and he saw, he had to believe. He asked Mandan Mishra – he was old, nearabout seventy – "I have come a very long way from South India to have a discussion with you, with a condition: If I am defeated, I will become your disciple, and if you are defeated, you will have to become my disciple. Naturally, when I become your disciple all my disciples will become your disciples and the same will be true if you become my disciple – all your disciples will become my disciples."

Old Mandan Mishra looked at the young man and he said, "You are too young and I feel a little hesitant whether to accept this challenge or not. But if you are insistent, then there is no way; I have to accept it. But it does not look right that a seventy year old man who has fought thousands of debates should be fighting with a young man of thirty. But to balance, I would suggest one thing" – and this was the atmosphere that has a tremendous value – "to substitute, I will give you the chance to choose the judge who will decide. So you find a judge. You are too young, and I feel that if you are defeated at least you should have the satisfaction that the judge was your choice."

Now where to find a judge? The young man had heard much about Mandan Mishra's wife. Her name was Bharti. She was also old, sixty-five. He said, "I will choose your wife to be the judge."

This is the atmosphere, so human, so loving. First Mandan Mishra gave him the chance to choose, and then Shankara chose Mandan Mishra's own wife! And Bharti said, "But this is not right,

I'm his wife, and if you are defeated you may think it is because I may have been prejudiced, favorable towards my husband."

Shankara said, "There is no question of any suspicion. I have heard much about your sincerity. If I'm defeated, I'm defeated. And I know perfectly well if your husband is defeated, you will be the last person to hide the fact."

Six months it took for the discussion. On each single point that man has thought about they quarreled, argued, quoted, interpreted, and after six months the wife said, "Shankara is declared victorious. Mandan Mishra is defeated."

Thousands of people were listening for these six months. It was a great experience to listen to these two so refined logicians, and this was a tremendous experience, that the wife declared Shankara to be the winner. There was great silence for a few moments, and then Bharti said, "But remember that you are only half a winner, because according to the scriptures the wife and husband makes one whole. I'm half of Mandan Mishra. You have defeated one half; now you will have to discuss with me."

Shankara was at a loss. For six months he had tried so hard; many times he had been thinking of giving up – the old man was really very sharp even in his old age. Nobody has been able to stand against Shankara for six months, and now the wife says his victory is only half. Bharti said, "But I will also give you the chance to choose your judge."

He said, "Where am I going to find a better judge than Mandan Mishra? You are such simple and fair and sincere people. But Bharti was very clever, more clever than Shankara had imagined, because she started asking questions about the science of sex.

Shankara said, "Forgive me, I am a celibate and I don't know anything about sex."

Bharti said, "Then you will have to accept your defeat, or if you want some time to study and experience, I'm willing to give you some time."

He was caught in such a strange situation; he asked for six

months and six months were given. "You can go and learn as much as you can because this will be the subject to begin with, then later on, other subjects. It is not easy," Bharti said, "to beat Mandan Mishra. But that half was easier! I am a much harder woman. If I can declare the defeat of my husband, you can understand that I am a hard woman. It is not going to be easy. If you feel afraid don't come back; otherwise we will wait for six months."

This atmosphere continued for thousands of years. There was no question of being angry, there was no question of being abusive, there was no question of trying to prove that you are right by your physical strength or by your arms or by your armies. These were thought to be barbarous methods; these were not for the cultured people.

Nietzsche was in a very wrong place in a wrong time; he was not understood by his contemporaries. Now, slowly, interest in him is arising; more and more people are becoming interested in him. Perhaps it would have been better for him to delay his coming a little. But it is not in our hands when to come and when to go. And people of his genius always come before their time. But he should have his respected place in the category of the Buddhas. That day is not far away.

When all other so-called great philosophers of the West will be forgotten, Friedrich Nietzsche will still be remembered, because he has depths which have still to be explored, he has insights which have been only ignored; he has just been put aside as a madman.

Even if he is a madman, that does not matter. What he is saying is so truthful that if to get those truths one has to become mad, it is a perfectly good bargain.

Osho,

Recently you spoke about the will to power. You explained the importance of having this will, this longing, to become a master over one's self. You also often declare that every desire is the basic reason for man's frustration. Can you please explain the difference between will and desire?

The difference between will and desire is great, although they appear almost similar.

Desire is always for things. More money, more prestige, more respectability, more knowledge, more virtue, a better place in the afterlife – these are all desires. Desires can be millions, because there are millions of things in the world which can become objects of desire. A desire always needs an object.

Will is not objective; it does not want something else to be added to it. Will is simply your very life force, which wants to assert itself in its totality, in its wholeness, to bring all the flowers that are hidden in you, to be yourself.

The will knows only one thing and that is you and your golden future. You, right now, are only seeds. But you can become great trees, reaching to the stars.

Vincent van Gogh, one of the most significant Dutch painters, was also thought of just like Nietzsche – a madman. He also had to live in a madhouse, and he was not a harmful man; his paintings were just not according to the ideas of people. Strange...in this world you are not even free to paint something according to your own idea, which is not harming anybody.

He had painted his trees so tall that stars were left far behind – they go above the stars. Naturally people used to ask him, "This is sheer madness. Where have you seen these trees going beyond the stars?"

And what was always his answer is immensely significant. He used to say, "To me, trees represent the will of the earth. The earth is trying to reach beyond the stars, and you will see one day that the earth has succeeded. It is just the beginning, that's why you don't see the trees that high. But I can see far away in the future."

But we cannot even forgive poets, we cannot forgive even visionaries for their harmless visions. But what a beautiful idea – that the earth wants to reach beyond the stars. That defines will.

Desire is always for possessions.

Will is always for consciousness.

Will is a life-force, a flame of your very being. It does not want anything else – it simply wants itself to be actualized in its totality. It does not want to remain a seed, it does not want just to remain a dream; it wants to become a reality, it wants to become an actual phenomenon.

I can understand your problem. It may have arisen in many people's minds, because I have always spoken against desire, and while speaking on Friedrich Nietzsche's *Zarathustra* I supported totally his idea of the will.

When on a rosebush flowers blossom, it is the will. They were hidden inside the bush and they were trying to come into manifestation – just as a Gautam Buddha is hidden in you, or a Zarathustra is hidden in you and is trying to come out. You are a seed. Once this idea settles in you, you will find inside the seed a serpent starts uncoiling itself – that is the will. Nietzsche has called it will to power. I myself would like to call it will to realization, will to actualization, will to become absolutely yourself.

Desire is a very dangerous thing, because you can get lost in desire and millions are lost. The jungle of desires is very thick, and there is no end; one after another you will find desires and desires and desires. And no desire is fulfilling. Every desire only gives you a new frustration, every desire gives you a new desire. But this whole process of desiring takes your energy away from becoming a will to realization, a will to bring your potential into flowering, into its ultimate expression.

Desire is going astray from will.

My effort here is to pull you back from your desires to one single-pointed will – the will that wants to know yourself, the will that wants to be yourself, the will that wants whatever is hidden in you to become manifest.

Mendel saves up for years to buy a really fine tailor-made suit, his very first, but after he has been out in it for an hour or so he notices there are things wrong with it. He goes back to the tailor.

"The arms are too long," says Mendel.

"No problem. Just hold your arms out further and bend at the elbows."

"But the trouser legs are too long."

"Right, no problem. Walk with your knees bent."

"The collar is too high; it is halfway up the back of my head."

"Okay. Just poke your head out further."

So Mendel goes out into the world with his first tailor-made suit. As he is passing a couple in the street the woman says, "Look at that poor man, he must have had polio."

The man says, "But what a fine suit he is wearing!"

Your desires may give you a fine suit, but they will also make you suffer from polio; everything will be wrong. Your desires will not allow you to be simply yourself, to be exactly your destiny.

Will is a longing to achieve one's destiny.

CHAPTER 6

Loneliness Is Aloneness Misunderstood

The average American
watches television five hours a day;
people are listening to the radio...
just to avoid themselves.
For all these activities, the only reason is —
not to be left alone; it is very fearful.
And this idea is taken from others.
Who has told you that to be alone is a fearful state?

Osho,

You said the other day that we are born alone, we live
alone and we die alone. Yet it seems as if from the day
we are born, whatever we are doing, whoever we are,
we seek to relate to others; in addition, we are usually
attracted to being intimate with one person in particular.
Would you please comment?

*T*he question that you have asked is the question of every human
being. We are born alone, we live alone, and we die alone. Aloneness
is our very nature, but we are not aware of it. Because we are not
aware of it, we remain strangers to ourselves, and instead of seeing
our aloneness as a tremendous beauty and bliss, silence and peace,
at-easeness with existence, we misunderstand it as loneliness.

Loneliness is a misunderstood aloneness. Once you misunderstand
your aloneness as loneliness, the whole context changes. Aloneness
has a beauty and grandeur, a positivity; loneliness is poor, negative,
dark, dismal.

Everybody is running away from loneliness. It is like a wound;
it hurts. To escape from it, the only way is to be in a crowd, to
become part of a society, to have friends, to create a family, to have
husbands and wives, to have children. In this crowd, the basic effort
is that you will be able to forget your loneliness.

But nobody has ever succeeded in forgetting it. That which is
natural to you, you can try to ignore – but you cannot forget it; it
will assert again and again. And the problem becomes more complex
because you have never seen it as it is; you have taken it for granted
that you are born lonely.

The dictionary meaning is the same; that shows the mind of
the people who create dictionaries. They don't understand at all the
vast difference between loneliness and aloneness. Loneliness is a gap.
Something is missing, something is needed to fill it, and nothing
can ever fill it because it is a misunderstanding in the first place.

As you grow older, the gap also grows bigger. People are so afraid to be by themselves that they do any kind of stupid thing. I have seen people playing cards alone; the other party is not there. They have invented games in which the same person plays cards from both sides.

Somehow one wants to remain engaged. That engagement may be with people, may be with work.... There are workaholics; they are afraid when the weekend comes close – what are they going to do? And if they don't do anything, they are left to themselves, and that is the most painful experience.

You will be surprised to know that it is on the weekends that most of the accidents in the world happen. People are rushing in their cars to resort places, to sea beaches, to hill stations, bumper to bumper. It may take eight hours, ten hours to reach, and there is nothing for them to do because the whole crowd has come with them. Now their house, their neighborhood, their city is more peaceful than this sea resort. Everybody has come. But *some* engagement....

People are playing cards, chess; people are watching television for hours. The average American watches television five hours a day; people are listening to the radio...just to avoid themselves. For all these activities, the only reason is – not to be left alone; it is very fearful. And this idea is taken from others. Who has told you that to be alone is a fearful state?

Those who have known aloneness say something absolutely different. They say there is nothing more beautiful, more peaceful, more joyful than being alone.

But you listen to the crowd. The people who live in misunderstanding are in such a majority, that who bothers about a Zarathustra, or a Gautam Buddha? These single individuals can be wrong, can be hallucinating, can be deceiving themselves or deceiving you, but millions of people cannot be wrong. And millions of people agree that to be left to oneself is the worst experience in life; it is hell.

But any relationship that is created because of the fear, because of the inner hell of being left alone, cannot be satisfying. Its very root is poisoned. You don't love your woman, you are simply using her not to be lonely; neither does she love you. She is also in the same paranoia; she is using you not to be left alone.

Naturally, in the name of love anything may happen – except love. Fights may happen, arguments may happen, but even they are preferred to being lonely: at least somebody is there and you are engaged, you can forget your loneliness. But love is not possible, because there is no basic foundation for love.

Love never grows out of fear.

You are asking, "You said the other day that we are born alone, we live alone and we die alone. Yet it seems as if from the day we are born, whatever we are doing, whoever we are, we seek to relate to others."

This seeking to relate to others is nothing but escapism. Even the smallest baby tries to find something to do; if nothing else, then he will suck his own big toes on his feet. It is an absolutely futile activity, nothing can come out of it, but it is engagement. He is doing something. You will see in the stations, in the airports, small boys and girls carrying their teddy bears; they cannot sleep without them. Darkness makes their loneliness even more dangerous. The teddy bear is a great protection; somebody is with them.

And your God is nothing but a teddy bear for grown-ups.

You cannot live as you are. Your relationships are not relationships. They are ugly. You are using the other person, and you know perfectly well the other person is using you. And to use anybody is to reduce him into a thing, into a commodity. You don't have any respect for the person.

"In addition," you are asking, "we are usually attracted to being intimate with one person in particular."

It has a psychological reason. You are brought up by a mother, by a father; if you are a boy, you start loving your mother and you start being jealous of your father because he is a competitor; if you are a girl, you start loving your father and you hate your mother because she is a competitor. These are now established facts, not hypotheses, and the result of it turns your whole life into a misery. The boy carries the image of his mother as the model of a woman. He becomes conditioned continuously; he knows only one woman so closely, so intimately. Her face, her hair, her warmth – everything becomes an imprint. That's exactly the scientific word used: it becomes an imprint in his psychology. And the same happens to the girl about the father.

When you grow up, you fall in love with some woman or with some man and you think, "Perhaps we are made for each other." Nobody is made for anyone. But why do you feel attracted towards one certain person? It is because of your imprint. He must resemble your father in some way; she must resemble your mother in some way.

Of course no other woman can be exactly a replica of your mother, and anyway you are not in search of a mother, you are in search of a wife. But the imprint inside you decides who is the right woman for you. The moment you see that woman, there is no question of reasoning. You immediately feel attraction; your imprint immediately starts functioning – this is the woman for you, or this is the man for you.

It is good as far as meeting once in a while on the sea beach, in the movie hall, in the garden is concerned, because you don't come to know each other totally. But you are both hankering to live together; you want to be married, and that is one of the most dangerous steps that lovers can take.

The moment you are married, you start becoming aware of the totality of the other person, and you are surprised on every single aspect – "Something went wrong; this is not the woman, this is not the man" – because they don't fit with the ideal that you are carrying within you. And the trouble is multiplied because the woman is carrying an ideal of her father – you don't fit with it. You are carrying the ideal of your mother – she does not fit with it. That's why all marriages are failures.

Only very rare marriages are not failures – and I hope God should save you from those marriages which are not failures, because they are psychologically sick. There are people who are sadists, who enjoy torturing others, and there are people who are masochists, who enjoy torturing themselves. If a husband and wife belong to these two categories, that marriage will be a successful marriage. One is a masochist and one is a sadist – it is a perfect marriage, because one enjoys being tortured and one enjoys torturing.

But ordinarily it is very difficult to find out in the first place whether you are a masochist or a sadist, and then to look for your other polarity…. If you are wise enough you should go to the psychologist and inquire who you are, a masochist or a sadist? and ask if he can give you some references which can fit with you.

Sometimes, just by accident, it happens that a sadist and masochist become married. They are the happiest people in the world; they are fulfilling each other's needs. But what kind of need is this? – they are both psychopaths, and they are living a life of torture. But otherwise, every marriage is going to fail, for one simple reason: the imprint is the problem.

Even in marriage, the basic reason for which you wanted to have the relationship is not fulfilled. You are more alone when you are with your wife than when you are alone. To leave husband and wife in a room by themselves is to make them both utterly miserable.

One of my friends was retiring; he was a big industrialist, and he was retiring because of my advice. I said, "You have so much and you don't have a son; you have two daughters and they are married in rich families. Now why unnecessarily bother about all kinds of worries – of business, and income tax, and this and that? You can close everything; you have enough. Even if you live one thousand years, it will do."

He said, "That's true. The real problem is not the business, the real problem is I will be left alone with my wife. I can retire right now if you promise me one thing, that you will live with us."

I said, "This is strange. Are you retiring or am I retiring?"

He said, "That is the condition. Do you think I am interested in all these troubles? It is just to escape from my wife."

The wife was a great social worker. She used to run an orphanage, a house for widows, and a hospital particularly for people who are beggars and cannot pay for their treatment. I also asked her in the evening, "Do you really enjoy all this, from the morning till the evening?"

She said, "Enjoy? It is a kind of austerity, a self-imposed torture."

I said, "Why should you impose this torture on yourself?" She said, "Just to avoid your friend. If we are left alone, that is the worst experience in life."

And this is a love marriage, not an arranged marriage. They married each other against the whole family, the whole society, because they belonged to different religions, different castes; but their imprints gave them signals that this is the right woman, this is the right man. And all this happens unconsciously. That's why you cannot answer why you have fallen in love with a certain woman, or with a certain man. It is not a conscious decision. It has been decided by your unconscious imprint.

This whole effort – whether of relationships or remaining busy in a thousand and one things – is just to escape from the idea that you are lonely. And I want it to be emphatically clear to you that this is where the meditator and the ordinary man part.

The ordinary man goes on trying to forget his loneliness, and the meditator starts getting more and more acquainted with his aloneness. He has left the world; he has gone to the caves, to the mountains, to the forest, just for the sake of being alone. He wants to know who he is. In the crowd, it is difficult; there are so many disturbances. And those who have known their aloneness have known the greatest blissfulness possible to human beings – because your very being is blissful.

After being in tune with your aloneness, you can relate; then your relationship will bring great joys to you, because it is not out of fear. Finding your aloneness you can create, you can be involved in as many things as you want, because this involvement will not anymore be running away from yourself. Now it will be your expression; now it will be the manifestation of all that is your potential.

Only such a man – whether he lives alone or lives in the society, whether he marries or lives unmarried makes no difference – is always blissful, peaceful, silent. His life is a dance, is a song, is a flowering, is a fragrance. Whatever he does, he brings his fragrance to it.

But the first basic thing is to know your aloneness absolutely.

This escape from yourself you have learned from the crowd. Because everybody is escaping, you start escaping. Every child is born in a crowd and starts imitating people; what others are doing, he starts doing. He falls into the same miserable situations as others are in, and he starts thinking that this is what life is all about. And he has missed life completely.

So I remind you, don't misunderstand aloneness as loneliness. Loneliness is certainly sick; aloneness is perfect health.

Ginsberg visits Doctor Goldberg. "Ja, you are sick."
"Not good enough. I want another opinion."
"Okay," said Doctor Goldberg, "you are ugly too."

We are all committing the same kinds of misunderstandings continually.

I would like my people to know that your first and most primary step towards finding the meaning and significance of life is to enter into your aloneness. It is your temple; it is where your God lives, and you cannot find this temple anywhere else. You can go on to the moon, to Mars....

Once you have entered your innermost core of being, you cannot believe your own eyes: you were carrying so much joy, so many blessings, so much love...and you were escaping from your own treasures.

Knowing these treasures and their inexhaustibility, you can move now into relationships, into creativity. You will help people by sharing your love, not by using them. You will give dignity to people by your love; you will not destroy their respect. And you will, without any effort, become a source for them to find their own treasures too. Whatever you make, whatever you do, you will spread your silence, your peace, your blessings into everything possible.

But this basic thing is not taught by any family, by any society, by any university. People go on living in misery, and it is taken for granted. Everybody is miserable, so it is nothing much if you are miserable; you cannot be an exception.

But I say unto you: You can be an exception. You just have not made the right effort.

Osho,

The other day, you talked about the third eye as a door for connecting with you and existence. Whenever I feel open, flowing, connecting with you, other people, nature or myself, I mostly feel it in my heart as silence and expanding spaciousness, and sometimes as radiating light. Beloved Osho, is this the same kind of experience you were talking about, or is there a difference between connecting through the third eye or the heart; or are there different stages?

What you are experiencing is in itself valuable, but it is not the experience of the third eye. The third eye is a little higher than your experience.

The way the mystics in the East have categorized the evolution of consciousness is in seven centers. Your experiences belong to the fourth center, the heart. It is one of the most important centers, because it is exactly in the middle. Three centers are below it and three centers are above it. That's why love is such a balancing experience.

Your description is, "Whenever I feel open, flowing, connecting with you, other people, nature or myself, I mostly feel it in my heart as silence and expanding spaciousness, and sometimes as radiating light. Is this the same kind of experience you were talking about?"

I was talking about the third eye, which is above the heart. There are three centers above the heart. One is in your throat, which is the center of creativity; one is between your two eyebrows, exactly in the middle, which is called the third eye. Just as you have two eyes to know the outside world...the third eye is only a metaphor, but the experience is knowing oneself, seeing oneself.

The last center is sahasrar, the seventh; that is at the top of your head. As consciousness goes on moving upwards, first you know yourself, and in the second step you know the whole universe; you know the whole and yourself as part of it.

In the old language, the seventh is "knowing God," the sixth is "knowing yourself," the fifth is "being creative," and the fourth is "being loving, sharing and knowing others." With the fourth, your journey becomes certain; it can be guaranteed that you will reach the seventh. Before the fourth, there is a possibility you may go astray.

The first center is the sex center, which is for reproduction – so that life continues. Just above it...the sex energy can be moved upwards, and it is a great experience; for the first time you find yourself self-sufficient.

Sex always needs the other. The second center is the center of contentment, self-sufficiency: you are enough unto yourself. At the third center you start exploring – who are you? who is this self-sufficient being? These centers are all significant....

The moment you find who you are, the fourth center opens and you find you are love.

Before the fourth the journey has started, but there is a possibility you may not be able to complete it. You can go astray. For example, finding yourself self-sufficient, contented, you can remain there; there is no need to do anything anymore. You may not even ask the question, "Who am I?" The sufficiency is so much that all questions disappear.

A master is needed in these moments, so that you don't settle somewhere in the middle without reaching the goal. And there are beautiful spots to settle...feeling contented, what is the need to go on? But the master goes on nagging you and wants you to know who you are; you may be contented, but at least know who you are. The moment you know who you are, a new door opens, because you become aware of life, of love, of joy. You can stay there; it is so much, there is no need to move any more. But the master goads you on, "Move to the fourth! Unless you find the purest energy of love, you will not know the splendor of existence."

After the fourth, you cannot go astray. Once you have known the splendor of existence, creativity arises on its own. You have known beauty; you would like to create it also. You want to be a creator. A tremendous longing for creativity arises. Whenever you feel love, you always feel creativity just as a shadow coming with it. The man of creativity cannot simply go on looking outside. There is much beauty outside...but he becomes aware that just as there is an infinite sky outside, to balance it there must be the same infinity inside.

If a master is available, it is good; if he is not available, these experiences will lead you onwards.

Once your third eye is opened, and you see yourself, the whole expanse of your consciousness, you have come very close to the temple of God; you are just standing on the steps. You can see the door and you cannot resist the temptation to go inside the temple and see what is there. There you find universal consciousness, there you find enlightenment, there you find ultimate liberation. There you find your eternity.

So these are the seven centers – just arbitrarily created divisions, so the seeker can move from one to another in a systematic way; otherwise, there is every possibility, if you are working by yourself, to get muddled. Particularly before the fourth center there are dangers, and even after the fourth center....

There have been many poets who have lived at the fifth center of creativity and never gone ahead – many painters, many dancers, many singers who created great art, but never moved to the third eye.

And there have been mystics who have remained with the third eye, knowing their own inner beauty; it is so fulfilling that they thought they had arrived. Somebody is needed to tell you that there is still something more ahead; otherwise, in your ignorance, what you will do is almost unpredictable.

Mike had decided to join the police force and went along for the entrance examination. The examining sergeant, realizing that the prospective recruit was an Irishman, decided to ask him a simple question. "Who killed Jesus Christ?" he asked.

Mike looked worried and said nothing, so the sergeant told him not to worry and that he could have some time to think about it. Mike was on his way home when he met Paddy.

"Well," said Paddy, "are you a policeman yet?"

"Not only that," says Mike, "but I am on my first case."

Man is such that he needs someone who has known the path and knows the pitfalls, knows the beautiful spots where one can remain stuck, and has compassion enough to go on pushing you – even against you – until you have reached to the final stage of your potentiality.

CHAPTER 7

Love: The Purest Power

To me God is only a symbol
and love is a reality.
God is only a myth —
love is the experience of millions of people.
God is only a word,
but love can become a dance in your heart.

Osho,

When you spoke about Nietzsche's concept of will, it was so much the opposite pole to the concept of will that the Nazis developed from the same source, and that is still so prevalent in the west. Could you speak about the difference?

*P*rem Pankaja, it is the destiny of the genius to be misunderstood. If a genius is not misunderstood, he is not a genius at all. If the common masses can understand, that means the person is speaking at the same level where ordinary intelligence is.

Friedrich Nietzsche is misunderstood, and out of this misunderstanding there has been tremendous disaster. But perhaps it was unavoidable. To understand a man like Nietzsche you have to have at least the same standard of consciousness, if not higher.

Adolf Hitler is so retarded that it is impossible to think that he can understand the meaning of Nietzsche; but he became the prophet of Nietzsche's philosophy. And according to his retarded mind he interpreted – not only interpreted, but acted according to those interpretations – and the second world war was the result.

When Nietzsche is talking about "will to power," it has nothing to do with will to dominate. But that is the meaning the Nazis had given to it.

"The will to power" is diametrically opposite to the will to dominate. The will to dominate comes out of an inferiority complex. One wants to dominate others, just to prove to himself that he is not inferior – he is superior. But he needs to prove it. Without any proof he knows he is inferior; he has to cover it up by many, many proofs.

The really superior man needs no proof, he simply is superior. Does a roseflower argue about its beauty? Does the full moon bother about proving its gloriousness? The superior man simply knows it, there is no need for any proof; hence he has no will to dominate.

He certainly has a "will to power," but then you have to make a very fine distinction. His will to power means: he wants to grow to his fullest expression.

It has nothing to do with anybody else, its whole concern is the individual himself. He wants to blossom, to bring all the flowers that are hidden in his potential, to rise as high as possible in the sky. It is not even comparative, it is not trying to rise higher than others – it is simply trying to rise to its fullest potential.

"Will to power" is absolutely individual. It wants to dance to the highest in the sky, it wants to have a dialogue with the stars, but it is not concerned with proving anybody inferior. It is not competitive, it is not comparative.

Adolf Hitler and his followers, the Nazis, have done so much harm to the world because they prevented the world from understanding Friedrich Nietzsche and his true meaning. And it was not only one thing; about every other concept too, they have the same kind of misunderstanding.

It is such a sad fate, one which has never befallen any great mystic or any great poet before Nietzsche. The crucifixion of Jesus or poisoning of Socrates are not as bad a fate, as that which has befallen Friedrich Nietzsche – to be misunderstood on such a grand scale that Adolf Hitler managed to kill more than eight million people in the name of Friedrich Nietzsche and his philosophy. It will take a little time…. When Adolf Hitler and the Nazis and the second world war are forgotten, Nietzsche will come back to his true light. He *is* coming back.

Just the other day, sannyasins from Japan informed me that my books are selling in their language at the highest rate and next to them are Friedrich Nietzsche's – his books are also selling. And just a few days earlier the same information came from Korea. Perhaps people may be finding something similar in them.

But Friedrich Nietzsche has to be interpreted again, so that all the nonsense that has been put, by the Nazis, over his beautiful philosophy can be thrown away. He has to be purified, he needs a baptism.

Little Sammy tells his grandfather about the great scientist, Albert Einstein, and his theory of relativity.

"Ah yes," says the grandfather, "and what does the theory have to say?"

"Our teacher says that only a few people in the whole world can understand it," the boy explains, "but then she told us what it means. Relativity is like this: if a man sits for an hour with a pretty girl, it feels like a minute; but if he sits on a hot stove for a minute, it feels like an hour – and that's the theory of relativity."

Grandpa is silent and slowly shakes his head, "Sammy," he says softly, "from this your Einstein makes a living?"

People understand according to their own level of consciousness.

It was just a coincidence that Nietzsche fell into the hands of the Nazis. They needed a philosophy for war, and Nietzsche appreciates the beauty of the warrior. They wanted some idea for which to fight, and Nietzsche gave them a good excuse – for the superman.

Of course, they immediately got hold of the idea of superman. The Nordic German Aryans were going to be Nietzsche's new race of man, the superman. They *wanted* to dominate the world, and Nietzsche was very helpful, because he was saying that man's deepest longing is "will to power." They changed it into will to dominate.

Now they had the whole philosophy: the Nordic German Aryans are the superior race because they are going to give birth to the superman. They have the will to power and they will dominate the whole world. That is their destiny – to dominate the inferior human beings. Obviously, the arithmetic is simple: the superior should dominate the inferior.

These beautiful concepts...Nietzsche could not ever have imagined they would become so dangerous and such a nightmare to the whole of humanity. But you cannot avoid being misunderstood, you cannot do anything about it.

A drunk who smelt of whiskey, cigars, and a cheap perfume,

staggered up the steps into the bus, reeled down the aisle, then plopped himself down on a seat next to a Catholic priest.

The drunk took a long look at his offended seat partner and said, "Hey father, I have got a question for you. What causes arthritis?"

The priest's reply was cold and curt, "Amoral living," he said, "too much liquor, smoking and consorting with loose women."

"Well, I'll be damned!" said the drunk.

They rode in silence for a moment. The priest began to feel guilty, that he had reacted so strongly to a man who obviously needed Christian compassion. He turned to the drunk and said, "I am sorry, my son. I did not mean to be harsh. How long have you suffered from this terrible affliction of arthritis?"

"My affliction?" the drunk said, "I don't have arthritis. I was just reading in the paper that the pope had it."

Now, what can you do? Once you have said something, then it all depends on the other person, what he is going to make of it.

But Nietzsche is so immensely important that he has to be cleaned of all the garbage that the Nazis have put on his ideas. And the strangest thing is that not only the Nazis but other philosophers around the world have also misunderstood him. Perhaps he was such a great genius that your so-called great men also were not able to understand him.

He was bringing so many new insights into the world of thinking, that even just a single insight would have made him one of the great philosophers of the world – and he has *dozens* of insights which are absolutely original, which man has never thought about. If rightly understood, Nietzsche certainly could create the atmosphere and the right soil for the superman to be born. He can help humanity to be transformed.

I have tremendous respect for the man, and also a great sadness that he was misunderstood – not only misunderstood, but forced into a madhouse. The doctors declared that he was mad. His insights were so far away from the ordinary mind that the ordinary mind felt very happy in declaring him mad: "If he is not mad, then we are too ordinary." He has to be mad, he has to be forced into a madhouse.

My own feeling is, he was never mad. He was just too much ahead of his time, and he was too sincere and too truthful. He said exactly what he experienced without bothering about politicians, priests and other pygmies. But these pygmies are so many and this man was so alone, that they would not hear that he was not mad. And the proof that he was not mad is his last book, which he wrote in the madhouse.

But I am the first man who is saying that he was not mad. It seems that this whole world is so cunning, so politically minded, that people say only things that bring reputation to them, which bring applause from the crowd. Even your great thinkers are not very great.

The book that he wrote in the madhouse is his greatest work, and is an absolute proof because a mad man could not write it. His last book is *The Will To Power*. He did not see it printed, because who is going to print a madman's book? He knocked on many publishers' doors, but was refused – and now everybody agrees that that is his greatest work. After his death, his sister sold the house and other things to publish the book, because that was his last desire, but he did not see it in print.

Was he mad? or are we living in a mad world? If a madman can write a book like, *The Will To Power*, then it is better to be mad than to be sane like Ronald Reagan, who is piling up nuclear weapons – there are thousands of people employed in creating nuclear weapons twenty-four hours a day. You call this man sane, and you call Friedrich Nietzsche mad?

An old Indian was sitting in a bar, when a long-haired, bearded, dirty hippie stormed into the bar and ordered a drink. The hippie's raunchy insults drove everyone else out of the bar, but the old Indian sat calmly watching. Finally the old hippie turned to him and said,

"Hey, red man, why the hell are you staring at me? Are you crazy, or something?"

"No," the Indian replied, "twenty years ago I was arrested for making love to a buffalo. I thought you might be my son."

Osho,

When you talked about the superman, you said, that the camel has to become a lion. I feel very attracted to that lion, but I am still afraid to get in contact with it. I have the feeling the lion in me has something to do with my power. How can I use my power without losing my love? How can I use my power and still stay with an open heart? To me, love and power seem to be contradictory. Is this so? Can you say something about this, please?

The question that you are asking is exactly the same as the question that Pankaja asked. You also have the same misunderstanding, although it is not related to Friedrich Nietzsche.

You are basically asking, "How can I use my power without losing my love? How can I use my power and still stay with an open heart? To me, love and power seem to be contradictory."

That's your misunderstanding.

Love and power are not contradictory.

Love is the greatest power in the world.

But you have to understand again: by power I don't mean power over others. Power over others is not love; power over others is pure hate, it is poison, it is destructive.

But to me, and to anyone who knows, love itself is power – and the greatest power, because there is nothing more creative than love. There is nothing more fulfilling than love, there is nothing more nourishing than love. When you are in love, all fears disappear, and when you become love yourself, even death becomes irrelevant.

Jesus is not very far away from the truth when he says, "God is love." Certainly God is power, the greatest power. I want to improve upon Jesus: I don't say God is love, I say *love is God*. To me God is only a symbol and love is a reality.

God is only a myth – love is the experience of millions of people.

God is only a word, but love can become a dance in your heart.

Your misunderstanding is that you think power means power over others. And it is not only your misunderstanding, Dhyan Agni, it is the misunderstanding of millions of people. And because of this misunderstanding they destroy the whole beauty of love. Instead of creating a paradise out of it, they create a hell for each other, because everybody is trying to dominate everybody else in the name of love – but deep down is the desire to dominate.

Love in itself is unconditional. It knows only giving, sharing; it does not know any desire for getting something in return. It does not ask for any response. Its joy and its reward is in sharing. And its power is in its sharing. It is so powerful that it can go on sharing with millions of people, and still the heart remains overflowing with love – it is inexhaustible. That is its power.

You are asking, "How can I use my power without losing my love?" If you want to dominate, then certainly you will have to lose your love. But if you want to love, you can love as powerfully as you want.

There is no contradiction between power and love. If there is a contradiction between power and love, then love will become powerless, it will become impotent, uncreative, weak; power will become dangerous, destructive – it will start to enjoy torturing people.

Love and power separate are the misery of the world. Love and power together, as one energy, can become a great transformation.

Life can become a blissfulness. And it is only a question of dropping a misunderstanding.

It is just as if you were thinking two plus two is equal to five, and then somebody points out to you that you are calculating wrongly: two plus two is not five, two plus two is four. Do you think many austerities will be needed to change your misconception? Will you have to stand on your head for hours to change your idea that two and two are four, or five? Or you will have to go on a fast unto death to change your misconception? Or you will have to renounce the world and all its pleasures because your calculation is wrong and you have to purify your soul first; otherwise how can you calculate rightly?

These are simple calculations, and a man of understanding can change them within a second. It is just a question of seeing where you have gone astray. Bring yourself back.

"I had the strangest dream last night," a man was telling his psychiatrist. "I saw my mother, but when she turned around to look at me, I noticed she had your face. As you can imagine, I found this very disturbing; and in fact I woke up immediately and could not get back to sleep. I just lay there in bed waiting for the morning to come and then I got up, drank a coke and came right over here for my appointment. I thought you could help me explain the meaning of this strange dream."

The psychiatrist was silent for a few moments before responding, "A coke? You call that breakfast?"

The poor fellow has come to understand the dream, why his mother's face has turned into his psychiatrist's face; but that is not the problem to the psychiatrist. To him the problem is: "A coke? You call that breakfast?"

But just watch people talking, and you will be amazed — everywhere there is misunderstanding. You are saying something, something else is understood; somebody else is saying something, you understand something else.

The world would be a more silent and peaceful place if people were saying only five percent of what they are saying now – although that five percent will cover absolutely everything that is essential. And I am not taking a very minimum point, that is the maximum. You can try it: speak only the essential, as if you are giving a telegram, so you have to go on choosing just ten words. And have you watched? Your telegram means more than your long letter, condensed. Be telegraphic and you will be surprised that in the whole day there are very few times when you have to speak.

One retired mathematician used to live in my neighborhood in a city. His whole life he had been a teacher, and it was very difficult for him to suffer retirement. His wife had not been on talking terms with him for years; "Because," she said, "He is such a bore! It is better not to talk with him. He immediately goes into mathematics."

No other neighbor was welcoming to him; one of my neighbors was worried about me because he used to come to me for hours. He was worried that that old fellow must be torturing me. He came to give me a suggestion.

He said, "I give you a suggestion how to get rid of this old man. Whenever you see him coming, just take your umbrella, stand on the door as if you are going somewhere, and he will ask, 'Where are you going?' and you can say that you are going somewhere."

I said, "You don't know that man! If I say I am going somewhere, he will say, 'I'm coming along,' and that will be more torturous. It is better here. And it is not a torture, I enjoy it, because I have nothing to say, I simply sit silently. He alone does everything. He talks and he goes on and on, and finally he thanks me and says, 'You are such a good conversationalist.' and I say, 'I am nothing compared to you, but I am learning just a little bit from you.'"

People don't want you to speak, they want you to listen. And if you learn a simple art of listening to people, so much misunderstanding in the world will be avoided.

The very elderly couple were listening to a religious revival on the radio. The preacher ended his stirring speech by saying, "God wants to heal you all. Just stand up, put one hand on the radio, then place the other on the part of the body that is sick."

The old woman tottered to her feet, put one hand on the radio and the other on her arthritic leg. The old man put one hand on the radio and one hand on his genitals.

The old woman snapped at him, "Fred! This preacher said God would heal the sick, not raise the dead!"

But you cannot avoid being misunderstood.

I don't know who has given you the idea that love and power are contradictory. Change it, because changing it will change you and your whole life.

Love is power, the purest power and the greatest power: Love is God. Nothing can be higher than that. But this power is not a desire to enslave others, this power is not a destructive force.

This power is the very source of creation.

This power is creativity.

And this power will transform you totally into a new being. It has no concern with anybody. Its whole concern is to bring your seeds to their ultimate flowering.

CHAPTER 8

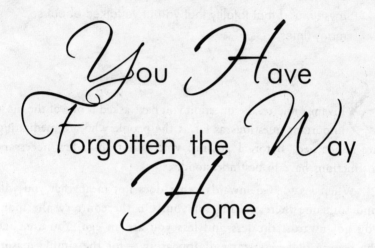

You Have Forgotten the Way Home

Happiness has not to be found somewhere else;
it was always with you,
but the cloud of suffering was covering it.
Happiness is our nature.
To say it in other words:
for suffering you have to make much effort,
for happiness you don't have to make any effort.
Just stop making the effort to create suffering.

Osho,

In my meditations, as I try to look more and more inside, I often feel that there is nobody. It is like falling into an endless black gap. And I feel a lot of tension, and wanting to run away. If there is no me inside, then whom should I love? Please help me find that love for myself, and that totality that you have talked about so many times.

Shivam Annette, the question you have asked is one of the most important questions as far as the people who are meditating are concerned. Before I go into your question, a few necessary distinctions have to be understood.

When I say, "Go inwards," that does not mean that you will find someone there waiting for you. On the contrary, the more you go inwards, the less and less you are an ego. You are, but the feeling of I-ness starts disappearing – for the simple reason that the I can exist only in reference to Thou. If the Thou is not present, the I starts melting.

Outside you are confronted with many Thous, they keep your I alive. But inside, there is no Thou; hence, there can be no I. That does not mean that you are not. It simply means you are in your purity – not in reference to somebody else, but just yourself, without any reference, in your absolute aloneness. Because our whole life we live as an ego, as an I, this disappearance of the I naturally creates fear and an effort to run away. Although it is natural, it is not right.

You have to go through this fear, darkness, anxiety, tension, because your I is dying. Up to now, you have remained identified with the I, so it seems as if you are dying. But just look at a single point: you are watching fear, you are watching the disappearance of I, you are watching tension, you are watching blackness, darkness, you are watching a feeling of nobodiness. This watcher is you.

Going inwards is to find the witness in its absolute purity, unpolluted by anything – just a pure mirror, not reflecting anything. If mirrors were thinkers – fortunately they are not – and if they were brought up always with somebody looking in them, that would have given them an idea of who they are. And for many years, always reflecting somebody, they would have created a certain image of themselves – that they are the reflectors.

Just visualize that one day suddenly nobody reflects in the mirror. The mirror will feel fear. The mirror will feel as if he is falling into a deep abyss, dark, dismal, into non-existence – who is he? His identity is lost just because nobody is looking in the mirror. The mirror has not changed, in fact the mirror is pure. But with this purity he has never been acquainted; nobody has introduced him to this purity.

Meditation takes you to your purity.

Your purity is witnessing, watching, awareness.

You have not asked, "Who is the watcher?" You are asking, "I find there is nobody."

Who finds it? – that's you! You will find nothingness, you will find nothing reflected in you; you will find emptiness. You have to change your focus from the object to your subjectivity. One thing is certain: the witness is present, and the inward journey is to find the witness – is to find the pure mirror of your being.

You say, "In my meditations, as I try to look more and more inside, I often feel that there is nobody." But you are not conscious at all that *you* are finding that there is nobody. But you are! Do you think you are going to meet yourself as somebody? Do you think you are going to meet somebody who will say, "Hello, Shivam Annette, how do you do?" That will really freak you out – "My God, I'm not one, I'm two!"

This feeling that there is nobody is absolutely right. You are on the right track. Just go on being alert that you are still there, watching. All these are objects – the nobody, the darkness, the fear, the tension…. "It is like falling into an endless black gap. And I feel a lot of tension and wanting to run away."

Watch all these things. They are just your old habits. You have never been into your own depths; hence the fear of the unacquainted, of the unknown. You have always been going around and around – but outside – and you have even forgotten the path to your inner home. In the beginning it will look like an endless black gap. Allow it. Blackness has a beauty of its own. Blackness is deep, is silent – enjoy it! There is no need to run away from it.

"If there is no me inside, then whom should I love?"

There is certainly no me inside anyone. But there is something else far more important: there is something which can only be called your am-ness, your is-ness – just your pure existence.

You call it *me*, because outside you need to refer to yourself.

Have you watched small babies? In the beginning they often refer to themselves by their name, "Johnny is hungry." They are far more accurate. But in a society they will be thought to be insane. "Johnny is hungry?" Why don't you say, "I'm hungry" "Johnny" gives the idea that somebody else is hungry. Johnny is your name to be used by others. You cannot use it when you are referring to yourself. Then you have to refer to yourself as 'I', 'me', but not your name."

It happened in Thomas Alva Edison's life...he was one of the greatest scientists. As far as numbers of inventions are concerned he is unparalleled – he invented one thousand things. It is almost impossible to find a thing which is not invented by Thomas Alva Edison. He was so much respected that nobody mentioned his name, just out of respect. His colleagues called him Professor, his students called him Sir, and obviously he didn't use his own name.

Then came the first world war, and for the first time rationing was introduced, and he went to the rationing shop. There was a queue; he was standing in the queue and when the man in front of him had left, the clerk shouted loudly, "Who is Thomas Alva Edison?" And Thomas Alva Edison looked here and there, where is Thomas Alva Edison? The clerk was also a little puzzled, because this man ought to be Thomas Alva Edison; it was his number. And the whole queue was also puzzled. They were looking at each other, what is the matter?

Finally one man from the back of the queue said to him, "Sir, as far as I remember, I have seen you. You are Thomas Alva Edison."

And Edison said, "If you say so, perhaps I am."

The clerk said, "Are you insane or what?"

He said, "Not insane, but I have not heard this name for almost thirty years. I have forgotten it. Nobody calls me by the name. My father died when I was very young, my mother died. Now it is a far, faraway memory. I can remember that something like Thomas Alva Edison used to be my name, but for thirty years nobody has mentioned it. It is good that that man recognized me; otherwise I don't think that on my own I would have been able to recognize it myself."

It is a rare case, but thirty years is a long time, particularly for a man like Edison whose life is so full of creativity. His thirty years are almost three hundred years in your life.

It is simply a social invention that you refer to others by their name, and you refer to yourself by I, me. But inside there is no other, and with the other gone, the me, the I, is gone.

But there is no need to worry. You will not find your I, but you will find something greater: you will find your is-ness, your existence, your being.

When I say "Love yourself," this is for those who have never gone inside, because they can always…they are bound to understand only a language of duality. Love yourself – that means you are dividing yourself into two, the lover and the loved. You may not have thought about it, but if you go inside you will not love yourself, you will be love.

You will be simply the energy called love.

You will be loving; you will radiate love. Love will be your fragrance.

Goldstein, who looked Jewish, was walking down a street in Berlin just before the war, when he accidentally collided with a stout Nazi officer.

"Schwein," bellowed the Nazi.

"Goldstein," replied the Jew with a courteous bow.

Sometimes you may need your name also; life gives strange situations. Goldstein did well. Rather than being offended, he introduced himself, just as the Nazi had introduced himself. But all these names can be used only on the outside.

Inside you are nameless, you are egoless. Inside you are just a pure existence – and out of that pure existence arises the aroma of love.

Osho,

Being with you, seeing your beauty, hearing your cozy voice, feeling your presence – this all uncovered again the deep longing in me for that which Zarathustra called 'the great noontide'. Is that enough? Does that lead me to the ultimate?

This is not enough. This will not bring you to what Zarathustra calls, "the great noontide", but it is a good beginning.

You are saying, "Being with you, seeing your beauty, hearing your cozy voice, feeling your presence – this all uncovered again the deep longing in me for that which Zarathustra called 'the great noontide'. Is that enough? Does that lead me to the ultimate?"

It is not enough, and it will not lead you on its own to the ultimate. You will have to understand something deeper on each point that you mention. "Being with you" is not enough; you have to be with yourself. Being with me may give you a taste, but that is not going to be enough nourishment. You have to learn, from that – being with yourself.

"Seeing your beauty"...these are good indications, but when are you going to see *your* beauty? I can only be an arrow. But the arrow is always pointing towards your center. The arrow may be beautiful, you may appreciate it, but that was not the purpose of the arrow. The purpose of the arrow was for you to move to where it was pointing.

You have to see *your* beauty.

You have not only to hear my voice; you have to hear the still, small voice of your own being.

It is a good beginning to experience my presence, but one should not stop at it. You have to experience *your* presence. That will bring in you what Zarathustra calls 'the great noontide'.

The master is just a milestone, on every milestone there is an arrow showing you – move on, you are coming closer to the goal. And when you come to the milestone where there is no arrow but zero, you have come home. That is the great noontide.

This is not going to happen just by itself; you will have to move a little, make a little effort. And the effort has to be very relaxed – that is the secret. We know efforts, but they become tensions, anxieties, worries.

You have to learn a different kind of effort – what Lao Tzu calls effortless effort – utterly relaxed, because you are not going anywhere. You are simply relaxing within yourself. You are not going to find some goal, some achievement far away which creates worries – whether you are on the right path or on the wrong path, whether you are moving in the right direction, whether the goal really exists or it is just a fiction that you have heard from others. With me one thing is clear – that you are not a fiction.

God may be a fiction and paradise may be a fiction.

You are a reality.

Relaxing within yourself simply means not going outwards, withdrawing all your energy which generally goes on moving outwards. Don't go anywhere – just be now and here. There is no question of tension, there is no question of any worry.

Silently you will slip into your own being and you will feel a great presence and you will hear a soundless sound – what the Zen people call "the sound of one hand clapping." You will see the most beautiful space which you cannot imagine, which you cannot even dream of. And it is so close by – just at the very center of you.

The journey is small, but it has to be done, and done in such a strange way that there is no doer – almost the way you fall asleep. You cannot be a doer, you cannot make any effort to bring sleep – that will be a disturbance. This entering into your own being and presence is almost like allowing it to happen.

That is the great effort which is effortless, which will bring the noontide and the ultimate experience. In a single word: meditation is equivalent to total relaxation. Just doing nothing, sitting silently, and the grass grows by itself.

> Osho,
>
> One line from Dostoevsky's work has impressed me much in my childhood. He says, "In suffering look for happiness." I used to think that nothing of value could be attained without sacrifice and hard work. After meeting you and drinking your message of love, life, enjoyment and celebration, I realize that my previous idea was quite masochistic and suicidal. I love Dostoevsky and all his works have been of immense value to me. But now I feel there is a depth of sadness in him, which he seems to stop – as if something of the opposite is missing. Could you please shed some light on this?

Fyodor Dostoevsky is a very special case – he was a genius. If one has to decide on ten great novels in all the languages of the world, he will have to choose at least three novels of Dostoevsky in the ten.

His insight into human beings and their problems is greater than your so-called psychoanalysts, and there are moments where he reaches the heights of great mystics. But he is a sick soul; he himself is a psychological case.

He needs all the compassion, because he lived in suffering, utter suffering. He never knew a moment of joy; he was pure anguish, angst. But still he managed to write novels which perhaps are the best in the whole literature of the world. *Brothers Karamazov* is so great in its insights that no *Bible* or *Koran* or *Gita* can be a competitor to it.

And this is the strange fact about him: that he was writing such great insights as if he was possessed, but he himself was living in hell. He created it himself. He never loved anybody, he was never loved by anybody. He never knew that there is something like laughter; he was sickly serious. I don't see that he ever felt even a single moment of blissfulness. There is nobody else in the whole history of man who was so sick, and yet had such clarity about things. He was a madman with a method.

You are saying, "One line from Dostoevsky has impressed me much in my childhood." He says, "In suffering look for happiness."

That statement will appeal to many people because many are suffering, and one can tolerate suffering only if one goes on looking for happiness; if not today then tomorrow, or the day after tomorrow. Suffering can be tolerated only through hope. Then one can suffer his whole life, just looking for happiness.

Your being impressed by the statement is dangerous. One should not look for happiness; one should look for the causes of suffering, because that is the way to come out of suffering. And the moment you are out of suffering there is happiness. Happiness is not something that you have to wait for. You can wait for infinity and happiness will not come to you, unless you destroy the causes of suffering.

I will not agree with the statement. I will say, "In suffering look for the causes of suffering." Don't waste your time about happiness; it is none of your business. You are suffering; suffering is your state. Look what is causing it – jealousy, anger, inferiority complex – what is causing it?

And the miracle is: if you can go into your suffering as a meditation, watching, to the deepest roots of it, just through watching, it disappears. You don't have to do anything more than watching. If you have found the authentic cause by your watching, the suffering will disappear; and if it is not disappearing, that means you are not watching deep enough.

So it is a very simple process and with a criterion: if your watching is deep enough...just the way you pull out a plant to look at its roots, it dies, because the roots outside the earth cannot survive. In the light is their death.

Suffering can exist only if its roots remain in the unconscious of your being. If you go deep down searching and looking for the roots, the moment you become conscious of the roots of suffering, suffering disappears. The disappearance of suffering is what you call happiness.

Happiness has not to be found somewhere else; it was always with you, but the cloud of suffering was covering it. Happiness is our nature.

To say it in other words: for suffering you have to make much effort, for happiness you don't have to make any effort. Just stop making the effort to create suffering.

"I used to think that nothing of value could be attained without sacrifice and hard work." That is the disease Christianity has been spreading all over the world. In fact, everything of authentic value is achieved by relaxation, by silence, by joy. The idea of sacrifice and hard work will create more suffering for you. But once the idea gets settled in your mind, your mind will go on telling you that you are suffering because you are not working hard enough, that your sacrifice is not total.

Hard work is needed to create things. Sacrifice is needed when you have something of value, truth, love, enlightenment. And when there is an attack by the mob on your experience, one is ready to sacrifice, but not to compromise.

Sacrifice is not in *finding* the truth; sacrifice is when you have found it – then you will be in trouble. Sacrifice is not in finding love, but when you have found it you will be in trouble. Then either compromise or sacrifice. The cowards compromise. The people who have guts sacrifice – but sacrifice is not a means to attain anything.

"After meeting you and drinking your message of love, life, enjoyment and celebration, I realized that my previous idea was quite masochistic and suicidal."

It is good that you understood something very significant. All your saints who have been sacrificing and working hard and torturing themselves, are just masochistic and suicidal. And because they are worshipped, they go on continuing more and more masochistic torture to themselves.

And the people who are worshipping them also have the same desire, but not the courage; they also want to be saints, perhaps in a future life. At least in this life they can worship the saints.

The whole past of humanity has been dominated by masochistic, sadistic, and suicidal people. That's why there is so much misery. To be blissful in this world looks as if you are committing a crime; to dance with joy amongst so many dead people all around...you cannot be forgiven.

I have always thought that Christianity became the greatest religion of the world because Jesus was on the cross. Just think, if he was with his girlfriend on the beach there would not have been any Christianity, although he would have enjoyed....

And why did it become the greatest religion? Almost half of humanity is Christian. Because he represents your deepest desire. You also want to be crucified, and in different ways you are crucifying yourself; in the name of duty, in the name of nations, in the name of the religion....

Jesus says, "Everybody has to carry his cross on his shoulders." But why? This will look very awkward – wherever you go you will be carrying your cross. But nobody has objected to it. Nobody has said, "Why?" And if I say that everybody has to carry his guitar they all condemn me! The whole world is against a single man who is not saying anything sick.

This is a sick idea, carrying your cross. Can't you carry anything else? Just a flowerpot? If you are determined to carry...then there are more beautiful things in the world. A cross is not something...just a bamboo flute will do, light in weight. And you can do something with it. You can play on it – a beautiful tune, a song; you can dance. What are you going to do with the cross? – except crucify yourself. So why carry it. Why not crucify it here and now? Unnecessarily carrying such weight....

Jesus was only thirty-three years of age, and he fell three times while he was carrying the cross – the cross was so heavy. And naturally, if it becomes the fashion that everybody has to carry his cross, you will see that people will be carrying heavier and heavier crosses, heavier than everybody else! You will feel embarrassed if you are carrying a small cross – are you childish or what? A heavy cross is needed so that you fall on the road many times and have many fractures....

But Christianity is masochistic. It does not know anything about enjoying life. It knows only about sacrificing life – sacrificing for some stupid fiction. It knows nothing of singing and dancing and celebration.

You say, "I love Dostoevsky and all his works have been of immense value to me. But now I feel there is a depth of sadness in him, which he seems to stop – as if something of the opposite is missing."

There is not only sadness in him, there is absolutely suicidal instinct; he is tired and bored with life itself. In his best book, *Brothers Karamazov*, one of the characters, Ivan Karamazov, makes a very significant statement. Perhaps Dostoevsky himself is speaking through him.

Ivan Karamazov says, "If there is a God and I meet him, I am going to return his ticket and ask him, 'Why did you send me life without asking me? What right do you have? I want to return the ticket to you.'" This is a suicidal instinct.

He lived very miserably and has always written that existence has no meaning, that it has no significance, that it is accidental, that there is nothing to find – no truth, no love, no joy. All his conclusions are wrong. But the man was tremendously capable, a great genius. Even if he writes things which are wrong, he writes with such art and such beauty that millions of people have been influenced by him – just like you, Jivan Mada.

The danger is: the words can be beautiful and the message can be poison, pure poison. His insights are deep – but they are always deep – to find more suffering in life, more misery in life. He is determined in all his works to prove that life is an exercise of utter futility. He influenced the contemporary philosophical movement of existentialism – he became a pioneer.

I also love him, but I also feel sad and sorry for him. He was a man who could have danced, who could have loved, who could have lived with tremendous totality and intensity. But he served death rather than life. Read him – there is nothing better to read – but remember you are reading a psychopath, a man who is deeply sick, incurably sick.

His whole work is just a dark night which knows no dawn.

CHAPTER 9

I Want You to Become the Dance

You should be more concerned
when I am answering the questions, because
they can change your reality.
I have to do both jobs: create the longing,
give a glimpse of the goal,
and then clean the path and grease your parts –
because you have never moved in many many lives,
you are sitting in a junkyard –
to put you back on the wheels and rolling.

Osho,

Nietzsche's maxim: "One is punished most for one's virtues" I see the truth of most clearly in you. But even a man who is virtuous by society's standards is subtly punished too, isn't he? – punished by jealousy and criticism. It is as if one is only meant to strive towards; to attain is an altogether different matter. Is this so?

*F*riedrich Nietzsche's maxim: "One is punished most for one's virtues" has a very deep and different meaning from what you have seen in it.

The man of virtue is not in any way a hypocrite; he is sincere, truthful. Society consists of hypocrites; they want virtue also to be a hypocrisy, and they have created false virtues which have no relation at all to any authentic virtuousness.

The people who conform to the society's idea of virtues are never punished; they are rewarded, they are respected. They are not stoned to death, they are not crucified. They are crowned as saints, as sages, as wise people; every kind of honor is given to them. But the basic condition is that they should conform to the idea of the society. They should not bother whether it is really virtuous; they should not even inquire.

Absolute surrender is needed by the society, a total enslavement. Only then the society gives respectability – only to the slaves, only to those who have committed spiritual suicide. They are not really virtuous people. Just look around in different societies so that you can have a sense of how real virtue and the so-called virtue of the societies are diametrically opposite.

In India you will find Hindu monks all getting fat and ugly because it is thought by the Hindus that to eat milk products is a virtue, because the cow is a holy animal. So the Hindu monk goes on eating milk products, goes on gathering fat – bigger the belly, bigger the saint. If you want to measure the height of the saint you have to measure his belly.

The Jaina monks eat only one time a day – and that too, standing. To make everything as uncomfortable as possible is a virtue. Now I cannot conceive what sin there is in sitting comfortably and eating. And because they have to eat only one time a day, they eat as much as possible – to compensate, because then they have to wait twenty-four hours again. So their bodies become thin and their bellies become big – but it is respected.

One of the sects of the Jainas believes that a saint is perfect only when he starts living naked. But what is the virtue in being naked? All the animals are naked. First these monks torture their bodies in every way. They cannot use anything except their own hands; for eating they will have to make a cup of their hands, they cannot use a plate. That is thought to be renunciation, great renouncing of the world and worldly things.

Then it goes to the extreme of stupidity. They cannot use razor blades, so they have to pull out their hairs with their own hands. It is such an ugly scene. Thousands of people, men, women, children, gather to see – this is a very special occasion, a very holy occasion – when a Jaina monk pulls out his hairs, beard, mustache. Tears are coming from his eyes. He is standing naked, surrounded by people; his whole body is a skeleton except the belly, and all these people are looking at the scene with such respect. They will take those hairs and make lockets of them – they are holy hairs. They will kiss the ground on which the saint was standing – it is holy ground.

But I don't see that there is any virtue in it. Certainly the man who is doing this act, performing this stupidity, is a masochist – and the people who have gathered there to see him do it are certainly sadists. They love to see people being tortured, and when somebody is torturing himself, that is a delicacy. Both are sick. But the masochist becomes a great saint and the sadists become followers.

Authentic virtue is a totally different thing. It needs a deep exploration of your own being, living according to your own insight, even if it goes – and most often it will – against the social norms, the ideals, and the conditioning.

Friedrich Nietzsche is saying, "One is punished most for one's virtues." But the virtues have to be your own, they have to be your own discoveries. And you have to be courageous and rebellious enough to live them, whatever the cost.

Socrates was asked by the judges, "We can forgive you if you stop speaking completely. What you think is truth is not accepted by the people amongst whom you have to live. They are offended by your truth. If you promise – and we can trust you, we know you are a man of your word – if you promise not to speak again, to just be silent, you can save your life."

The answer that Socrates gave is to be remembered forever by all those who, in some way, are interested in truth. He said, "I'm living only to speak the truth. Life was given to me by existence to experience truth, and now I'm repaying life by spreading the truth to those who are groping in the dark. If I cannot speak then I don't see any point – why should I live? My life and my message of truth are synonymous. Please don't try to seduce me. If I am alive I will speak."

The judges were at a loss. One of the judges said, "You are too stubborn, Socrates."

Socrates said, "It is not I who is stubborn; it is truth, it is virtue which is stubborn. Truth knows no compromise. It is better to die than to be condemned forever because I compromised for a small life. I'm already old; death will come anyway. And it is far more beautiful to accept death, because then death also becomes meaningful. I'm accepting it on the grounds that even death cannot stop me from speaking."

Society has virtues. There are hundreds of societies in the world, so naturally there are hundreds of different kinds of virtues. Something is virtuous in one society and the same thing is unvirtuous in another society.

For example, the whole world economy depends on the system of charging interest. A society becomes richer if the money moves faster and does not remain stuck in one hand, but the money can move faster only if there is some incentive. Why should I give my money to somebody else unless I can earn something out of it? Interest is nothing but a strategy to make the money move from one hand to another hand. And the faster the money moves, the richer the society becomes.

Mohammedans are poor because interest is condemned by their religion as a sin. To take interest or to give interest is a great sin. Now Mohammedans can never be rich; or if they become rich, they have to be condemned by the society. They cannot take loans from the banks because interest will have to be paid. Mohammedanism is the world's second largest religion after Christianity, and they have remained poor for a single reason: that interest is thought to be a sin.

No other society thinks interest is a sin. What is the sin in it? You take somebody's money, you have to pay something; otherwise why should he give his money to you? Interest is just a kind of rent. But the Mohammedan considers interest to be so unvirtuous that anybody who commits the sin loses all respect in the society. The same person will gain respect in any other society because he will become richer – and richness is respected.

The vegetarians are not willing to see a simple fact, that not a single vegetarian has received, up to now, a Nobel prize. Forty percent of Nobel prizes go to the Jews, which is simply out of proportion to their numbers; sixty percent go to the rest of the world and forty percent to the Jews alone. And why have vegetarians not been able to find a single Nobel prize? The reason is in their food, because it lacks a few vitamins which are absolutely necessary for intelligence to grow. It is virtuous, in a vegetarian society, not to eat meat – but you are losing your intelligence.

Substitutes could have been found and I have been for thirty years continually telling vegetarians, "You should start eating unfertilized eggs. They are absolutely vegetable because there is no life in them. And they contain all the vitamins that intelligence absolutely needs; otherwise you will remain retarded."

Vegetarians stopped asking me to speak at their conferences; they became my enemies, and I was simply suggesting to them something that is purely scientific and in their favor. But they would rather listen to their tradition; they will not see the facts.

The virtues that society's concepts create are just manufactured by man's mind. If you agree with them you will be rewarded greatly. But what Nietzsche is saying is not about those virtues which are acceptable to any society, but about those virtues which an individual finds in the clarity of his own intelligence, in the silences of his own heart, in the understanding of his own being – and follows them. He will be crucified, he will be stoned to death, because he will not be acceptable to the crowd.

You are saying, "Nietzsche's maxim: 'One is punished most for one's virtues' I see the truth of most clearly in you. But even a man who is virtuous by society's standards is subtly punished too, isn't he? – punished by jealousy and criticism."

No, he is not punished by jealousy or criticism. He is certainly punished by his own virtue – that is another thing – because he will have to do something stupid, he will have to torture himself, he will have to go against his own intelligence. Only then can he fulfill the demands of the society that he should be virtuous.

But these saints and virtuous people are not punished by jealousy and criticism. Criticism is for those who are not following the virtuous; jealousy is for those who are enjoying life and are not being ascetics. The virtuous people are punished, they are punished by their own virtue, but their egos are so immensely satisfied that they are ready to do *anything* – they can even commit suicide.

Jainism is the only religion in the world where even suicide is considered a virtue. Of course it has to be done in a certain methodological way: one has to fast unto death. It is a very torturous, long awaiting, because a healthy person can live without food for ninety days. And those ninety days, continuous hunger and waiting for death…and people around him are singing religious songs and worshipping him. His pictures are printed in the newspapers with great respect, as though he is doing something very spiritual; he is leaving the condemned body. And even today, people do it.

So they *are* punished, but by their own virtue, not by others. Do you think anybody will feel jealous that somebody is committing suicide? Do you think somebody will criticize him? His worshipers will kill whoever criticizes him.

"It is as if one is only meant to strive towards; to attain is an altogether different matter."

That's true. Society talks about, scriptures talk about, great virtues of truth, of love, of silence, of peace, of brotherhood. But they are only to be talked about; you are not supposed to *practice* them. Yes, in the name of love you can kill as many people as you want. Millions of people have been killed in the name of Christian love; millions of others have been killed in the name of peace, by the Mohammedans.

These beautiful words are just decorative. They give you a good feeling that you have such a beautiful philosophy to live by, such beautiful, distant stars to reach – but don't try to reach to those stars, because a man of truth will not be acceptable in society!

The society lives by lies, so many lies that the man of truth is going to expose it – he is a danger. The man of love cannot be acceptable because the society lives by hate: one nation hates another, one religion hates another, one color hates another. There are so many groups, sects, cults and they are all hating each other and are ready to destroy each other. Just talk about love, write about love, but don't practice – because a man of love is dangerous. That means he will be against you whenever he sees any hatred, any anger.

For a man of love, nationality is nothing but a beautiful name for hatred. Religious organizations are nothing but sophisticated ways of hating others who don't belong to your organization, to your herd, to your crowd.

Friedrich Nietzsche is right; his whole life's experience is condensed in that small statement. He suffered for his virtues.

The Italian priest was preaching about sex and morality to his congregation. "Sex is-a dirty", he shouted. "I wanna see only good-a girls today. I wanna every virgin in-a church to-a stand up."

Not a soul moved. Then after a long pause a sexy looking blond holding an infant in her arms got to her feet. "Virgins is-a what I want," said the outraged priest.

"Hey father," she asked, "you expect a two month old baby to stand by herself?"

I was in Greece and one of my sannyasins, Amrito, who was my hostess, told me that virginity is the most important quality preached by the Greek Orthodox church. I said, "But are there virgins in Greece?"

She said, "That is a different matter. I have not come across any virgins."

As a doctrine it is beautiful, but in reality virginity should not be a virtue; it is going against nature. In fact, a man who has any intelligence should not marry a girl who is a virgin; you should expect some experience.

When you employ a servant you ask, "What are your qualifications? Bring all your certificates." You are going to marry a woman for your whole life; you should at least think that if she has remained a virgin that means no man was attracted to her up to now, so why are you being stupid? First ask how many people she has been in love with. The more experienced she is the better companion she will prove to be, because experience is always valuable. Experience is a virtue in every field!

Osho,

Whilst you were speaking on Kahlil Gibran and Zarathustra, your words seemed to penetrate without my interpretation directly to the center of my being. I experienced an attunement, a communion happening as nectar that was filling my being. Sometimes, without sobbing, tears simply poured from my eyes, and after almost every discourse I felt for a long while in touch with something far beyond what I know of as myself. With questions and answers this does not happen. I still feel that special whatever-it-is that comes when sitting with you, but not with the depth of intensity I have just described. What is the difference?

*T*he question you have asked raises many other questions too. I would like to cover all the implications in short, because it is important not only to you but for everyone else here.

The first thing: as far as I am concerned, the question-answer sessions are more significant because they relate to you, they relate to your growth. Certainly you are groping in darkness, trying to find a way. You cannot ask questions of the heights of Zarathustra, of Kahlil Gibran – and I have to answer your reality.

Listening to Zarathustra and Kahlil Gibran is a good and great entertainment: you may sob and you may have tears and you may feel great, but it is all hot air! You remain the same – nothing changes in you. I speak sometimes on Buddha, on Chuang Tzu, on Zarathustra, just to give you an insight into the heights people have reached, just to make you aware of those distant stars. They are not so distant as they look – people like us have reached there. It is within your grasp.

That is the reason why, on Zarathustra and Buddha and Bodhidharma and a thousand others, I have spoken: to create a longing in you. But just the longing is not enough. Then I have to give you the path; then I have to sort out the mess that you are, and put your fragments, which are spread all over the space...to find out where your legs are and where your head is and put them all together, and somehow push you on the path.

The question-answer sessions are concerned with you, your growth, your progress – the place where you are. And the discourses on Zarathustra or Kahlil Gibran are concerned with the places where you should be – but you are not yet there.

So I disagree with you. I can understand that you enjoy the dream that is created when one is hearing about Buddha.... You have nothing to do; you are just listening to great poetry, listening to a great song, listening to great music, seeing a great dance. But you are not singing, you are not becoming the poetry, you are not becoming the dance. And I want you to *become* the dance; I want you to reach to the greatest heights that anybody has ever reached.

So I have to keep a balance, talking about the dreamlands and then talking about the dark caves where you are hiding, very reluctant to come out in the light. You want to hear about light and you enjoy, but you remain hiding in your dark cave. You want to hear about strange lands, beautiful stories and parables, but it is mere entertainment.

You should be more concerned when I am answering the questions, because they can change your reality. I have to do both jobs: create the longing, give a glimpse of the goal, and then clean the path and grease your parts – because you have never moved in many many lives, you are sitting in a junkyard – to put you back on the wheels and rolling.

The second job is difficult, and not very juicy either. But it is absolutely necessary. Secondly, I have to remind you of one thing. When I was speaking on Zarathustra...it is a very complicated affair, because I was not speaking directly on Zarathustra; I was speaking on a Zarathustra who is an invention of Friedrich Nietzsche. All the great insights are given by Nietzsche to Zarathustra.

Zarathustra...many times his original books have been brought to me, and they are so ordinary that I have never spoken on them. Nietzsche has used Zarathustra only as a symbolic figure, just as Kahlil Gibran was using Almustafa, which was a completely fictitious name. Nietzsche has used a historical name, but in a very fictitious way. He is putting his insights into the mouth of Zarathustra.

So first you should remember it is Nietzsche's Zarathustra; it has nothing much to do with the original Zarathustra. And secondly, when I am speaking on it, I don't care what Nietzsche means, and

I don't even have any way to know what he means; the way he used Zarathustra, I am using him! So it is a very complicated story. It is my Nietzsche, and via Nietzsche it is my Zarathustra. So whatever heights you are flying in have nothing to do with Zarathustra.

I have been speaking on hundreds of mystics, but it is always that I am speaking. And I know perfectly well that if by chance, somewhere, I meet these people, they are going to be very angry. They are going to be really enraged and say, "I never meant that." But my problem is, "How can I know what you had meant?" I can only mean what I mean. So whether it is Zarathustra or Buddha or Jesus or Chuang Tzu, once they pass through me they have my signature on them. You are always listening to me.

When I am answering your questions I am more concerned with your growth, with your actual problems; they are more earthly. So don't be deceived; many people have been deceived. I have been reminding you, but people's memories are not great.

I was speaking on Gautam Buddha in Varanasi and one Buddhist, a very renowned scholar in Buddhism, said to me, "I have been reading the same scriptures. But you have revealed such great depths and heights that I was never aware of; you have confirmed my faith in Gautam Buddha."

I said, "If you don't get angry with me...you should confirm your faith in me."

He said, "What?"

I said, "Yes, because whatever you were reading was perhaps exactly what Buddha meant, and the depths and heights I am talking about are *my* experiences."

But what to do? There are idiots all over the world. If you want Buddhist idiots to listen to you, you just have to say the name "Buddha" and that's enough; then you can say anything you want. If you want Hindus to listen to you, you have to talk about Krishna.

I am always talking about myself; I cannot talk about anybody else – how can I? Five thousand years ago, what was Krishna thinking, what was in his mind?...but when they listen to me they think, "My God, we were not aware that Krishna had such depths, such heights." Krishna had nothing. Those heights and those depths are my experiences that I am hanging on anybody; these people function like hooks, I simply hang my idea on them.

And even great scholars...this man was Bhikkshu Jagdish Kashyap; he was dean of the faculty of Buddhism in the University of Varanasi, a very learned man. But when I said this to him, he became a permanent enemy. I said, "What happened to the heights and to the depths?"

People are much more concerned with names. If I say to you that "Zarathustra said this," you listen with great attention. The very name Zarathustra looks so ancient, so prophetic, that he must have said something...and trust me, I know him, he is a poor guy. But don't tell this to anybody! This is just a private conversation with you.

Michelangelo was painting the ceiling of the Sistine Chapel. He was getting tired of lying on his back, so he rolled over and saw an old woman praying, down in the chapel. He leaned over the edge of the scaffold and shouted, "I'm Jesus Christ! I'm Jesus Christ! Listen to me and I will perform miracles!"

The Italian lady looked up and clasping her rosary answered back, "Shut up-a your mouth. I'm talking to your mother!"

Michelangelo must have been thinking that he was joking with the old woman, but he was at a loss when he heard this. Of course, a mother is a mother, and you should not interfere between two old women talking...just go on and play outside!

So don't be disturbed. If you want I can go on talking about any historical, mythological, fictitious figure; I can create my own fictions. Do you think all the stories that I have told you have happened? They should have happened! – they are so significant. But if I tell you that I am just making up this story, you will not be very interested; you will not be flying high.

Once in a while I want you to fly high, but it is just an imaginary flight. Really, I want you to be one day actually on those heights but for that, practical work is needed, pragmatic work is needed.

Just for you to fly a little high....

Goldstein, a string merchant from New York, was trying desperately to sell some of his goods in Alabama, but wherever he went he kept encountering anti-Semitism. In one department store the manager taunted him: "All right, Goldstein. I will buy some of your string – as much as reaches from the top of your nose to the tip of your Jewish prick."

Two weeks later, the manager was startled to receive a shipment containing eight hundred cartons of grade-A string. Attached was a note: "Many thanks for your generous order. Invoice to follow. Signed: Jacob Goldstein, residing in New York, circumcised in Kiev."

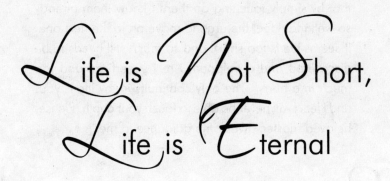

CHAPTER 10

Life is Not Short, Life is Eternal

In existence do you see any hurry?
Seasons come in their time,
flowers come in their time,
trees are not running to grow fast
because life is short.
It seems as if the whole existence
is aware of the eternity of life.

Osho,

You once told me to open all my windows so I could
have the sunrise in the East, and the sunset in the West.
I feel so many possibilities inside me that I often don't
take enough time to explore them in depth; rather, I feel
that by simply touching on them I know them already
so well that I feel the urge to move on to the next one.
It seems life is too short, and so much still needs to be
discovered and developed. Am I superficial and too
much in a hurry? The only continuity in my life is you,
and I feel I will never be able to touch your depth. Please,
beloved master, give some guidance to me.

*E*verybody has to go according to his own heart feeling; if you
feel at ease to move from one thing to another, it is perfectly
right for you. The whole question is that whatever you do should be
a deep pleasure, without any tension. If you force yourself to explore
any possibility more deeply, you may create tension in yourself. If
it feels enough, that touching a certain possibility has given you
enough juice to move on, then move on. Perhaps that is natural;
to you that is your natural pace.

One should never go against one's nature. That is the only sin,
according to me, to go against one's nature; and the only virtue
is to go with your nature in total harmony. And never compare
yourself with others; everybody is different, and everybody's
liking is different. Once you start comparing, thinking that, "Somebody
is going deeper into things, moving more slowly, and I am moving
faster," then tension will arise in you: "Perhaps I am hurrying too
much." All these tensions arise out of comparison.

Remember one thing: You have to be in tune with your own
nature, not in tune with anybody else. So always feel within yourself.
If it is pleasant, do it. If it feels tense, forced, then it is not for you.
Don't do it.

Always go with the river of life. Never try to go against the current, and never try to go faster than the river. Just move in absolute relaxation, so that each moment you are at home, at ease, at peace with existence.

The second thing you have to remember is that life is not short; life is eternal, so there is no question of any hurry. By hurrying you can only miss. In existence do you see any hurry? Seasons come in their time, flowers come in their time, trees are not running to grow fast because life is short. It seems as if the whole existence is aware of the eternity of life.

We have been here always, and we will be here always – of course not in the same forms, and not in the same bodies. Life goes on evolving, reaching to higher stages. But there is no end anywhere, and there has been no beginning anywhere either. You exist between a beginningless life and an endless life. You are always in the middle of two eternities on both sides.

Your conditioning has given you the idea of one life. The Christian idea, the Jewish idea, the Mohammedan idea – which are all rooted in the Jewish conception that there is only one life – has given the West a tremendous madness for speed. Everything has to be done in such a hurry that you cannot enjoy doing it, and you cannot do it in its entire perfection. You somehow manage to do it and rush to another thing.

The Western man has been living under a very wrong conception: It has created so much tension in people's minds that they can never be at ease anywhere; they are always on the go, and they are always worried that one never knows when the end is coming. Before the end they want to do everything. But the result is just the opposite; they cannot even manage to do a few things gracefully, beautifully, perfectly.

Their life is so much overshadowed by death that they cannot live joyously. Everything that brings joy seems to be a wastage of time. They cannot just sit silently for an hour, because their mind is saying to them, "Why are you wasting the hour? You could have done this, you could have done that."

It is because of this conception of one life that the idea of meditation never arose in the West. Meditation needs a very relaxed mind, with no hurry, with no worry, with nowhere to go...just enjoying moment to moment, whatever comes.

In the East, meditation was bound to be discovered, just because of the idea of life's eternity – you can relax. You can relax without any fear, you can enjoy and play your flute, you can dance and sing your song, you can enjoy the sunrise and the sunset. You can enjoy your whole life. Not only that, you can enjoy even dying, because death too is a great experience, perhaps the greatest experience in life. It is a crescendo.

In the Western concept, death is the end of life. In the Eastern concept, death is only a beautiful incident in the long procession of life; there will be many, many deaths. Each death is a climax of your life, before another life begins – another form, another label, another consciousness. You are not ending, you are simply changing the house.

I am reminded of Mulla Nasruddin. A thief entered into his house; Mulla was sleeping, not really, just with closed eyes, in between opening them and seeing what the thief is doing. But he did not believe in interfering in people's work. The thief was not interfering with his sleep, why should he interfere with his profession? Let him do it.

The thief was a little concerned that this man seemed to be strange. As he was carrying everything out of the house, sometimes something fell from his hands and there was noise, but Mulla remained completely asleep. A suspicion arose in the thief's mind that this type of sleep is possible only if a man is awake: "What a strange man that he does not say anything; I'm just emptying his whole house!." All the furniture went out, all the pillows went out, everything that was in the house went out.

And when the thief was collecting everything, binding them to carry home, he suddenly felt, "Somebody is following me." He looked back, it was the same man who was asleep. He said, "Why are you following me?"

Mulla said, "No, I'm not following you; we are changing the house. You have taken everything. Now what am I going to do in this house? So I am also coming."

This at-easeness is the Eastern way; even with death the East has followed the idea…just changing the house.

The thief was worried; he said, "Forgive me, take your things."

Mulla said, "No, there is no need. I was thinking myself to change the house; it is almost in ruins. You can't have a worse house than this, and anyway I am a very lazy man. I need somebody to take care of me, and when you have taken everything, why leave me alone?"

The thief became afraid that…he had been stealing his whole life. He had never come across such a man. He said, "You can take your things."

Mulla said, "No, there is not going to be any change. You will have to carry the things, otherwise I am going to the police station. I am behaving like a gentleman, I am not calling you a thief, but just a man who is helping me to change the house."

There is no hurry, so your idea of a short life is a dangerous idea. That's why even though the East is very poor, there is no despair, there is no anguish. The West is rich, but the richness has not brought anything to its spirituality, or its growth; on the contrary, the West is very tense. It should be more relaxed, it has all the comforts of life.

But the basic problem is that deep down the West knows that life is such a short thing; we are standing in a queue, and every moment we are coming closer to death. Since we were born, we started the journey towards the graveyard. Every moment life is being cut – becoming shorter and shorter. This creates a tension, an anguish, an anxiety. All the comforts, all the luxuries, all the riches become meaningless, because you cannot take them away with you. You will have to go into death alone.

The East is relaxed. First, it does not give death any importance; it is just a change of form. Second, because it is so relaxed, you become aware of your inner riches, which will be going with you – even beyond life. Death cannot take them away.

Death can take everything that is outside you and, if you have not grown your inner being, naturally there will be fear that you cannot save anything from death; it will take everything that you have. But if you have grown your inner being, if you have found peace, blissfulness, silence, joy, which are not dependent on anything outside, if you have found your garden of being and seen the flowers of your own consciousness, the question of fearing death does not arise at all.

Again I say to you, remember only one thing: You are an immortal being. Right now, it is not your experience; right now, if you love me, if you have any trust in me, you can accept it as a hypothesis – not as a belief, but a hypothesis to experiment with.

I never want anybody to accept anything from me as a belief, but only as a hypothesis. Because I know the truth of it, I need not enforce belief and faith on you. Knowing the truth I can say to you, "It is just for experiment, a temporary hypothesis," because I am absolutely certain that if you experiment, your hypothesis will change into your own knowing – not in a belief, not in a faith, but in a certainty. And only certainties can save you. Beliefs are boats made of paper.

One should not think that one can cross the ocean of existence on a boat made of paper. You need a certainty...not a belief, but a truth that is experienced by yourself. Not somebody else's truth, but your own. Then it is a joy to go into the unknown, uncharted ocean; it is a tremendous excitement and ecstasy.

But always keep in tune with your own nature.

Some trees grow slowly, some trees grow fast; there is nothing special in growing fast or in growing slowly. One thing is similar to both trees – they are both following their natures. It is only man who looks all around, starts comparing, and gets into unnecessary anxieties.

Whenever you feel a problem, look within your heart. If you are at ease, you are on the right path. Your heart is the criterion. If it is disturbed, that means you have to change the path; something has gone wrong, you have gone astray.

The heart is your guide. When it is completely in harmony with nature, there is a beautiful dance and a music in your heart. When you go away from nature the music becomes just noise, the dance becomes disturbed. These are the signs and the language of the heart to make you aware whether you are going right or wrong.

You don't need any guidance from anybody. Your guide is within yourself.

Osho,

Yes, you have disturbed my slumber; now, waking to a morning sun, birds sing and leaves dance in the breeze. Sitting in your garden is so sweet. Sitting with you, there is more and more joy each day. Is this juice in your presence increasing so much these days, or am I just now noticing what's been here all along?

What you are experiencing now has always been here, but you were not here. For the first time you are also here – that's why you are noticing.

You may have come here many times, but it was only a coming of your physical body. Your mind was wandering somewhere else, your being was not here. Now you have known the knack to be here and now, and the juice that you are feeling will go on growing, because your presence will go on becoming more and more crystallized.

The juice has always been here, the flowers have always been blossoming here, the cool breeze was always blowing here, the trees and the sun rays…but you were blind.

For the first time you have opened your eyes, for the first time your senses have become alive. The more alive they become, the more profound are the experiences waiting for you. It all depends on your sensitivity, your awareness, your being silently just here and now.

It is possible that there may be somebody else who is not feeling any juice, who is not feeling anything at all, and he will go with the idea that there is nothing. This is how your mind befools you; it never allows you to be aware of your blindness, your unawareness, your unattentiveness. On the contrary, if somebody says to such a person, "You have missed something," he will retort, "You are hypnotized! I am a rational man; you have allowed yourself to be hypnotized and you have forgotten all rationality."

People protect their blindness, protect their unconsciousness, they protect their misery; anything that is *theirs* – it may be hell – they will protect it.

But to be really with me, you have to put all your defenses away, you have to be vulnerable – because we are not here to fight with each other. We are here to have a deep rapport, a deep accord, a harmony in which all differences dissolve…and there are not so many people, but a single silence, a single peace that passeth understanding.

Those who cannot put their defenses away need all the compassion. They may think that they are rational beings, but they are really unconscious beings. Eyes don't need reason, because eyes can see light without any reason; only blind men think about light, reason about light – for or against, believe in light, disbelieve in light – but the man who has eyes neither believes nor disbelieves, he is neither for nor against. He simply knows: light is there. It has to be enjoyed, not argued about.

You are in a state in which I want everybody to be. But people are so strange!

I have heard…

A great astronomer was concluding his lecture at the synagogue: "…And some of my colleagues believe that our own sun will probably die within four or five billion years."

"How many years did you say?" asked Mrs. Siegel, from the back of the room.

"Four or five billion," replied the scientist.

"Phew," said Mrs. Siegel. "I thought you said million."

People are very strange...as if she has understood! It does not matter in existence – four billion or four million – but perhaps million is the biggest number she knows. If it is four *billion*, no problem.

If you are listening with your mind there will come many such moments; if you are not listening with the mind but with the heart, there will not come any such moment. And listening with the heart is the only true listening.

Ronald Reagan came home and found his wife Nancy in bed with his very best friend, Edwin Meese.

"Hey, what do you think you are doing?"

"See," Nancy said to Meese, "I told you he was stupid. Now he can see everything and he is asking, 'What is going on?'"

Your experiences are fresh. This is the beauty of the inner experiences, that they always remain fresh. You cannot make them mechanical. Tomorrow and the day after tomorrow, whenever you will be here...the same perfume, the same presence, the same juice – but with a new taste, with a deeper understanding, with a greater sensitivity.

In the spiritual life nothing becomes old, it always remains fresh. And its freshness keeps you, even to the last breath of your life, young.

The mystic always dies young. His age may be a hundred years or a hundred and twenty years, it does not matter. He always dies young because his sources of life are continuously being refreshed; a fresh breeze is passing through him, fresh rays of the sun are passing through him, fresh moonlight and fresh stars are always arising in him.

You are blessed. Don't lose track. You have come to the right point. Become more and more centered on that point.

Osho,

I have managed to tie up my camel. The lion roars in distant, unknown jungles, the child is not yet conceived, and the stubborn mule goes nowhere. Can you comment?

*Z*arathustra has no idea about a stubborn mule; you seem to belong to a totally different category. You are neither a camel, nor a lion, nor a child – you are a mule. And with the mule there are many difficulties.

Have you ever thought that the mule cannot conceive a child? Mules don't give birth to children; they are cross-breeds between donkeys and horses. They have all that is the worst in donkeys and all that is worst in horses. But one thing is good about them: they don't leave a new generation, they simply die.

I would like you to consider again. Look into a mirror...because Zarathustra has absolutely categorized, and there is no place for the mule. You will find a camel in the mirror.

And you say, "I have managed to tie up my camel." If you *have* managed to tie up your camel, then the only criterion to prove it will be the lion's roar. But you are saying, "The lion roars in distant unknown jungles." The camel has to *become* the lion...the camel has the capacity to become the lion.

These are metaphors that Zarathustra has used. The moment the camel rebels against slavery, he becomes a lion, and suddenly there is the roar! One of the most beautiful experiences is to hear the lion roar. And the process is such that if the mule becomes the lion...

the lion is only a passage, a bridge. The child is always there. It is not a question of conceiving a child; everybody is pregnant, born pregnant with the child, just the right opportunity....

In the camel the right opportunity is not there; in the lion *is* the right opportunity for the child to be born. But rather than going the simple way, you are stuck with some mule, a stubborn mule. Do you know any other kind? All mules are stubborn, that is their great quality.

But recognize exactly where you are. No man is a mule, because man is not a cross-breed. You have to begin with the camel. And you are not supposed to hear the lion roar faraway, "in distant unknown jungles." That lion's roar will not help. The roar has to come from your deepest heart. And in that very roar you will become, for the first time, aware that the child *is* coming.

The child is our destiny.

One has to become, finally, as innocent as a child, full of wonder and surprise, full of trust and love, absolutely in tune with existence. That's what is meant by the child. These are metaphors. But I can understand what you mean by, "the stubborn mule goes nowhere."

The pope stood before a hushed crowd of attentive Italian villagers. "My flock, you must-a not use-a the pill," he warned.

Just then a beautiful young *signorina* stepped forward and said, "Look – you no play-a the game, you no make-a the rules!"

A simple thing: You don't play the game – you don't have the right to make the rules. This is the quality of the mule; he does not like to move even an inch, wherever he is. In that sense our minds can be compared to mules.

You can watch your mind; it does not want to change anything. Every change means difficulty, readjustment, rearrangement – but no change signifies death. I would like you to remember that the mind is a dead machine, it is simply a biocomputer. It resists all change, it is against evolution, and all the evolution that has happened in the world has happened through the people who were courageous enough to put the mind aside.

Putting the mind aside is what I mean by meditation. Mind is a mule; meditation is an eagle, flying to the farthest horizon across the sun, always ready to go into the unknown.

If the mule goes nowhere, get down from the mule. What is the need to go on sitting on the mule and looking stupid? Get down from the mule! It is better to walk on your own feet – at least you can move, you can evolve to a better state of consciousness.

The whole religion can be condensed in one single word, and that is meditation. And meditation is a simple way to get down from the mule, to get down from the mind. Let the mind remain where it is; you start moving without it. And once you are not thinking through the mind, you will be able to understand Zarathustra's categories. You will find yourself first a slave in thousands of ways – a slave of your tradition, a slave of your education, a slave of your religion, a slave of all kinds of superstitions. You will find so many slaveries. Just a little courage, and let the camel revolt against any enslavement.

All the great teachers of the world have been insisting for a revolution against the slavery that keeps your spirit in a *status quo*. And once the slavery is thrown away, the camel goes through the metamorphosis, becomes a lion. He had always been a lion; he became a camel because of the slavery.

And the moment he becomes a lion – courageous and brave, ready to go into the unknown, ready to be alone – the child is not faraway. The second metamorphosis will happen; you will find the lion turning into a child. And the child is the ultimate state of liberation.

The innocence of the child is his wisdom; the simplicity of the child is his egolessness. The freshness of the child is the freshness of your consciousness, which never becomes old, which always remains young. It has passed through thousands of bodies: they became young, they became old, they died. But the consciousness continues, a young river, fresh, dancing towards the ocean. The wondering eyes of the child is the opening of your being to all the great mysteries of existence.

The scientist also tries to discover the mysteries and their secrets, but his method is violent; it is more a rape than a love. He dissects, he attacks. The behavior of the scientist with nature is not human; it is very inhuman.

The child and the sage also come to know the mysteries of existence, but in a way that can be called only playfulness, that can be called only loving radiation. And existence itself is eager to open its heart to the loving child, to open its secrets to the wondering eyes of the child.

Lao Tzu says, "The moment you drop knowledge, you become wise."

The moment you stop inquiring into the mysteries of existence, existence itself opens up all its doors, invites you. And to enter the mysteries of existence as a guest is dignified. To attack nature, to force nature is barbarous. Science is still barbarous, and science will remain barbarous unless it learns to be meditative too. Only meditation can change the barbarousness of science and can make it an innocent love affair with existence.

That will be a golden future: when science becomes a love affair with existence – not a struggle, not a conflict, but a deep harmony, a friendship.

Up to now, even the greatest thinkers like Bertrand Russell talk in terms which are barbarous. He has written a famous book; the title is *The Conquest Of Nature*. The very idea of conquering nature is ugly. We are *part* of nature; how can the part conquer the whole? Can you conceive that my left hand can conquer me? And we are such a small part of existence that the very idea of conquering it is quixotic.

But a different science is certainly needed; this science has failed. The old religion has failed. It has not delivered salvation to humanity, it has not brought what it has promised – blissfulness, benediction, godliness. All its promises have proved lies.

And now I want to say, science has also failed. In conquering nature, it has only created destructive weapons, atomic energy, nuclear missiles. Rather than conquering nature, it has succeeded in preparing a graveyard of the whole planet. Science has failed. It has not been able to serve life for the simple reason that the very idea of conquering is barbarous and violent.

We have to find a new religiousness and a new scientific approach, and they cannot be two different things. They can be two sides of one coin: Applied to the inner consciousness, it becomes religiousness; applied to the objective world, it becomes science.

But the basic reality is innocent, wondering, and loving eyes…a friendship, a harmony, a love affair.

CHAPTER 11

The Sacred Makes You Speechless

These are the mysteries of life:
when you cannot say,
the urge becomes more and more powerful to say it.
The musician says in his own way,
the poet says in his own way,
the painter says in his own way,
but nobody succeeds —
something remains beyond all expression.

Osho,

I have heard you say that Gautam Buddha's work came to an end when he became enlightened, and you started your work after your enlightenment. Could you say something about this?

One of the most important things to be remembered by all is the way you have started your question. The question is, "I have heard you say." Usually, people drop the first part. They simply say, "You have said this." And there is such a great difference between the two, such an immense difference that it is unbridgeable, and needs a great understanding.

Whatever you hear is not necessarily the thing said; what is said is not necessarily what you hear. The obvious reason is that I am speaking from a different space of being, and you are hearing from a totally different space. In the transmission, many things change.

It is always a sign of understanding to remember that whatever I have said may be totally different than what you have heard. Your question should be about what you have heard, because how can you ask a question about something which you have not heard?

Gautam Buddha, in his whole life, never allowed people to write down what he was saying. His reason was that if you are writing it down, your attention becomes divided. You are no longer total. You have to hear and you have to write, and what he is saying is so subtle that unless you are total, you are going to miss it. So rather than writing it down, try with your totality and intensity to approach your heart, to let it sink within you.

He spoke for forty-two years continuously. After his death, the first question was to write down whatever the disciples remembered; otherwise it would have been lost to humanity. They did a great service, and also a great disservice. They wrote down...but they came to see a strange phenomenon – that everybody had heard something different. Their memory, their remembrance, was not the same.

Thirty-two schools sprang up, proclaiming, "This is what Buddha has said." Only one man – a man to be remembered forever, his closest disciple, Ananda – who was not even enlightened before Buddha died.... Just out of his humbleness, knowing, "I was unenlightened, how can I hear exactly what comes from an enlightened consciousness? I am going to interpret it, I am going to mix it with my own thoughts, I am going to give it my own color, my own nuance. It cannot carry within me the same meaning it has brought, because I don't have yet those eyes that can see and those ears that can hear." Out of this humbleness, the memories that he remembered and wrote down became the basic scriptures of Buddhism. They all start with "I have heard Gautam Buddha say."

And all the thirty-two philosophical schools – they were great scholars, far greater than Maitreya, than Ananda, far more capable to interpret, to bring meanings to things, to make systems out of words – those thirty-two schools slowly, slowly became rejected. And the reason for their rejection was that they had missed a single beginning: "I have heard...." They were saying, "Gautam Buddha said" – the emphasis was on Gautam Buddha.

Ananda's version is the universally accepted version. Strange... there were enlightened people, but they remained silent because what they had heard was not possible to be expressed. And there were unenlightened philosophical geniuses who were very articulate, and they wrote great treatises – but they were not accepted. And the man who was not enlightened, not a great philosopher, but just a humble caretaker of Gautam Buddha, his words have been accepted. The reason is, these beginnings – "I have heard.... I don't know whether he was saying it or not. I cannot impose myself on him. All that I can say is what echoed in me; I can talk about my mind – not the mindless silence of Gautam Buddha."

Buddhist scriptures, in this way, are the only scriptures in the world which have this quality of the great difference between the master and the disciple, between one who has arrived and one who is trying to arrive.

You are asking, "I have heard you say that Gautam Buddha's

work came to an end when he became enlightened, and you started your work after your enlightenment."

It is one of those strange incidents of history, where the obvious is completely ignored. I have talked, discussed, with a few very great scholarly Buddhist monks. One was Bhikkshu Sangharakshita. He was an Englishman, but while he was young, searching, he found that Christianity had nothing to give and became a Buddhist. When I met him, he had become very old. He used to live in the Himalayas, in Kalimpong. He has written great books on Buddhism with such love and such insight that one feels full of awe.

I have been discussing many times with Bhikkshu Ananda Kausalyayan, who is the most prominent Buddhist scripture scholar and who has written much with depth and profundity. And the third man was Doctor Bhikkshu Jagdish Kashyap. He was the head of the great Institute of Buddhist Studies.

None of these three people have noticed the difference – that Ananda's version is humble and truer because he is saying what is reflected in his being, and he can authoritatively say only that. When I pointed it out to them, they were all surprised – "We have been studying our whole life, but we never thought that this has any significance. We always thought that it is just the way Ananda writes."

And when I said to them, "No Buddhist, except a few Zen masters, are going to agree with me...." The whole of Asia is Buddhist. In different countries it has taken different shapes, different rituals. But one thing is similar everywhere – that Buddha worked for six years, hard enough to attain enlightenment. He attained enlightenment after six years of hard work – this is just accepted.

But when I came to see the life of Gautam Buddha, I was simply amazed, because in a way it can be said that he attained his enlightenment after six years of hard work, but that is not the whole truth. It is not even a small fragment of the truth. The truth is, he attained enlightenment only when he dropped all desire for it, all work for it, all hope for it.

This gap between the hard work and relaxing and dropping the idea that anything like truth exists…. He had done everything that was told to him, and yet no silence had descended on him. He had not been able to enter into his innermost being. He had knocked on all the doors, but no door was opened. His work was so total and intense that he could not conceive that there was anything more to be done.

I have been to the small river Niranjana, by the side of which he had become enlightened one full-moon night. That day, the most important experience happened – which is not even talked about by the Buddhists, by the followers. It does not look important, they are not to be blamed. He had tortured his body, he had been fasting for months, and he had become so weak…and Niranjana is a very small river. He had got into the river for his morning bath, but even the smallest river and its current was too much; he started going down with the river. He could not manage to get out of it. He hung to the root of a tree.

That moment was momentous. Hanging to the root of the tree in the river, a thought arose in him, "What kind of stupid life have I been living? All this asceticism, all this arduous effort, has led me nowhere to truth, but only to weakness. It has not given me an abundance of life; it has brought me closer to death. How is this kind of discipline, which is being taught by all the schools, going to help me cross the ocean of life and reach the further shore?"

A question mark about his whole lifestyle, and in a clear moment, in a transparent moment on that morning – the sun was rising – something changed in his whole being. He had renounced his kingdom; in that moment he renounced his renunciation too. He had renounced *this* world; in that moment he renounced *that* world too. He had renounced ambition, power, prestige – and now he saw that in a subtle way even the effort to achieve enlightenment is nothing but ambition, that it is also a desire. A desire for a more eternal life, desire for truth, but anyway it is also a desire.

As he struggled to get out of the river, that desire was also dropped. He rested under a bodhi tree. For the first time in his whole life he was utterly relaxed. There was nowhere to go, nothing to find, no effort to be made. And amazingly, the silence that he was seeking started descending on him like rain.

By the evening he was a totally changed man – calm and cool, at home, at ease. The center that he was searching for – he laughed about it, because the seeker himself was the sought. He had been doing something absurd. The center of his being was not something separate from himself. Unless all desires disappear, all ambitions disappear – unless you have nothing to do, nothing left to be done; you are just sitting, peacefully....

He found the center.

He *was* the center.

There was no object anywhere else.

One of the most important Danish philosophers, Soren Kierkegaard, has said that "Subjectivity is all." You can call it religion, you can call it truth, you can call it nirvana. But your own subjectivity, your own being....

And by the evening, a beautiful incident happened. It was a full-moon night – it has just passed here, one or two days ago; it was the same full-moon night – a woman in the nearby village.... In India people worship trees, they worship animals, they worship stones, they worship mountains, they worship the sun, the moon. On the surface it looks very childish, but deep down the question is not what you worship; the question is that you *worship*. Whether it is the sun or the moon or a tree or a river, these are only excuses; the real thing is worship. That woman was a worshiper of the tree under which Gautam Buddha was sitting.

The moon had risen...this is the strongest moon in the whole year, the most beautiful. And Gautam Buddha was looking almost like a god under the tree in the silence of the forest, by the side of the river – particularly to that woman. She had asked the tree something and her desire had been fulfilled, and so she had promised that she would come with delicious food to offer to the god of the tree. She thought perhaps the god of the tree had come out of the tree and was sitting and waiting.

And Buddha was hungry; he had not eaten for many days, so when she offered – her name was Sujata – he accepted. He slept for the first time in these six years of torturous search, without any tension, without any dreams. Just a silence was the only experience that was becoming deeper and deeper; his sleep was becoming *samadhi*. When there are no thoughts, no desires, and the mind is quiet, sleep becomes *samadhi*; it becomes enlightenment.

And in the morning, when he opened his eyes…just visualize… nowhere to go, nothing to achieve. And as he saw the last star disappearing in the sky, he saw himself also disappearing in the sky. This he called *nirvana*, disappearing. He became absent, just a pure silence, a nothing…a joyful silence, a silence that has a song in it, a silence which is an invisible dance.

This was the day of his enlightenment. Buddhist scholars for twenty-five centuries have thought that he achieved this state because of those six years of arduous effort. I differ from them absolutely. And they have not been able to prove to me…and they think that I am crazy because they think that if it were true, then in twenty-five centuries people would have seen it. But I say that he attained enlightenment because he dropped the desire to attain it.

I said Gautam Buddha's work came to an end when he became enlightened. He worked too hard. I have never worked for enlightenment; I have never followed any discipline, any scripture, any religion, any ascetic path. Where Buddha reached after six years of arduous effort, I found myself there from the very beginning – sitting under a tree, relaxed. People used to think – my teachers, my friends – that I must be mad. Even sometimes I used to think, "Perhaps they are right, because everybody has ambition; I don't have any. Everybody wants to become this and that, and I want simply to sit silently and not to do anything, and just be myself."

Enlightenment to Buddha was the culmination of his whole work. My work started after my enlightenment. I have never searched for it. It is one of those mysteries which have no explanation. It knocked on my door, and I said to it, "Come in, it is open." I have not even taken the trouble to open the door. I have left it open always.

The day I became enlightened, then my work began. My work is you; Gautam Buddha's work was himself.

I have lived for you.

I have no other reason to be alive, because all that life could give to me, it has given to me without asking. It has been very generous to me. But after my own enlightenment, I felt the first urge in my being – that this is so simple, so natural, that it should happen to everybody. And unless it happens to everybody, the world is going to remain in misery and in suffering. Gautam Buddha was enlightening himself; I have been enlightening others. So where his work was completed, my work starts.

> Osho,
> Whenever I try to write what I would like to tell you before going back to the West, I find myself as speechless as Lancelot. It is more than gratitude, more than love, more than you and me. And yet, some longing to convey this feeling is there, strong, and doesn't go; there is a quiet sadness and a burning fire. Beloved master, how can I express the immensity that has filled me so many times when sitting in your presence and living in your buddhafield?

The moment it happens it is always more than love, it is always more than joy, it is always more than gratitude, because life is more than you and more than me. It is so multi-dimensional, it is so vast…. Only if you are not aware of it, are you capable to express your feelings. But the moment awareness enters in your life, explanations start disappearing, expressions become impossible, because whatever you can say falls very short.

There have been many people on the earth who have achieved the ultimate, but we don't even know their names for the simple reason that the moment they achieved, they became dumb – the silence was so deep, they could not find a way to convey what had happened to them.

There are many mystics in the world, but very few masters. Every mystic is not a master. It is a rare combination of articulateness, of using words in such a way that they carry wordlessness in them, to say things in such a way as if nothing has been said, to be in such a way as if you are not. And the more you are absent, the more you are a pure presence.

You are asking me, "Whenever I try to write what I would like to tell You before going back to the West, I find myself as speechless as Lancelot."

You are fortunate. It is part of blissfulness to be so silent; you know something has to be said, but there is no way to say it. You know there is a great blissfulness overflowing you, a gratitude in your heart, and it does not look right not to express them. But all words are so earthly, and all these experiences are so unearthly, that there is no way of translating them. Even the great masters who tried to convey something of the inexpressible had to find strange ways.

Just the other day, I received the news of a man in the part of Kashmir occupied by Pakistan. He is one hundred and twenty-five years old, and he has joked about death three times. This was the third time.

He dies; doctors declare that he is dead and there is great mourning – friends and relatives, and preparations – and at the final moment when they are taking him to the graveyard, he opens his eyes and he starts laughing! The first time he did it people thought, "It may have been just a coma, and we were misled." The second time they were more alert not to be deceived by the old fellow; in every way they made certain that he was dead. But still, the same thing happened: at the last moment, just when they were putting him into the grave, he said, "Wait!" He said, "Can't you see the joke?"

And he has performed it now again at the age of one hundred and twenty-five. This is his way, a strange way of saying to you that life is eternal and death is just a joke. He is saying it by his own life. And this time he has said, "Now I am very old, and I cannot go on doing this strategy for long, so perhaps this is the last time. Remember – the fourth time I may be *really* dead."

But they said, "We can't believe you. Every time you say, 'Next time I may be really dead.'"

He is showing the eternity of life and consciousness. He is a master. Without words, he is saying what the *upanishads* have said: Amritasya putrah – "You are sons and daughters of eternity." But his way of saying it is far more significant, because words can be used in a very poetic way and still they may not be true, they may not be the experience of the poet. But this man knows how to go deep – so deep into himself that there is no medical way to find out that he is still alive.

Speechlessness is bound to happen with anything that you can experience but you cannot bring to words. You see a beautiful sunset – what can you say? You see a bird on the wing in the sky – so beautiful, just the expression of freedom – but what can you say? And whatever you say will always fall short of the target.

Only mundane things can be said.

The sacred makes you speechless.

Because "it is more than gratitude...." You say "gratitude" and you certainly feel you have not said it; the word is so small and the experience is so big – and yet there is a great longing to convey the feeling.

These are the mysteries of life: when you cannot say, the urge becomes more and more powerful to say it. The musician says in his own way, the poet says in his own way, the painter says in his own way, but nobody succeeds – something remains beyond all expression.

That something beyond expression is God, is truth, is enlightenment, is liberation. But these words also don't say it; they only indicate – just fingers pointing to the moon.

You are right, "There is a quiet sadness and a burning fire...how can I express the immensity that has filled me so many times when sitting in Your presence and living in Your buddhafield?"

You will have to go through an alchemical change. That sadness is beautiful; it is not misery, it is just the sadness of experiencing the beyond and the inability to express it. And the burning desire to express it turns into creativity – you can paint, you can sing, you can dance; you can find your own way somehow to indicate the beyond, and the burning fire will not be a torture to you. It will become a great joy of creativity.

So don't make it sadness, and don't make it a suffering. Feel blessed! Change it into a great laughter. It is only a question of getting out of the bed from the right side.

The Mother Superior of the convent awoke in a happy mood, dressed and set off to visit her flock. "Good morning, Sister Augusta. God bless you. Are you happy at your work?"

"Yes, Reverend Mother, but I am sorry to see you got out of bed on the wrong side this morning."

The Mother Superior ignored the remark, and passed on to another nun. "Good morning, Sister Georgina. You look pleased with yourself."

"I am, Reverend Mother, but it is a pity you got out of bed on the wrong side today."

The Mother Superior, greatly puzzled, moved on to a young novice, "Tell me, little sister, do you also feel I got out of bed on the wrong side?"

"I am afraid so."

"But why? Am I not as happy as a songbird? and pleasant to you all?"

"Yes, Mother, but you are wearing Father Vincenzo's slippers."

CHAPTER 12

That Beyondness is You

There are things which have to be done,
and there are things which have not to be done.
Things that can be done are ordinary, mundane,
mediocre, of the objective world.
Things which happen, and cannot be done,
belong to a superior, higher order of existence.

Osho,

These days, looking inside, I do not find a personality with certain characteristics, but rather an ever-changing flux, totally unpredictable. It makes life in this body feel very fragile, vulnerable and momentary – a feeling which extends itself to everything around me, shaking me to the roots.

*M*an is not one, man is many: man is a multitude, a crowd. The feeling of being a personality is a mirage. It arises because you never go in, and you never face the crowd. Perhaps to avoid the crowd, you never go in.

You are living outside your own home and the home is being occupied by your neighbors, many of whom are dead. And when I say many, I mean many! – centuries, queues of old and dead people are living within you; hence, when for the first time one enters on the path of meditation, the first encounter shakes one to the very roots. One sees many faces and many people – except one face, except the one individual that he is.

Most people, out of fear, simply run out again and get engaged in things so that they can forget what is happening within themselves. To find oneself alone needs such courage because the moment you find yourself alone you have to face a multitude, a crowd. Each in the crowd pretends to be your real self, and there is no way for you to find out who is your real individual. Millions of people live their lives without meditation for the simple reason that they cannot cope with this encounter.

The method is very easy. Bodhidharma used to say to his disciples, "When you enter into yourself you will find many pretenders who look almost like you. Some of them are even better than you, because they have been practicing your act, your part, for years – or perhaps for lives. You have to behave the way the elephant behaves when a crowd of dogs starts barking: the elephant goes on without even bothering, as if there is nobody...You have to be an elephant and treat the crowd within you as if they are barking dogs."

In India it is now becoming a rare scene, but in my childhood it was an everyday scene because all the Maharajas, and there were many, and all the great religious leaders, and they were many, all had many elephants. In fact, a religious leader's religiousness was measured by how many elephants he had, because to keep an elephant is not easy; it is very costly.

It was an everyday scene – the elephants passing on the road and the dogs barking. A strange feeling arises when you see a dog bark at the elephant; the elephant pays not even the smallest attention – as if there is nobody, nothing is happening. And if you look at the face of the dog, you can understand the meaning of the word *despair*... "This fellow is strange: we are barking, so many dogs, and he is going his way as if nothing is happening."

Soon those dogs start disappearing – "What is the point? The elephant seems to be an idiot, or maybe he is deaf, but not our equal. Perhaps he does not understand our language, but whatever the reason, the task is hopeless."

Bodhidharma is right; the meditator has to behave like an elephant. And he will be surprised: all those who are surrounding his inside – many facades, many voices – start becoming distant. Soon a moment comes when they are so far away that it seems you have only seen them, heard them, in a dream. And as they go, receding...a great silence, a tremendous tranquillity settles in your being.

Your question is, "These days, looking inside, I do not find a personality with certain characteristics, but rather an ever-changing flux, totally unpredictable. It makes life in this body feel very fragile, vulnerable and momentary – a feeling which extends itself to everything around me, shaking me to the roots."

It appears as if it is a curse – it is not.

The roots that can be shaken are not *your* roots, and that which is fragile, that which is momentary, does not belong to you. Only one thing belongs to you in this whole experience: that is the watcher, the witness. Who is witnessing the fragileness, the ever-changing flux of personalities? Who is watching the shaking of the roots? Certainly he is beyond all of it.

That beyondness is yours.

That beyondness is you.

That is your individuality, that is your being.

Settle in that witnessing, and all that you are feeling disturbed by will disappear. It is just the first encounter of entering into oneself. Don't go back; go deeper into it.

Ginsberg sits down in a Moscow cafe and orders a glass of tea and a copy of Pravda.

"I will bring the tea," the waiter tells him, "but I can't bring a copy of *Pravda*. The Soviet regime has been overthrown and *Pravda* is not published anymore."

"All right," says Ginsberg, "just bring the tea."

The next day, Ginsberg comes to the same cafe and asks for tea and a copy of *Pravda*. The waiter gives him the same answer.

On the third day, Ginsberg orders the same and this time the waiter says to him, "Look, sir, you seem to be an intelligent man. For the past three days you have ordered a copy of *Pravda* and three times now I have had to tell you that the Soviet regime has been overthrown and Pravda is not published anymore."

"I know, I know," says Ginsberg, "but I just like to hear you say it!"

It is good news that you don't exist as a personality. You should rejoice – rejoice in the fact that you are only the witness, the watcher, because that is the only thing which is eternal and immortal. It is the only thing which cannot be transcended by any more beautiful experience, any deeper ecstasy, any greater enlightenment.

Just let this personality, this fragileness, this momentariness, this fear, this trembling of the roots, not be identified with yourself. Remain aloof, a watcher on the hills, and soon the whole scene changes.

The pope lay dying. His doctor called the cardinals together and announced, "We can only save his life with a heart transplant."

"We must tell the people," said one of the cardinals, "perhaps a donor will volunteer to give his heart for the pontiff."

An announcement was made and thousands gathered beneath the pope's balcony shouting, "Take-a my heart, take-a my heart!"

The cardinals now had to decide on the person who would donate his heart to the holy father. "We will drop a feather from his holiness' head," said the head cardinal. "Whosoever it lands upon will be the lucky person."

As the feather floated down from the balcony, from the multitudes below came, "Take-a my heart – phew! Take-a my heart – phew!"

It is one thing to say, "Take-a my heart," but when it comes so close, "Phew!" Everybody wants to know his inner reality, but you will have to lose something; you will have to pay for it.

There is nothing in existence available without payment. If you want to know yourself, you will have to drop all false identities. They are your investments, they are your power, they are your prestige, they are your religion, they are your qualifications. It is difficult to drop them; it feels like death.

Certainly meditation is a death, a death of all that is false in you. And only then, that which is not false is experienced. That experience is resurrection – a new life, the birth of a new man.

Osho,

I am most aware of a big fear or guilt in me when I sit with you, and I am longing so much to be totally open to you. Recently I could feel the serpent rolled up in the bottom of me, sleeping, and the door, the third chakra still closed. My heart wants to fly with you. Is there anything I can do?

hat is fear? There are fears and fears; I am not talking about them. I am talking about the most fundamental fear – all other fears are faraway echoes of the basic fear – and that fear is of death. Life is surrounded by death. You see every day somebody dying – something dying; something that was alive a moment before is dead.

Each death reminds you of your own death.

It is impossible to forget your own death; every moment there is a reminder. So the first thing to be understood is that the only possibility of getting rid of fear is to get rid of death. And you can get rid of death, because death is only an idea, not a reality.

You have only seen other people dying; have you ever seen yourself dying? And when you see somebody else dying, you are an outsider, not a participant in the experience. The experience is happening inside the person. All that you know is that he is no longer breathing, that his body has become cold, that his heart is no longer beating. But do you think all these things put together are equivalent to life? Is life only breathing? Is life only the heartbeat, the blood circulating and keeping the body warm? If this is life, it is not worth the game. If only my breathing is my life, what is the point of going on breathing?

Life must be something more. To be of any value life must have something of eternity in it; it must be something beyond death. And you can know it, because it exists within you. Life exists within you – death is only an experience of others, outside observers.

It is simply like love. Can you understand love by seeing a person being loving to someone? What will you see? They are hugging each other, but is hugging love? You may see they are holding hands together, but is holding hands love? From the outside, what else can you discover about love? Anything that you discover will be absolutely futile. These are expressions of love, but not love itself. Love is something one knows only when one is in it.

One of the greatest poets of India, Rabindranath Tagore, was very much embarrassed by an old man who was his grandfather's friend. The old man often used to come because he lived in the neighborhood, and he would never leave the house without creating trouble for Rabindranath. He would certainly knock on his doors, and ask, "How is your poetry going? Do you really know God? Do you really know love? Tell me, do you know all these things that you talk about in your poetry? Or are you just articulate with words? Any idiot can talk about love, about God, about the soul, but I don't see in your eyes that you have experienced anything."

And Rabindranath could not answer him. In fact he was right. The old man would meet him in the marketplace and hold him and ask him, "What about your God, have you found him? Or are you still writing poetry about him? Remember, talking about God, is not knowing God."

He was a very embarrassing person. In poets' gatherings, where Rabindranath was very much respected – he was a Nobel prize winner – that old man was bound to reach. On the stage, before all the poets and worshipers of Rabindranath, he would hold him by his collar and would say, "Still it has not happened. Why are you deceiving these idiots? They are smaller idiots, you are a bigger idiot; they are not known outside the land, you are known all over the world – but that does not mean that you know God."

Rabindranath has written in his diary: "I was so much harassed by him, and he had such penetrating eyes that it was impossible to tell a lie to him. His very presence was such that either you had to say the truth, or you had to remain silent."

But one day it happened…Rabindranath had gone for a morning walk. In the night it had rained; it was very early morning and the sun was rising. In the ocean it was all gold, and by the side of the streets water had gathered in small pools. In those small pools also the sun was rising with the same glory, with the same color, with the same joy…. And just this experience – that in existence there is nothing superior and nothing inferior, that all is one whole – suddenly triggered something in him. For the first time in his life he went to the old man's house, knocked on the door, looked into the eyes of the old man and said, "Now, what do you say?"

He said, "Now there is nothing to say. It has happened. I bless you."

The experience of your immortality, of your eternity, of your wholeness, of your oneness with existence is always possible. It only needs some triggering experience.

The whole function of the master is to create a situation in which the experience can be triggered; and suddenly the cloud of death disappears and there is all sunshine – tremendous life, abundant life, life full of song and full of dance.

So the first thing, Amrita, is to get rid of death. All fears will disappear. You don't have to work on each single fear; otherwise it will take lives and still you will not be able to get rid of them.

You say, "I am most aware of a big fear...."

Everybody is more or less aware of the big fear, but the fear is absolutely rootless, baseless. And you say "...or guilt in me, when I sit with You."

The fear is natural, because death is known by everybody around. Guilt is not natural; it is created by religions. They have made every man guilty – guilty of a thousand and one things, so burdened with guilt that they cannot sing, they cannot dance, they cannot enjoy anything. The guilt poisons everything.

Sitting with me it becomes more clear to you, because I am a stranger amongst you; I don't have any guilt. Guilt is an absolutely non-existential thing. It is the conditioning of religions.

Sitting with me, everything inside you starts becoming clear by contrast: Here is a man who has no guilt, a man who has no fear, a man who is absolutely alone in this whole world – a single man against the whole world. All your guilt that ordinarily remains unconscious, because you are living with the same kind of people, with the same kind of conditioning....

Being with me is being with a mirror.

And to see yourself and the mess that you are carrying within you, is certainly saddening. But it is also important, because if you become aware of it, it can be dropped. Guilt is an idea accepted by you. You can reject it, and it can be rejected because it is not part of existence. It is part of some stupid theology, of some old primitive religion.

You are saying, "and I am longing so much to be totally open to You." And you become afraid because the closer you become, the more open you become, the more you feel yourself full of guilt, sadness, misery, condemnation. You have been humiliated so much. All the religions have conspired against innocent human beings to make them guilty, because without making them guilty they cannot be made into slaves. And slaves are needed. For a few people's lust for power, millions of people are needed to be enslaved. For a few people to become Alexander the Great, millions have to be reduced to a sub-human status.

But all these are simply conditionings in the mind, which you can erase as easily as writing in the sands on a beach. Just don't be afraid, because those writings you have accepted as holy, you have accepted as coming from very respectable sources, from great founders of religions. It does not matter. Only one thing matters: that your mind should be completely cleaned, utterly empty and silent.

There is no need of Moses or Jesus or Buddha to reside inside you. You need a totally silent, clean space. And only that space can bring you not only to me, but to yourself, to existence itself.

"Recently I could feel the serpent rolled up in the bottom of me, sleeping, and the door, the third chakra, still closed. My heart wants to fly with you. Is there anything I can do?"

There are things which have to be done, and there are things which have not to be done. Things that can be done are ordinary, mundane, mediocre, of the objective world. Things which happen, and cannot be done, belong to a superior, higher order of existence.

If you are feeling that you would like your love to grow, to blossom, then wait with deep longing – as a seed. The longing has to be the seed. And the waiting, the patient waiting for the time when the spring comes and seeds start changing from dormant beings into alive, active blossomings....

The longing is there.

Just waiting is needed.

And the waiting should not be impatient, because impatient

waiting means you don't trust existence. And your impatience cannot bring the spring a single moment earlier. On the contrary, your impatience may block the door for the spring to come to you.

Just remain available, with a deep longing, just like a thirst in every cell of your body, a passion.

And spring has always come.

Your spring will also come.

You need not do anything else.

Just long as lovingly, as intensely, and wait as patiently, as possible.

The religions of the world have given so many diseases to man that they are uncountable. One of the diseases is that they have made every man ambitious for reward – if not in this world then in the other world. They have made man so greedy, and at the same time they are all talking against greed. But their whole religion is based on greed.

Don't let your longing be a greed.

Your longing should be a love affair.

Your longing should not be a sad state but a joyful state, just as a pregnant mother. Your longing makes you pregnant. You can feel the child inside you which is growing every day, and each moment becomes a reward – not that your reward will be delivered in heaven.

Religions have done such harm that they cannot be forgiven. They have taken away all dignity of man – his joy of longing, of love, his pleasure in waiting, his trust that the spring will come. They have taken everything away from you. You will be rewarded only if you do certain rituals which have no relationship, no relevance. Now, going around a statue seven times – what relevance can there be that you have earned virtue?

There are people who are continuously counting beads. I have seen people who are tending their shop and their hand is holding the beads so others should not see. It looks strange that you are haggling about the price of a certain thing with a customer and at the same time moving the beads, so they keep their hands and their beads in a bag so you cannot see. But anybody can see – why should one have one's hand in a bag?

So the religion is going on inside the bag; outside they are haggling for the price and everything, and trying to cheat and exploit – lying. And inside, how many times they have moved the beads – means they have earned that much virtue. Virtue is the coin in heaven – how much virtue have you in your bank account?

In Tibet they have done even better than counting beads. They have made small prayer wheels; each spoke represents one bead. So they go on doing all kinds of work, their prayer wheel by their side, and just once in a while they move it. And it goes on moving; when it slows down, they again give a push....

When I first came to know a lama with his prayer wheel I said, "You are stupid. Just plug it into the electricity. It will go on eternally, irrespective of whether you are alive or dead!"

But the lama could not understand that I was making a laughingstock of him. He said, "Your idea is great, because then we are completely free; otherwise this is a hindrance and everything – you cannot do anything wholeheartedly." Even making love, they are moving their prayer wheel – both the wife and the husband, they both have their prayer wheels. Now, it is very difficult: in the first place, the exercise of love is difficult – such primitive gymnastics! – and on top of it you have to go on moving those prayer wheels.

A simple and innocent religion would have changed the whole earth. But the cunning priests would not allow a pure and innocent and childlike religion, with wondering eyes, with joy, not bothering about stupid ideas about heaven and hell but living each moment with great love.

And waiting for more – not desiring, but by waiting, deserving, creating more and more space, silence, so that the spring comes. And not only a few flowers, but so many flowers....

One of the Sufi mystics has a small poem about it: "I had waited long for the spring – it came. And it came so abundantly, with so many flowers, that there was not a place left where I could make a nest for myself."

Life gives abundantly; you just have to be a recipient. But never wait for any reward.

Three men die on the same day and go to heaven. One by one they are interviewed by Saint Peter, who asked the first man how many times he had made love: "Never! I am a virgin," is the first guy's answer. Saint Peter gives him a Mercedes Benz to get around in, and poses the same question to the second man. "Only once," he says, "on my wedding night."

Giving him the keys to a Toyota, Saint Peter turns and asks the third man how often he has made love in his life. "I have gotten laid so many times I have lost count," the fellow confesses. And Saint Peter gives him a bicycle.

Not too much later, the first man is driving around in his Mercedes Benz when he sees something so extraordinary that he turns his head to look. He crashes headlong into a tree, and when he comes to, in Heaven Hospital, the angel doctors and police are standing by his bedside, waiting to find out what caused the accident.

"It was shocking, simply shocking!" whispers the poor man, "I saw Pope John Paul on roller skates."

All your old religions are based on reward and punishment, on more and less. Even on the last night when Jesus is departing from his disciples they ask only one question – "Certainly in heaven you will be standing at the right hand of God, but what about us? Who will be standing next to you? And what are going to be our positions?" It is shocking to think that the man they had loved, lived with, is going to be crucified tomorrow – it is almost certain – but their whole concern is about their position. This is the corruption that religions have put into man's mind.

I want you to be absolutely innocent of all religious corruption and pollution. Have a silent, loving mind, waiting for more to happen. Life is so much that we go on exploring it – but we cannot exhaust it. The mystery is timeless.

CHAPTER 13

Nothing Goes Right Without Meditation

Meditation is your own exploration.
You are searching to know exactly what constitutes you:
what is false in you and what is real in you.
It is a tremendous journey from the false to the real,
from the mortal to the immortal,
from darkness to light.

Osho,

I feel a strong connection between death and meditation, a fascination and a fear. When I sit with you, it is somehow safe to close my eyes and meditate; when I am alone, it is frightening. Please comment.

*T*here is not only a strong connection between meditation and death, but they are almost the same thing – just two ways of looking at the same experience.

Death separates you from your body, from your mind, from all that is not you. But it separates you against your will. You are resisting, you don't want to be separated; you are not willing, you are not in a state of let-go.

Meditation also separates all that is not you from your being and reality – but the resistance is not there; that is the only difference. Instead of resistance, there is a tremendous willingness, a longing, a passionate welcome. You want it; you desire it from the very depth of your heart.

The experience is the same – the separation between the false and the real – but because of your resistance in death, you become unconscious, you fall into a coma. You cling too much in death; you don't allow it to happen, you close all the doors, all the windows. Your lust for life is at the optimum. The very idea of dying frightens you from the very roots.

But death is a natural phenomenon and absolutely necessary too – it has to happen. If the leaves don't become yellow and don't fall, the new leaves, the fresh and young will not come. If one goes on living in the old body, he will not be moving into a better house, fresher, newer, with more possibilities of a new beginning. Perhaps he may not take the same route as he has taken in his past life, getting in a desert. He may move into a new sky of consciousness.

Each death is an end and a beginning.

Don't pay too much attention to the end. It is an end to an old, rotten, miserable life style, and it is a great opportunity to begin a new life, not to commit the old mistakes. It is a beginning of an adventure. But because you cling to life and you don't want to leave it – and it has to happen by the very nature of things – you fall unconscious.

Almost everyone, except those few people who have become enlightened, dies unconsciously; hence they don't know what death is, they don't know its new beginning, the new dawn.

Meditation is your own exploration.

You are searching to know exactly what constitutes you: what is false in you and what is real in you. It is a tremendous journey from the false to the real, from the mortal to the immortal, from darkness to light. But when you come to the point of seeing the separation from the mind and the body, and yourself just as a witness, the experience of death is the same. You are not dying...a man who has meditated will die joyfully because he knows there is no death; the death was in his clinging with life.

You say, Sagar, "I feel a strong connection between death and meditation." There is. In the ancient scriptures of this land, even the master is defined as death because his whole function, his whole work is to teach you meditation. In other words, he is teaching you to die without dying – to pass through the experience of death, surprised that you are still alive; death was like a cloud that has passed; it has not even scratched you. Hence the fascination, and the fear. The fascination is to know the mysterious experience everybody has to pass through, has passed through many times, but became unconscious. And the fear – that perhaps death is only the end and not another beginning.

It happened, just in the beginning of this century, that the King of Varanasi was to be operated on; the operation was major. But the King was very stubborn and he wouldn't take any kind of anesthesia. He said, "You can do the operation, but I want to see it happen; I don't want to be unconscious."

The doctors were puzzled. It was against medical practice...such a major operation was going to be too painful; the man might die because of the pain. Surgery needs you to be unconscious.

Perhaps the science of surgery has learned the art of anesthesia from the experience of death, because death is the greatest surgery. It separates you from your body, from your heart, and you have remained identified with all this for seventy years, eighty years. They have become almost your real self. The separation is going to be very painful, and there is a limit to pain.

Have you ever noticed? – there is no unbearable pain. The words *unbearable pain* exist only in language – all pain is bearable. The moment it becomes unbearable, you fall unconscious. Your unconsciousness is a way to bear it.

If he had been an ordinary man, the doctors would not have listened to him – but he was a king, and a very well-known king, known all over the country as a great wise man. He persuaded the surgeons, "Don't be worried, nothing is going to happen to me. Just give me five minutes before you start your operation so that I can arrange myself into a meditative state. Once I'm in meditation, I am already far away from the body. Then you can cut my whole body into pieces – I will be only a witness, and a faraway witness, as if it is happening to somebody else."

The moment was very critical; the operation had to be done immediately. If it was not done immediately, it might cause death. There were only two alternatives: either to operate and allow the patient to remain conscious, or not to operate, but follow the old routine of science. But in that case, death was certain. In the first case, there was a chance that perhaps this man could manage, and he was so insistent...finding no way to persuade him, they had to operate.

That was the first operation done without anesthesia, in a state of meditation. The king simply closed his eyes, became silent. Even the surgeons felt something changing around the king – the vibe, the presence; his face became relaxed like a small baby, just born, and after five minutes they started the operation. The operation took two hours, and they were trembling with fear; in fact, they were not sure that the king would survive – the shock might be too much. But when the operation was over, the king asked them, "Can I open my eyes now?"

It was discussed in the medical field all over the world as a very strange case. The surgeons asked him what he did. He said, "I have not done anything. To meditate is my very life. Moment to moment I am living in silence. I asked for those five minutes because you were going to do such a dangerous operation that I had to become absolutely settled in my being, with no wavering. Then you could do anything...because you were not doing it to me. I am consciousness – and you cannot operate on consciousness, you can operate only on the body."

You say, "When I sit with you, it is somehow safe." There is really no difference whether you sit with me or you sit alone – it is just a mind security, the idea that the master is present so there is no harm to take the jump. If something goes wrong, somebody is there to take care of it.

In meditation, nothing goes wrong – ever.

Without meditation, everything is going wrong.

Nothing goes right without meditation; your whole life is going wrong. You live only in hope, but your hopes are never fulfilled. Your life is a long, long tragedy. And the reason is your unawareness, your unmeditativeness.

Meditation looks like death, and the experience is exactly the same. But the attitude and the approach is different, and the difference is so vast that it can be said that meditation is life and death is just a dream.

But this is the function of a mystery school, where many people are meditating, where a master is present. You feel safe, you are not alone. If something goes wrong, help will be available immediately. But nothing goes wrong.

So meditate while you are sitting with me, and meditate in your aloneness. Meditation is the only thing with an absolute guarantee that nothing goes wrong with it. It only reveals your existence to yourself

– how can anything go wrong? And you are not doing anything; you are really stopping doing everything. You are stopping thinking, feeling, doing – a full stop to all your actions. Only consciousness remains, because that is not your action, it is you.

Once you have tasted your being, all fear disappears, and life becomes a totally new dimension – no longer mundane, no longer ordinary. For the first time you see the sacredness and the divineness not only of yourself, but of all that exists. Everything becomes mysterious, and to live in this mystery is the only way to live blissfully; to live in this mystery is to live under blessings showering on you like rain. Each moment brings more and more, deeper and more profound blessings to you. Not that you deserve them, but because life gives them out of its abundance – it is burdened, it shares with whomsoever is receptive to it.

But don't get the idea that meditation is death-like, because death has no good associations in your mind. That will prevent you experiencing consciousness – "It is death-like." In fact, it is a *real* death. The ordinary death is not a real death, because you will be again joined with another structure, another body. The meditator dies in a great way; he never again becomes imprisoned in a body.

An Italian missed a day at work and the foreman wanted an explanation.

"Where have you been?" he asked.

"It was-a my wife. She give-a birth to a wheelbarrow."

"If you can't do any better than that," said the foreman, "I'm gonna have to fire you."

"I think-a I got it wrong," said the Italian. "My wife, she's in-a bed having a push chair."

"That's it, wise guy," shouted the foreman, "You are fired!"

The Italian went home and asked his wife, "Hey, what was wrong with you yesterday?"

"I told-a you, I had-a miscarriage."

"I knew it was-a something with-a wheels-a on it."

There are misunderstandings piled upon misunderstandings in you. Some misunderstandings can be tremendously harmful. Getting the association of meditation and death identified in your mind is one of the greatest harms that you can do to yourself. Although you are not wrong, your associations with the meaning of death are such that they will prevent you from getting into meditation.

That is one of the reasons I want to make death more and more associated with celebration rather than with mourning, more and more associated with a change, a new beginning, rather than just a full stop, an end. I want to change the association. That will clear the way for meditativeness.

And if you are feeling, here with me, silent and meditative – still alive, more alive than ever – then there is no need to be afraid. Try it in different situations, and you will always find it a source of great healing, a source of great well-being, a source of great wisdom...a source of great insight into life and its mysteries.

Osho,

When someone like Nietzsche or Gertrude Stein dies – a genius who would probably have become enlightened if they had met a master – what sort of consciousness do they carry into the next life, and what was it that in their previous lives allowed them to experience such a huge potential, such a great flowering, and such a great knack? Was it the idea of wanting to go their own way without a master?

There are many things in your question. First, you ask, "When someone like Nietzsche or Gertrude Stein dies – a genius who would probably have become enlightened if they had met a master – what sort of consciousness do they carry into the next life?

The first thing to be understood is that consciousness has

nothing to do with genius. Everybody can be a Gautam Buddha. Everybody cannot be a Michelangelo, everybody cannot be a Friedrich Nietzsche.

But everybody can be a Zarathustra, because the spiritual realization is everybody's birthright. It is not a talent like painting, or music, or poetry, or dancing; it is not a genius either. A genius has tremendous intelligence, but it is still of the mind.

Enlightenment is not of the mind, it is not intellect; it is intelligence of a totally different order. So, the first thing to remember is that it is not only people, like Friedrich Nietzsche who have missed the journey towards their own selves; they were great intellectuals, geniuses unparalleled – but all that belongs to the mind. And to be a Gautam Buddha, a Lao Tzu, or a Zarathustra is to get out of the mind, to be in a state of mindlessness. It does not matter whether you had a big mind or a small mind, a mediocre mind, or a genius; the point is that you should be out of the mind. The moment you are out of the mind, you are in yourself.

So the strange thing is that the more a person is intellectual, the farther he goes away from himself. His intellect takes him to faraway stars. He is a genius, he may create great poetry, he may create great sculpture. But as far as you are concerned, you are not to be created, you are already there.

The genius creates, the meditator discovers.

So, don't make a category of Nietzsche and Stein and Schweitzer separate from others. In the world of mind, they are far richer than you, but in the world of no-mind, they are as poor as you are. And that is the space which matters.

Secondly, you ask, "What sort of consciousness do they carry into the next life?" They don't have any consciousness to carry into another life. They have a certain genius, a certain talent, a certain intelligence; they will carry that intelligence into another life, but they don't have consciousness.

Consciousness is an altogether different matter. It has nothing to do with creativity, it has nothing to do with inventiveness, it has nothing to do with science or art; it has something to do with tremendous silence, peace, a centering – they don't have it. So the question of carrying a certain consciousness into the next life does not arise; they don't have it in the first place. What they have, they will carry into the next life. They will become greater geniuses, they will become better singers, they will become more talented in their field, but it has nothing to do with meditation or consciousness. They will remain as unconscious as you are, as anybody else is.

It is as if you all fall asleep here; you will be dreaming. Somebody may have a very beautiful dream, very nice, very juicy, and somebody may have a nightmare. But both are dreams. And when they wake up, they will know that the beautiful dream and the nightmare are not different – they are both dreams. They are non-existential, mind projections.

When an ordinary man meditates, he comes to the same space of blissfulness as Nietzsche or Albert Einstein or Bertrand Russell. That space of blissfulness will not be different, will not be richer for Bertrand Russell because he is a great intellectual. Those values don't matter outside of the mind; outside of the mind, they are irrelevant.

This is great and good news because it means a woodcutter or a fisherman can become Gautam Buddha. An uneducated Jesus, an uneducated Kabir, who doesn't show any indication of genius, can still become enlightened, because enlightenment is not a talent, it is discovering your being. And the being of everyone is absolutely equal. That is the only place where communism exists – not in the Soviet Union, not in China.

The only place where communism exists is when somebody becomes a Gautam Buddha, a Zarathustra, a Lao Tzu. Suddenly all distinctions, talents of the mind, disappear. There is only pure sky where you cannot make any distinctions of higher and lower.

And you are asking, "What was it that in their previous lives allowed them to experience such a huge potential?"

You are growing every moment in whatever you are doing. A warrior will attain a certain quality of warriorness, a sharpness of the sword, and he will carry that quality into the next life. A mathematician will carry his mathematical intelligence to higher peaks in another life. That's why people are so different, so unequal, because in their past lives everybody has been doing different things, accumulating different experiences, molding the mind in a certain way. Nothing is lost, whatever you are doing will be with you like your shadow. It will follow you, and it will become bigger and bigger.

If Nietzsche is a great philosopher, he must have been philosophizing in his past lives – perhaps many, many lives – because such a genius needs a long, long philosophical past.

But the same is true about everybody. Everybody has a certain talent, developed or undeveloped; it depends on your decision, on your commitment. Once you are committed, you have accepted a responsibility to grow in a certain direction. Even whole races of people have developed in different directions, not only individuals.

For example, the Sikhs in India are not different from Hindus. They are only five hundred years old, following an enlightened man, Nanak. They became a different sect – but they are Hindus. And for these five hundred years, a strange phenomenon has happened, which has not happened anywhere else in the world. You cannot find in a Jewish family that one person is a Christian; you cannot find in a Mohammedan family that one person is a Hindu. But for five hundred years it has been a convention that in Punjab, where Sikhs dominate, the eldest son of the family should become a Sikh. He still remains in the family. His whole family is Hindu – his father is Hindu, his wife may be Hindu; he is a Sikh.

And the strangeness is that just by being Sikhs, the whole character of those Hindus has changed. Hindus have become cowards in the name of nonviolence; they are boiling with aggression within but, nonviolence is the ideal. Sikhs don't believe in nonviolence; neither do they believe in violence – they believe in spontaneity.

A certain situation may need violence and a certain situation may need nonviolence; you cannot make it a principle of life. You have to remain open, available, and responsive to the moment. And there is no difference of blood – the differences are such that one can only laugh at them – but they have created a totally new race.

Any Hindu can become a Sikh, any Mohammedan can become a Sikh, because the change is very simple. You have to have long hair, you cannot cut your beard or mustache; you have to use a turban, and you have to keep a comb in your turban; you have to wear a steel ring, a bracelet, just to show that you are a Sikh, and you have to carry a sword. You always have to wear underwear.

How these things have changed people is a miracle, because the Sikh is totally different from Hindus in his behavior. He is a warrior; he's not cowardly. He's more sincere, more simple, more of the heart.

It happened...I was going to Manali, the mountainous part, and it had rained, and the driver of my limousine was a Sikh. He started becoming afraid. The road was very small, the limousine was very big. The road was slippery; there were water pools collected on the road. At a certain point it looked very dangerous. A great river was flowing by, thousands of feet down – and just a small road. He stopped the car, went out, and sat there. And he said, "I cannot move anymore, it is simply going into death."

I said, "Don't be worried, you just sit; I will drive."

He said, "That is even more dangerous! I cannot give you the key."

I said, "This is very strange, because we have been traveling the whole night, twelve hours; now we are in the middle."

I tried to explain to him, "Even going back, you will have to travel twelve miles, twelve hours again on the same dangerous road. Whether you go backwards or you go forwards, it is the same."

He said, "It is not the same, because the road that we have passed, we have survived – I can manage. But ahead it seems to be simply committing suicide – I cannot go."

At that very moment, the inspector general of Punjab, who was coming to participate in the camp, came in his jeep. Seeing me standing there, and the limousine and driver sitting there, he said, "What is the matter?"

I said, "It is good you have come at the right moment; this driver is not ready to move ahead."

The inspector general of Punjab was also a Sikh. He came close to the driver and told him, "You are a Sikh. Have you forgotten this? Just get into the car."

And strangely enough, he immediately got into the car. We moved. I asked him, "What happened? I have been arguing with you...."

He said, "It is not a question of argument. I am a Sikh! I am supposed not to be afraid, and I had forgotten it."

Just a slight idea can change not only the individual, it can change the whole race.

We have seen how Adolf Hitler created in Germany a race of warriors as nobody has done ever before, just by giving them the idea that "you are the purest Aryans, that you are born to rule all over the world." And once the idea got into their minds, he almost conquered the world. For five years, he went on conquering. People became so afraid that a few countries simply gave way to him without fighting. What was the point of fighting with those people? They were superhuman. These ideas also are carried from one life to another.

In India there are sudras, untouchables. For five thousand years they have been condemned, oppressed, as nobody else in the whole world. I used to go to their functions and they would not let me sit with them. I would tell them, "You are as human as anybody else, and in fact you are doing a service which is far more valuable than any prime minister or any president of any country. The country would be more peaceful without these presidents and prime ministers, but without you, the country cannot live. You are keeping the country clean, you are doing the dirtiest jobs; you should be respected for it."

They would listen to me, but I could see that they were not ready to accept the idea that they are equal to other human beings. For five thousand years they have not revolted against such oppression, such humiliation – just they go on carrying it from one life into another life; it becomes more and more ingrained.

You are asking, "Was it the idea of wanting to go their own way without a master?" No, they had no idea of the great experience that happens between a master and a disciple. They have never consciously decided to go on their own way.

In fact in the West, masters have not existed. There have been saviors. They are not masters; they don't help you to become enlightened, they help you to remain unenlightened. Just believe in them and they will save you, you are not to do anything. The West has known prophets, messengers of God, but the West has not known masters. It has known mystics, but the mystics have remained silent in the West seeing that they will not be understood.

It is the atmosphere of thousands of years in the East that has made a few people take courage, and say things which cannot be said. It was the long heritage that allowed a few mystics to become masters. The West has missed completely a whole dimension of life.

The East has also missed many things – it has missed the scientific mind, it has missed the technological progress. It has remained poor, it has been invaded very easily by anybody, because its whole soul was devoted towards only one thing – everything else was irrelevant: Who rules the country does not matter, what matters is whether you are enlightened or not. Whether you are rich or poor does not matter, what matters is whether you know yourself or not – a single-pointed devotion. And because of this, the East has a climate of its own.

As you enter into the Eastern climate, you suddenly feel a difference. The West is more logical; the East is more loving. The West is more of the mind; the East is more of mindlessness, of meditation.

No, they have not missed a master; the very idea was non-existent to them. Even today, millions of Western people are unaware of the fact of masters, disciples, meditations. It is only the younger generation – and that too a very small portion of it – which has entered into the Eastern dimension, and has been shocked that the real richness is not of the outside world, the real richness is of the inside.

Ginsberg is dying. "Call the priest," he says to his wife, "and tell him I want to be converted into the catholic religion."

"But Max, you are an orthodox Jew all your life. What are you talking about? You want to be converted?"

Ginsberg says, "Better one of them should die than one of us."

People have lived as Jews, as Christians, as Mohammedans, but people have not lived as simply religious.

In the East also, only a very few people have lived in pure religiousness. But only those very few people have filled the whole of the East with a fragrance which seems to be eternal.

God asked Moses to choose whatever promised land he wished. After weighing several factors, Moses settled on California. But Moses, according to legend, had a speech impediment and he begin to answer, "C...C...."

Whereupon God said, "Canaan, that wasteland? Well, okay Mo. If you want it, you got it."

Poor Moses, because of a speech impediment got Canaan, which is now Israel – its old name is Canaan.

But from the very beginning in the Western mind, the desire was for California. He could have asked for Kashmir where finally he came and died; he could have asked for the land of Gautam Buddha.

But the East has appealed only to those who are called by psychologists "introverts"; and the West has appeal for those who are known as extroverts. Going Eastward means going inward; going Westward means going outward.

For thousands of years, authentic seekers have been coming to the East. They have found a certain magnetic pull; where so many people have meditated, they have created a tremendous energy pool. Being in that atmosphere, things become simpler, because the whole atmosphere is supportive, is a nourishment.

I have been around the world, and I have seen how the West is absolutely unaware of the Eastern grace. How is it that the Western man is unaware of himself? He's thinking of the farthest star, but not about himself. The East has remained committed to a single goal – to be oneself, and to know oneself. Unless you know yourself, and you are yourself, your life has gone to waste; it has not blossomed, it has not flowered. You have not fulfilled your destiny.

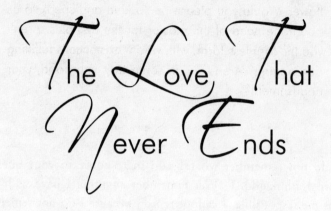

CHAPTER 14

The Love That Never Ends

That which is beyond the mind in you,
it is possible to attain and never lose it.
Love is always up and down,
one moment joyful, another moment sad.
But the love that we are talking about —
love between two spirits, between two beings —
only begins, it never ends.

Osho,

Once, in Kathmandu, I asked you about the need of
the disciple for a master. Then I asked you if the master
needs the disciple, and you showered on me some words
that I received in tears, like petals of an unknowable
flower. Would you please be so kind and speak to us
about the need of the master for the disciples. Aren't
you the formless form, with whom existence is fulfilling
our longing? Aren't we, in some way, your food, your
nourishment?

I do not remember what I said in response to your question
in Kathmandu. I never remember anything I have said. That
keeps me responsible. I cannot repeat, because I do not remember.
I can only respond to the question, and to the questioner in this
very moment.

Between Kathmandu and this moment, neither you have remained
you, nor I have remained I. And so much water has gone down the
Ganges, that any repetition is always out of date. Any repetition is
dead, is not alive.

That's how the whole of humanity is only pretending to live,
but deep down is dead, because it has forgotten the language of
response. It knows only the language of reaction. It reacts according
to the memory. It does not respond according to the awareness of
the moment, of the need here and now. It is full of the past.

There is no present in millions of people around the world.
Millions of people live without knowing the taste of the present.
And when you are full of the past you are a graveyard. Howsoever
beautiful the past may be, it is still dead. And beauty is meaningless
if it cannot dance, if it cannot sing, if it cannot even breathe.

I am here, you are here, why bring Kathmandu in? I don't know
what Kathmandu means in Nepalese, but in Hindustani we have a

phrase which immediately reminds one of Kathmandu. The phrase is *kath ke ullu*. It means, "You are an owl. And that too not real, but made of wood." I don't know what Kathmandu means; Kath certainly means wood....

Why bring Kathmandu in? You really want to listen to the same answer again, but it is impossible. You will have to forgive me, because I don't remember a single word. Kathmandu is almost as far away as the farthest star, as if it happened in some other life.

While we are alive, why waste your time? You can ask a new question and you can receive a new response. The new will be fresher, and the new will be better. The new will be more mature.

But people have lived to live in the past. It has become almost a second nature to them. It is very difficult to drag them out of their graves and tell them, "You are not dead yet. Start breathing, you are still alive."

An elderly Jewish man walks into a jewelry store to buy his wife a present. "How much is this?" he asks the assistant, pointing to a silver crucifix.

"That is six hundred dollars, sir," replies the assistant.

"Nice," says the man, "and how much without the acrobat on it?"

People cannot forgive the past, people cannot forget the past. Two thousand years have passed, but Jesus is not yet acceptable to the Jewish mind. Not a single Jew in two thousand years has repented that crucifying Jesus was a criminal act, and that he finds himself also part of the conspiracy. You will be surprised to know that not a single Jewish scripture even mentions the name of Jesus. It is so unworthy. Such is our approach to life....

I will take your question as fresh, because we are not in Kathmandu. And I will answer you in this moment, responding to your question and to you. I am not in the habit of quoting myself.

You are asking, what is the need of the disciple for a master, and vice versa – what is the need of a master for a disciple? Condensed to its essentialness, the question is, "Does love exist in the lover or in the beloved? Or does love exist in the harmony of both?"

Only in those rare moments, when there is no "I" and no "thou," love blossoms. It does not exist in the lover, it does not exist in the beloved, it exists in the disappearance of their separation.

That's why all lovers are disappointed, because they cannot remain organically one for more than a few seconds. Just a small thing and the separation returns; it was just waiting. If in twenty-four hours you can find twenty-four seconds of organic unity and harmony, you should think yourself immensely blessed, tremendously rich.

The same is the situation between the disciple and the master. Something higher than love, something deeper than love and togetherness exists in those moments of silence, those moments of communion, when the disciple forgets that he is separate from the master, when the disciple melts and merges into the master.

The master is already merged into existence. Merging into the master you are really merging with existence itself. The master functions only as a door, and a door is an emptiness; you pass through it.

The master is the door to the beyond.

And the beyond exists in the organic unity, in the communion, in the merger, in the melting of the master and the disciple. It is the highest form of love. It is the greatest prayer, the deepest gratitude, and the most ecstatic experience available to human consciousness.

The master is missing something when he is alone; he is like an ocean into which no rivers melt. A disciple is certainly just a nobody without a master. With a master, he becomes the whole existence. Both are fulfilled in a togetherness. And because this togetherness is not of the body, not of the mind, but of that which is beyond the mind in you, it is possible to attain and never lose it.

Love is always up and down, one moment joyful, another moment sad. But the love that we are talking about – love between two spirits, between two beings – only begins, it never ends.

The masters ordinarily will not accept what I am saying, but if they don't accept it they are insincere. And if they are insincere, what kind of masters are they?

The masters have been pretending that they don't need anything – they don't need you, they don't need your eyes, they don't need your heartbeat, they don't need your love, they don't need your merger and meeting. That is an egoistic attitude. And anybody who pretends that he needs nothing is only a teacher, not a master. He himself needs to be a disciple. He has heard many beautiful truths, but he has not known anything on his own.

A true master, out of his sincerity, out of his humbleness, will accept the simple fact that he is not beyond any need. Of course, his needs are of a very spiritual kind.

He cannot live unless he can share. Even to exist is impossible for him – he loses all meaning – unless he can wake up people who are fast asleep, unless he can make people who are miserable become transformed into dancing roses. In their fulfillment he becomes again and again enlightened.

His enlightenment is not an incident: the authentic master is becoming continuously enlightened each moment. His enlightenment is a progress, an eternal progress; otherwise, the world would have been far more poor. It is already poor.

If Gautam Buddha needed nothing, then for forty-two years walking the whole land, talking to people, knowing perfectly well that they cannot understand, is an arduous task. Why is he doing it? He is helpless, he has to do it. It comes as an intrinsic part of his own enlightenment.

Before, it was a longing to become enlightened. Now it is a longing to make the whole world enlightened.

Osho,

I love the way you speak so intimately to sannyasins who have been with you for a long time, remembering Veena with photographic clarity and whether someone else's hands were cold or warm, and where he used to stand to greet you. The intimacy of you acknowledging us is such an incredibly beautiful gift it makes me weep. Could you say something about acknowledgment?

One of the most important secrets of life is that the something can be of immense spiritual value, and the same thing can be a great hindrance for your growth.

Such is acknowledgment. It can arise out of your ego – to be acknowledged – then it is dangerous. Then it is going to strengthen that which is false in you and block the doors for the real to open up.

But if it arises out of a simple, innocent heart – not as a nourishment to the ego but just as a blissful recognition that you are also there, that you are also in existence, that you are accepted as you are, that you are respected as you are – then acknowledgment can become a tremendous experience and transformation.

It all depends on you, what you make of it.

There are people whom I feel afraid to recognize – not that it is going to do any harm to me, but because it is going to do harm to them. I can see in their eyes, in their faces, a deep desire, a greed to be recognized. I ignore it. But there are people who are simply here – just enjoying. It is more than enough that they are breathing the same air, that they are sitting under the same roof, that they are surrounded by the same trees.

I am reminded of a strange story about Ananda, one of Gautam Buddha's most intimate disciples.

And he was not only a disciple, he was also his elder cousin-brother. Just the fact that he was more deeply related with Gautam Buddha, the fact that blood is thicker than water, the fact that, "Not only I am related, he is younger in age to me," became a hindrance.

Forty-two years he remained with Buddha, but could not attain enlightenment. And many, many others came and became enlightened. It was the day when he was taking initiation that he had asked Gautam Buddha, "I have come to be initiated. After initiation I will be your disciple. Right now I am your elder brother." And in India, even cousin-brothers, if they are elder, have to be respected just like your real brothers.

Ananda said, "I want you to remember three conditions, and give me a promise that you will not go against your word, because after initiation your order will be my life, your word will be my law – then I cannot say anything. So just before initiation I want three promises. As your elder brother you have to respect my desires."

Sariputra, one of Gautam Buddha's earliest disciples, said to Ananda, "Don't be stupid, these promises will become hindrances for your growth. These conditions will prohibit all for which you are taking the initiation. You are saying, 'I am going to become your disciple,' but deep down you will never be a disciple. You will always know that you are the elder brother, and those three conditions will always make you certain about it."

Initiation has to be taken unconditionally, but Ananda was not going to listen to an ordinary sannyasin. Sariputra was one of the wisest disciples of Gautam Buddha, but in the eyes of Ananda he was nobody. Ananda was a king, had his own kingdom; Sariputra was just a commoner. Ananda said to him, "You keep quiet. It is a question between two brothers, you need not interfere."

After forty-two years Ananda wept when Gautam Buddha was dying. And he said, "I did not listen to Sariputra. I was ignorant, I insisted. Those conditions were nothing but an enhancement of my ego."

The first condition was, "I will always remain with you. You cannot send me anywhere else to spread the word." Second, "I can ask any question. You cannot say to me, 'Wait, and when the time is right you will receive the answer.' No, you will have to give me the answer immediately." And third, "If I bring a friend – even if it is in the middle of the night, and I wake you up – you will have to receive him and answer his questions."

Gautam Buddha laughed. There are very few occasions when he laughed – in his whole life maybe three or four occasions. He laughed, laughed at the stupidity of human ignorance. What he was asking was just meaningless, and what he was losing he was not aware of.

Buddha said, "You are my elder brother. I have to obey you, respect you. Your conditions are accepted. You will never find a fault. I give my promise – but I am giving it with a very heavy heart, because you don't know what you are missing. You are thinking you are becoming special, and this is the place where you have to become humble."

But a blind man is a blind man. He took initiation only after those conditions were accepted. And he wept tears of blood, because he remained always with a subtle ego: "I have a certain speciality amongst ten thousand disciples. Nobody has any promise from Gautam Buddha except me."

But the people who had no promise, their promises were fulfilled. Those who had come without asking anything and surrendered themselves, they attained. He remained lagging behind. He could not believe it: "What is the matter? Very junior people have attained to liberation, and I am one of the most senior persons. And I am the closest."

But closest only physically. He slept in the same room in which Gautam Buddha slept. He moved just behind him like a shadow, and he felt greatly proud of his specialness. He was acknowledged by Gautam Buddha and by everybody else; but his acknowledgment became his fault, his failure.

Never desire acknowledgment. Enjoy when it comes, relish it, dance...but when it comes on its own, not asked for. The master always recognizes – but only those who will be helped by it. And he ignores those who will be helped by his ignoring them. Perhaps they will come to an understanding of why they are being ignored: because they want to be special, because they want to be acknowledged.

Drop that! If you cannot drop, even with a master, then what kind of discipleship is it? What kind of initiation have you taken? Now leave it to him. If he feels that you need being ignored, he will ignore you – and you have to be thankful for it. And if he feels you need acknowledgment he will acknowledge you, and you have to be thankful for that too. But it should not be a demand on your part.

The moment you demand you miss the intimacy, the deep spiritual connection. You fall far away, because the desire is not of your being, it is of your ego, of your personality – which is not you, which is your enemy. This enemy has to be crucified.

Without ego, without any sense of "I", you will know the innocence of a child. Then the whole starry sky and its freedom is yours.

A smart New York career girl married Stefano, a handsome young Italian farmer. She was not too happy with his social manners, and started trying to improve him immediately. Throughout the wedding reception she continuously corrected his mistakes, telling him what to say, which knife to use at the table, and how to pass the butter.

Finally, the celebrations were over, and they were in bed at last. Stefano fidgeted between the sheets, unsure of himself, but finally he turned towards his new wife and stuttered, "Could you pass the pussy please?"

It is better to recognize whatever you are: ignorant, uneducated, knowledgeable, moralistic, puritan, egoist – it is better to recognize whatever you are.

There is no need to hide yourself from the master.

The function of the master is not to improve upon you, but to transform you – and these are two different processes.

To reform you means to decorate you, to polish you; to transform means to help you die as an ego and be born as an innocent child, who knows no idea of "I-ness".

Only the childlike consciousness is capable of understanding all that is beautiful in life, all that is great in existence. And the whole existence is full of greatness, full of glories. This is the only existence there is; its beauty, its truth, is the only beauty and the only truth. But they are available only to the innocent people. Blessed are the innocent, for theirs is the kingdom of God.

CHAPTER 15

Most People Return Unopened

Everybody hesitates to ask, and the reason
and the rationalization are two different things.
The reason for feeling hesitation is
that one does not want to show one's ignorance,
and every question shows your ignorance.
One hopes that some other stupid person
is going to ask the question.

Osho,

It feels so hopeless. I feel ashamed to have been a sannyasin for ten years and still be in this state. I hesitate to ask for your help, because even your words become mechanical in me after a few repetitions. Would you please comment?

*I*t is not yet hopeless enough. Just make it a little more hopeless. There comes a point in hopelessness where you stop hoping.

Hopelessness is still deep down nothing but hope. Let the hope fail completely and totally, and a dramatic experience arises out of that space when you don't have any hope – because hope is another name of desire, another name of expectation, another name of ambition. And before you can realize yourself, all desires, all expectations, all ambitions must have failed you, must have left you alone. Hoping nothing, desiring nothing, expecting nothing – where will you be? There is no way to go out.

Hope is a way of going out, desire is a way of going away, ambition is a way to avoid going in. On the path, to be utterly hopeless, so hopeless that you stop hoping…suddenly you are in – without taking a single step.

Hope is a kind of opium; it keeps you intoxicated. To tolerate the miserable present, your eyes remain fixed on a faraway star: your hope. Millions of people live without finding themselves – not because of any sin that Adam and Eve committed, or that they committed in some of their past lives. The sin is that people go on looking in the future and the present goes on passing by. And the present is the only reality; the future is a dream, and howsoever sweet, dreams never come true.

Self-realization is not a dream. It is a realization in the present moment of your own being. So don't be worried; you are on the right path, becoming hopeless. Go on more and more, exhaust hopelessness. Come to the optimum hopelessness. Then hope disappears automatically.

And when there is no hope, you are.

When there is no hope, the present is.

An old spinster died, and her two old friends went to a stone mason to have a gravestone made. "And what message would you like to have on the stone?" asked the mason. "Well," said one of the old maids, "It's quite simple really. We would like 'She came a virgin, she lived a virgin, and she died a virgin.'"

The mason replied, "You know, you ladies could save a lot of money by just saying, 'Returned unopened.'"

Most of the people return unopened, and nobody is responsible except themselves.

You are asking, "It feels so hopeless...." Not yet; otherwise even this question would not have arisen. There is still hope. You say, "I feel ashamed to have been a sannyasin for ten years, and still be in this state." That is your ego feeling hurt; otherwise you would feel humble, not ashamed. What is there to be ashamed of?

Life is not a small thing. It is so vast, and we are so small. The ocean is so big, and we have to swim in it just with our own small hands. Only those people who never start swimming and go on standing on the bank looking at others, should feel ashamed. One who has started swimming...ten years is nothing much, even ten lives are short.

One should be so patient. It is your impatience that is feeling ashamed; it is your ego that is feeling ashamed. You should feel humble – humble before the vastness of existence, humble before the mysteries of life...just humble, a nobody. And in that humbleness, the ocean becomes small and your hands become bigger.

You say, "I hesitate to ask for your help...."

You go on saying things which you don't mean. If you really hesitate, then why are you asking? In fact, hesitation is your question.

You should ask a little more so that you can open up, so that you can become more exposed. Don't go on hiding yourself. What is the hesitation in asking? And you go on rationalizing everything within yourself; you have rationalized your hesitation.

Everybody hesitates to ask, and the reason and the rationalization are two different things. The reason for feeling hesitation is that one does not want to show one's ignorance, and every question shows your ignorance. One hopes that some other stupid person is going to ask the question; just wait...because the human reality is one, and human problems are one, and the search for oneself is one. So some day somebody is going to ask the question that you cannot gather courage to ask yourself.

But I want you to remember that even in asking there is something valuable. In asking, you are exposing your ignorance; in asking, you are accepting that you don't know; in asking, you are dropping your so-called knowledgeability.

To ask a question is more important than the question itself. The question may be anything – xyz – but the very asking is significant. It brings you closer to me, and it brings you closer to all other sannyasins, the fellow travelers. You don't remain closed, afraid that somebody may know that you know not. Exposing yourself – that you are ignorant – all fear disappears. You become more human, and you become more intimate with everyone who is a fellow traveler, because the same is his situation. That is the reason why one hesitates.

But rationalizations are a totally different thing. You rationalize that, "I hesitate to ask for your help because even your words become mechanical in me after a few repetitions."

What is the need of repeating them? One repeats a thing because one wants to make it mechanical. In your mind, there is a robot part; if you repeat a certain thing, the robot part takes it over. Then you don't have to think about it; the robot part goes on doing it. You are unburdened of thinking, you are unburdened of responsibility. And the robot part is very efficient; it is mechanical. It has its use, and it has its misuse.

When you are working in the ordinary world, the day to day world, if you have to remember every day where your house is, who your wife is…if you have to search every day in the crowd looking into every face – who is your wife? – it will become a little difficult. The robot part takes over. It knows the way home; you need not think on every turn whether to go right or to go left. You go on listening to the radio, and your hands will go on turning the steering wheel exactly to your own porch.

If one has to think about everything, life will become too clumsy. Once in a while, it happens with a few people, who don't have a very strong robot part – and these are the people who are very intelligent – that their whole energy moves into intelligence, and their robot part is left starving.

Thomas Alva Edison is one of the cases to be considered. He was leaving and going to an institute to deliver a lecture on some new scientific project he was working on. Saying good-bye to his wife, he kissed her and waved to his maid. His chauffeur could not believe his eyes – because he had kissed the maid, and he was waving to the wife. His robot part was very, very small; his whole life energy was devoted to scientific investigations where a robot part is not needed.

One day, he was sitting and working on some calculations, and his wife came with the breakfast. Seeing him so much involved, she left the breakfast by his side, thinking that when he sees it, he will understand why she has not disturbed him. Meanwhile, one of his friends came. Seeing him so much absorbed, he also felt not to disturb him. Having nothing else to do, he ate the breakfast, and left the empty dishes by his side. When Edison looked up and saw his friend, he looked at the empty plate and said, "You came a little late. I have finished my breakfast. We could have shared it."

The friend said, "Don't be worried."

You say that everything becomes mechanical in you after a few repetitions. But why repeat? The repetition is a method to make a thing mechanical. Always do something fresh, something new, if you do not want to get caught in repetitions. But in ordinary life, repetitions are perfectly good.

As you enter into the world of higher consciousness, repetitions are dangerous. There you need always a fresh mind, an innocent mind, which knows nothing and responds to a situation not out of the mechanical, robot part of your mind, but from the very living source of your life.

Here we are not concerned about the mundane world. Our concern is to raise the consciousness.

Don't repeat, don't imitate. Remember one thing: you have to respond always in a fresh way. The situation may be old, but *you* are not to be old. You have to remain young and fresh. Just try new responses. They will not be as efficient as mechanical responses, but efficiency is not a great value in spiritual life...freshness is.

A rabbi and a minister were sitting together on a plane. The stewardess came up to them and asked, "Would you care for a cocktail?"

"Sure," said the rabbi. "Please bring a Manhattan."

"Fine, sir," said the stewardess. "And you Reverend?"

"Young lady," he said, "before I touch strong drink, I would just as soon commit adultery."

"I've missed," said the rabbi. "As long as there is a choice, I will have what he's having."

People are imitative and imitation is bound to be unintelligent. They want to do exactly the things which others are doing. That destroys their freshness. Do things in your own style; live your life according to your own light. And even if the same situation arises, be alert to find a new response.

It is only a question of a little alertness, and once you have started enjoying...and it is really a great joy to respond to old situations always in a new way, because that newness keeps you young, keeps you conscious, keeps you non-mechanical, keeps you alive.

Don't be repetitive. But when I am saying don't be repetitive, I don't mean in the ordinary life, in the marketplace; there, repetition is the rule. But in the inner world, the freshness of your response is the law.

Osho,
I have noticed that when you leave the discourse and pass through the door, you often look to your left. Are you simply saying "hello" to the ghost?

I have to. That room, Anando's room, has so many ghosts. I had not told Anando when she came into the room for the first time – but how long can you hide a fact? The ghosts started declaring themselves. In the middle of the night, they would wake her. They would knock – she would jump out of her bed. And she was afraid to tell anybody what was the matter. Finally she gathered courage and asked me, "What is the matter? Suddenly, in the middle of the night, somebody knocks, and if I don't jump up, he tries to pull my leg."

I said, "Nothing to be worried about. It is a very nice assembly of ghosts." I keep them in Anando's room just so they can also listen to the discourse – in fact, it is their room. They are not ghosts, they are the hosts – Anando is the guest. But she was very much afraid I said, "You don't be afraid. Start introducing yourself to them."

She said, "But what will others think?"

I said, "Nobody is there in the middle of the night."

She said, "That's right." So she introduced herself: "I'm a nice Australian girl and I don't want any trouble." And now she has even started making a bed in the bathroom, in the bathtub, with cozy blankets and many clothes for the ghosts, so they can rest there.

I have to pass that room just because of those fellows. Just a "hello" is needed. And now it has become known to a few people. Milarepa is asking, "Why, when you enter the room, do you l ook to the left and say, 'Hello'?" Mukta has even approached Anando to say, "I enjoy the company of ghosts. I would like to invite them for tea – just to be friendly with them."

But Anando is very much afraid. She has to talk to them every night. I have asked her whether they answer. She said, "They never answer."

I said, "They will not answer because they don't exist. You have to create them; it is a very creative dimension."

Nirupa became interested, because everybody wants to know mysterious things. She stayed with Anando, and she also heard the knocks. She said, "My God, they are!" But in fact, all those knocks are made by Milarepa. It is by arrangement with me, just to keep a place in the commune for nice ghosts.

You can create ghosts very easily. Anything else is very difficult because it needs some material. Ghosts are absolutely immaterial. It just needs a good imagination, and Anando has a good imagination. And it is a good exercise to talk to the ghosts, because you can be more truthful than you can be with human beings – it is a good meditation. You can tell them secrets which you cannot tell to anybody else, because they are not going to spread rumors. You can trust them; they are your own creation.

Slowly, slowly Anando will make it a meditation – it is becoming one by and by. I am giving her as much encouragement as possible. There is nothing to be afraid of, because ghosts don't exist anywhere – Anando's room included. But to have a good company of ghosts, and to talk with them, can be transformed into a meditation, as if you are talking to your own different selves.

Every man has many selves. He can make each self a ghost, and then it is easy to talk to them. And just one step more – talk from your side and answer from *his* side. Between this conversation, between you and the non-existential ghost, you will find treasures hidden within yourself, secrets and mysteries of which you were not aware before.

So Anando's room is a special room. When you walk through it, never forget to say hello to the ghosts.

Goldstein applies for membership in the Communist Party, and he is requested to answer a few questions.

"Who was Karl Marx?"

"I don't know," replies Goldstein.

"Lenin?"

"Sorry, I don't know him either."

"What about Leonid Brezhnev?"

"Never heard of him."

"Are you playing games with me?" asked the official. "Not at all," says Goldstein. "Do you know Herschel Salzberg?"

"No," says the official.

"What about Yankl Horovitch?"

"Never heard of him."

"Sammy Davidovitch?"

"No."

"Well," says Goldstein, "I guess that's the way it goes. You have got your friends, I have got mine."

People think Anando lives alone – she has such a beautiful congregation! Right now I am telling her to have some conversations, and soon you will see her addressing the congregation. There will be nobody, but she will enjoy her own revelations. And one thing is good about ghosts: you can say anything to them, in any language; right or wrong, it does not matter.

Ghosts are almost like God. People are praying all over the world every morning, every evening, to a God. And it is not that their prayer is absolutely useless – although there is no God. If they are praying with tears in their eyes and love in their hearts, and a feeling of gratitude surrounding them, whether God exists or not is not the point. The prayer changes the person. It gives him a new experience. God was just an excuse.

So are the ghosts of Anando's room an excuse for her to stand up and address the congregation. I think tonight she's going to do it, and enjoy it, and tell those poor fellows...because they are so old. Somebody may have died thousands of years before. Just visualize a few skeletons sitting around you – it is an exercise in visualization – and then start addressing them, "Brothers and sisters...." And you will not be surprised that they applaud, they laugh, at exactly the right moments.

Milarepa has another question. He is afraid that Anando's ghosts are just underneath his room, and someday they may start moving around the house. You need not be afraid, Milarepa, because I have asked a few ghosts...they are afraid of you! So you remain courageous. Even if you feel some ghost has entered, behave as if nobody has entered. Go on playing on your guitar a little louder. Ghosts don't particularly like the contemporary music because they are not contemporary – they are very classical people.

Two Italians were watching a jet fly overhead.

"Hey, that's-a the pope up-a there," declared one.

"How you know-a that?" asked the other.

"That's-a easy" replies the first. "The airplane-a, said TWA on it. That means Top Wop Aboard."

Milarepa, you can write on your door TWA: Top Wop Aboard. And don't be afraid of the ghosts. I am always here. If some ghost plays tricks on you, you can just inform me, because I have such an intimacy with everything in life – ghosts and gods, trees and rivers, mountains and clouds – that I will prevent them...Don't Disturb the Musician!

You are allowed to be present in the court of Anando. She is my legal secretary, and if you want to learn about law, she can teach you things. I don't think that any ghost is interested in things like law – so technical. But they are interested in Anando. She is very juicy!

Osho,

When I saw you the other morning, you seemed so totally fresh, so new, so radiant – deeper, and higher, and vaster than ever before. What has happened to you in these days of silence?

*T*here are many things that have not been told by the mystics to people, just so that they don't freak out. One of the things is the moment you become aware, conscious, reaches which were unknown to you before become available. Your contact with the body becomes loose, particularly after enlightenment.

The general understanding is that you will be more healthy. You are in an inner sense more healthy, but as far as your body is concerned, you become more fragile. So whenever I have a great opportunity of being sick, I use it – just resting under my blankets, being utterly silent. I love to be sick, to tell you the truth, because then I can sleep twenty hours, at least. It is sleep to the outside people; but to me it is a deep meditation.

So, because both my arms and their joints are in bad shape, I cannot even participate in your rejoicing and in your music, I have been resting completely. And whatever I do, I do totally. That may have given you the idea that I looked "totally fresh, new, radiant – deeper and higher and vaster than ever before."

I am always the same. But as you become more and more centered inward, even to look outside is a strain on the eyes, even to speak a word is a strain because effort has to be made. Otherwise the silence cannot be translated in any way and conveyed to you.

So whenever I get some chance.... For example, when I was in American jails for twelve days, all I did was sleep for twenty hours, waking up twice to take a bath and to eat something, and then go to sleep again. When I came out of the jail, the jailer said, "You are my first experience of someone...from when you entered, till now when you are coming out, I can compare: You are looking so radiant, so fresh."

I said to him, "Jail life suits me!"

He said, "What?"

I said, "Yes, because there is no disturbance."

Each of your presidents, your prime ministers, your senate members should be given a chance every year, at least for twelve days, to be in jail. They will all feel nourished. They just have to know the art: take it easily. Easy is right.

An American from Texas is visiting France, and feeling thirsty, he stops at a house along the road. "Can you give me a drink of water?" asked the Texan.

"Of course," says the Frenchman.

"What do you do?" asks the Texan.

"I raise a few chickens," says the Frenchman.

"Really," says the Texan. "I'm also a farmer. How much land do you have?"

"Well," says the Frenchman. "Out front it is fifty meters, as you can see, and in the back we have close to a hundred meters of property. And what about your place?"

"Well," says the Texan proudly. "On my ranch, I have breakfast, and I get into the car, and I drive and drive, and I don't reach the end of the ranch until dinnertime."

"Really," replied the Frenchman. "I once had a car like that."

It all depends how you take it.

Margaret Thatcher, Francois Mitterand, and Ronald Reagan were lunching together. Naturally, they talked about their respective heartaches.

Margaret Thatcher said, "I have thirteen undercover agents and one of them is a double agent, but I don't know which."

Mitterand spoke up, "I have thirteen mistresses and one of them is cheating on me, but I don't know which."

Reagan said, "I have thirteen cabinet ministers, and one of them is intelligent – but I don't know which."

CHAPTER 16

Life is an Eternal Incarnation

The whole Western mind has become
the mind of a tourist who is carrying two, three cameras,
and rushing to photograph everything
because he only has a three-week visa.
And in three weeks, he has to cover
the whole country — all the great monuments.
There is no time for him to see them directly;
he will see them at home, at ease, in his album.

Osho,

Sometimes in discourse, I suddenly come to consciousness and realize that I don't know where I've been, and yet the discourse is coming to a close. Your words were coming through, but I'm not sure if I was awake. If I'm not conscious, am I asleep? Are these the only two possibilities? Is there some stage in-between? How to tell the difference?

*M*ary Catherine, the question you have asked is the question everybody needs the answer for. Man is asleep, but it is no ordinary sleep; he is asleep with open eyes. His sleep is spiritual, not physical.

Just as in physical sleep your consciousness is filled with dreams, in spiritual sleep your consciousness is filled with thoughts, desires, feelings – a thousand and one things.

It is not that you are unconscious in the sense of being in a coma; you are unconscious in the sense that your consciousness is covered with too much dust. It is exactly like a mirror: if covered with many layers of dust, it will lose the quality of reflecting, will lose the quality of being a mirror. But the mirror is there; all that is needed is to remove the dust. Your consciousness is there – even while you are physically asleep your consciousness is there, but now more covered than when you are awake.

You are asking, "If I'm not conscious, am I asleep? Are these the only two possibilities? Is there some stage in between? How to tell the difference?"

You are not unconscious in the sense a person falls into a coma; you are not conscious in the sense a Gautam Buddha is conscious. You are in between. A thick layer of thoughts does not allow you to be in the present. That's why, while you are listening to me, you are listening and yet the listening is very superficial – because deep down there are so many thoughts going on. You are listening but it is not reaching you, and as I stop speaking, suddenly you realize that you have been listening, certainly, but you have not understood it. It has not penetrated you; it has not become part of your being. Something has prevented it, like a China Wall. Those thoughts are transparent, but they are thicker than any China Wall can be.

You are neither asleep nor awake, you are in between – awake as far as your day to day mechanical activities are concerned, and asleep as far as a clear consciousness is concerned. A pure consciousness, a deep innocence like an unclouded sky, is absent.

The pope was sitting with his cardinals signing papers and proclamations. The phone rang and his secretary answered. "Your holiness," she said. "It is about the abortion bill. A reporter wants to talk to you."

"Don't bother me," the pope interrupted.

"But he wants to know what you are going to do about the bill."

"Just pay it," the pope replied. "Pay it quick!"

In what position will you put the pope? Asleep or awake? He is in between; he has heard the word bill, but he has interpreted it in his own way. He has forgotten completely that the bill is about abortion, and certainly he has not been aborted, and he has not to pay any bill.

But this is the situation of us all. We hear what we want to hear; we hear only that which adjusts with our preconceived notions, prejudices.

You will be surprised to know...the scientific research is almost unbelievable: it says ninety-eight percent of what you hear is prevented from reaching to you – ninety-eight percent! Only two percent reaches you. It has to pass through so many thoughts, conceptions, beliefs, conditionings, and they go on cutting it according to themselves. By the time it reaches you, it is something totally different than was said, than was heard. It is a long process of screening, and we are all screening. If something falls in tune with our mind – that means with our past – we hear it. But if it goes against it, we certainly hear the sound but we miss the meaning.

To listen is a great art.

People only hear; very few people are able to listen.

One man had reached Gautam Buddha. He was a well-known philosopher of the day and he had defeated many philosophers in discussions about the ultimate, the truth, God. He had come to defeat Gautam Buddha too – that would be the crowning victory. He had brought with him five hundred chosen disciples to see Gautam Buddha defeated.

But Gautam Buddha asked a very strange question. He asked, "Do you understand the meaning and the difference between hearing and listening?"

The man was at a loss. He had come to discuss great things, and this was a small matter. And there was no difference...as far as language is concerned, dictionaries are concerned, hearing is listening. The man said, "There is no difference at all, and I had hoped you would not ask such an ordinary question."

Gautam Buddha said, "There is a great difference. And unless you understand the difference, there is no possibility of any dialogue. I will say something; you will hear something else. So if you really want to have a dialogue with me, sit by my side for two years. Don't speak a single word, just listen. Whatever I'm telling others, be unconcerned; I'm not telling you. So you need not be worried about whether it is true or untrue, whether you have to accept it or not. You are just a witness; your opinion is not required.

"After two years, you can have the dialogue, the discussion you have come for. And I would love to be defeated, so this is not to postpone defeat; it is just to make the dialogue possible."

At that very moment, Mahakashyap – a great disciple of Gautam Buddha; perhaps the greatest – laughed. He was sitting under a tree far away, and the philosopher thought, "That man seems to be mad. Why is he laughing?"

Buddha said, "Mahakashyap, this is not mannerly; even for an enlightened man this is not right."

Mahakashyap said, "I don't care about right and wrong; I'm just feeling sorry for the poor philosopher."

And he turned to the philosopher and said to him, "If you want to have a discussion, have it right now; after two years, there will be just silence and no dialogue. This man is not trustworthy. He deceived me; I also came with the same idea as you, to defeat him, and he cheated me. He said, 'Sit down for two years by my side, and listen. Learn first the art of listening. And because you are not concerned at all, your mind need not function.'

"And two years is a long time; the mind starts forgetting how to think, how to function. The very presence of Gautam Buddha is so peaceful, so silent, that one starts rejoicing in the silence. And to listen to his words...which are not addressed to you, so you are not worried whether they agree with your prejudices, your philosophy, your religion – with you – or not. You are indifferent. You listen to him as if you are listening to the birds singing in the morning when the sun rises.

"And two years...the mind disappears. And although those words are not addressed to you, they start reaching to your heart. Because the mind is silent, the passage is open – the door is open, the heart welcomes them. So if you want to ask anything, if you want to challenge this man, challenge now. I don't want to see another man cheated again."

Gautam Buddha said, "It is up to you; if you want to defeat me now, I declare my defeat. There is no need to talk. Why waste time? You are victorious. But if you really want to have a dialogue with me, then I'm not asking much, just two years to learn the art of listening."

The man remained for two years, and even forgot completely that after two years he had to challenge Gautam Buddha for a debate. He forgot the whole calendar. Days passed, months passed, seasons came and went away, and after two years he was enjoying the silence so much that he had no idea that two years had passed.

It has to be remembered that time is a very elastic thing. When you are in suffering, time becomes longer; suddenly all the watches and clocks of the world start moving slowly – a great conspiracy against a poor man who is in suffering. Time moves so slowly that sometimes one feels as if it has stopped.

You are sitting by the side of someone you love who is dying, in the middle of the night; it seems time has stopped, that this night is not going to end, that your idea that all nights end was a fallacy...this night is not going to have a dawn, because time is not moving.

And when you are joyful – when you meet a friend after many years, when you meet a beloved, a lover for whom you have waited long – suddenly, again the conspiracy. All the clocks, all the watches, start moving faster; hours go like minutes, days go like hours, months go like weeks. Time is elastic: time is relative to your inner condition.

The man had enjoyed those two years of silence so deeply that he could not conceive that two years had passed. Suddenly, Buddha himself asked him, "Have you forgotten completely? Two years have passed; this is the day you had come two years ago. Now if you want to challenge me to a debate, I'm ready."

The man fell to the feet of Gautam Buddha.

And Mahakashyap laughed again, and said, "I had told you, but nobody listens to me. I have been sitting under this tree for almost twenty years, preventing people from falling into the trap of this man; but nobody listens to me. They fall into the trap, and each person gives me two occasions to laugh."

The man went, after touching Gautam Buddha's feet, to touch the feet of Mahakashyap too, saying, "I am grateful to you. I have learned the distinction between hearing and listening. Hearing had made me a great knowledgeable man, and listening has made me innocent, silent – a peace that passeth understanding. I don't have any questions, and I don't have any answers; I am utterly silent. All questions have disappeared, all answers have disappeared. Can I also sit by your side under the tree?" he asked Mahakashyap.

Mahakashyap said, "No, I don't accept disciples; that is the business of Gautam Buddha – you just go there. Don't crowd around my tree, because even here there is nothing to listen to, only once in a while a laughter when somebody comes and I see that he's falling into the trap. You have fallen into the trap; now be initiated, become a sannyasin."

Not only did the man become a sannyasin, his five hundred followers who were also sitting and listening for two years, had also become silent.

Mary Catherine, you are well-educated; perhaps too much – well-read; perhaps too much. Your mind is so full of thoughts. Those thoughts are creating a state which is neither consciousness nor unconsciousness. Everything seems to be so full of noise in you that if I shout, perhaps my words may reach you – but what about my whispers? And truth cannot be shouted, it can only be whispered. In fact, it can be said only in silence; even whispering is too much verbiage.

Put your educated mind aside. Here you have to be innocent, like small children playing on the beach making castles of sand, running after butterflies, collecting seashells, looking at everything with so much wonder that each and every thing in existence becomes a mystery.

Listening to me is only a beginning; then you have to listen to the trees, to the mountains, to the moon, to the faraway stars – they all have messages for you. To the sunrises, to the sunsets... they all have been waiting for so long. Once you start listening, the whole existence starts speaking to you. Right now you only speak to yourself, and nobody listens.

Three Soviet citizens – a Pole, a Czech, and a Jew – were accused of spying and sentenced to death. Each was granted a last wish.

"I want my ashes scattered over the grave of Karl Marx," said the Pole.

"I want my ashes scattered over the grave of Lenin," said the Czech.

"And I," said the Jew, "want my ashes scattered over the grave of Comrade Gorbachev."

"But that is impossible!" he was told. "Gorbachev is not dead yet."

"Fine," said the Jew, "I can wait."

You should not wait.

Start from this moment to listen, to be silent, because the next moment is not certain. Gorbachev may die, may not die. Tomorrow it may not be so easy as it is today, because in twenty-four hours you will have gathered more garbage in your head; so the sooner the better, because you cannot sit silently. If you don't start now, you will be doing something or other....

Don't postpone it. Every postponement is suicidal – particularly of those experiences which belong to the beyond.

Osho,

In Western society, at least, youth is considered to be everything, and to a certain extent, it seems this is as it should be if we are to continue growing in every dimension of life. But the natural corollary of that is that as one moves away from youth, birthdays are no longer a cause for congratulations, but are an embarrassing and unavoidable fact of life. It becomes impolite to ask someone their age; gray hair is dyed, teeth capped or replaced entirely, demoralized breasts and faces have to be lifted, tummies made taut, and varicose veins supported – but under cover. You certainly don't take it as a compliment if someone tells you that you look your age. But my experience is that as I become older, each year is only better and better; yet nobody told me this would be so, and you never hear people singing the praises of growing older. Would you, for the benefit of your middle-aged sannyasins, speak on the joys of growing older?

The question you have asked implies many things. First, the Western mind is conditioned by the idea that you have only one life – seventy years, and youth will never come again. In the West, the spring comes only once; naturally, there is a deep desire to cling as long as possible, to pretend in every possible way that you are still young.

In the East, the older person was always valued, respected. He was more experienced, he had seen many, many seasons coming and going; he had lived through all kinds of experiences, good and bad. He had become seasoned; he was no more immature. He had a certain integrity that comes only with age. He was not childish, carrying his teddy bears; he was not young, still fooling around thinking that this was love.

He had passed through all these experiences, had seen that beauty fades; he has seen that everything comes to an end, that everything is moving towards the grave. From the very moment he left the cradle, there was only one way – and it is from cradle to the grave. You cannot go anywhere else; you cannot go astray even if you try. You will reach to the grave whatever you do.

The old man was respected, loved; he had attained a certain purity of the heart because he had lived through desires, and seen that every desire leads to frustration. Those desires are past memories. He had lived in all kinds of relationships, and had seen that every kind of relationship turns into hell. He had passed through all the dark nights of the soul. He had attained a certain aloofness – the purity of an observer. He was no longer interested in participating in any football game. Just living his life, he had come to a transcendence; hence, he was respected, his wisdom was respected.

But in the East, the idea has been that life is not just a small piece of seventy years in which youth comes only once. The idea has been that just as in existence everything moves eternally – the summer comes, the rains come, the winter comes, and the summer again; everything moves like a wheel – life is not an exception.

Death is the end of one wheel and the beginning of another. Again you will be a child, and again you will be young, and again you will be old. It has been so since the beginning, and it is going to be so to the very end – until you become so enlightened that you can jump out of the vicious circle and can enter into a totally different law. From individuality, you can jump into the universal. So there was no hurry, and there was no clinging.

The West is based on the Judaic tradition which believes only in one life. Christianity is only a branch of the Jews. Jesus was a Jew, born a Jew, lived a Jew, died a Jew; he never knew that he was a Christian. If you meet him somewhere and greet him with, 'Hello, Jesus Christ', he will not recognize who you are addressing because he never knew that his name is Jesus and he never knew that he is Christ. His name was Joshua, a Hebrew name, and he was a messiah of God, not a Christ. Jesus Christ is a translation in Greek from Hebrew. Mohammedanism is also a by-product of the same tradition – the Jews.

These three religions believe in one life. To believe in one life is very dangerous because it does not give you chances to make mistakes, it does not give you chances to have enough experience of anything; you are always in a hurry.

The whole Western mind has become the mind of a tourist who is carrying two, three cameras, and rushing to photograph everything because he only has a three-week visa. And in three weeks, he has to cover the whole country – all the great monuments. There is no time for him to see them directly; he will see them at home, at ease, in his album.

Whenever I remember the tourists, I see the old women rushing from one place to another – from Ajanta to Ellora, from Taj Mahal to Kashmir – in a hurry, because life is short.

It is only the Western mind which has created the proverb that time is money. In the East, things go slowly; there is no hurry –

one has the whole of eternity. We have been here and we will be here again, so what is the hurry? Enjoy everything with intensity and totality.

So, one thing: because of the idea of one single life, the West has become too concerned about being young, and then everything is done to remain young as long as possible, to prolong the process. That creates hypocrisy, and that destroys an authentic growth. It does not allow you to become really wise in your old age, because you *hate* old age; old age reminds you only of death, nothing else. Old age means the full stop is not far away; you have come to the terminus – just one whistle more, and the train will stop.

I had an agreement with my grandfather. He loved his feet to be massaged, and I had told him, "Remember, when I say 'comma,' that means be alert; the semi-colon is coming close. When I say 'semi-colon,' get ready because the full stop is coming close. And once I say 'full stop,' I mean it." So he was so much afraid of "comma" that when I would say, "Comma," he would say, "It is okay, but let the semi-colon be a little longer. Don't make it short and quick!"

Old age simply reminds you, in the West, that a full stop is coming close – prolong the semi-colon. And who are you trying to deceive? If you have recognized that youth is no longer there, you can go on deceiving the whole world. But you are not young, you are simply being ridiculous.

I have heard…two so-called young people got married – so-called because both were pretending to be young; youth had gone down the drain a long, long time ago. They went for a honeymoon with suitcases, with the tags, "Just married." But both were afraid. There was no joy on their faces, only the fear of exposure.

Immediately they entered the hotel room, and closed the doors; the man immediately got into bed, under the blanket, and told the wife, "Put the light off while you are in the bathroom. I will wait in darkness; I like darkness."

The wife said, "Why do you like darkness? I cannot, because you are a stranger to me. We just met on the beach; I don't know who you are, you don't know who I am. I want to keep the light on the whole night."

The man said, "I will not be able to sleep."

The woman said, "But at least until I come out of the bathroom, keep the light on."

And that struggle is always the beginning of every honeymoon, the fight.... Because the woman started insisting, "Why you are so stubborn that the light should be put out?"

The man said, "You are going to know anyway, so what is the point of fighting?"

He threw the blanket away and showed that one of his legs was false.

He said, "I did not want you to know it."

The woman said, "But it is good."

She threw off her wig, took out her teeth, and told the man, "My breasts are also false. So now there is no need to be afraid of the light."

He said, "Now there is no need to be afraid of anything. Now just come on, have a headache, and go to sleep; the honeymoon is over."

People are trying to remain young, but they don't know that the very fear of losing youth does not allow you to live it in its totality.

And secondly, the fear of losing youth does not allow you to accept old age with grace. You miss both youth – its joy, its intensity – and you also miss the grace, and the wisdom, and the peace that old age brings. But the whole thing is based on a false conception of life.

Unless the West changes the idea that there is only one life, this hypocrisy, this clinging, and this fear cannot be changed.

In fact, one life is not all; you have lived many times, and you will live many times more. Hence, live each moment as totally as possible; there is no hurry to jump to another moment. Time is not money, time is inexhaustible; it is available to the poor as much as to the rich. The rich are not richer as far as time is concerned, and the poor are not poorer.

Life is an eternal incarnation.

What appears on the surface is very deep-rooted in the religions of the West. They are very miserly in giving you only seventy years. If you try to work it out, almost one third of your life will be lost in sleep, one third of your life will have to be wasted in earning food, clothes, housing. Whatever little is left has to be given to education, football matches, movies, stupid quarrels, fights. If you can save, in seventy years' time, seven minutes for yourself, I will count you a wise man.

But it is difficult to save even seven minutes in your whole life; so how can you find yourself? How can you know the mystery of your being, of your life? How can you understand that death is not an end?

Because you have missed experiencing life itself, you are going to miss the great experience of death, too; otherwise, there is nothing to be afraid of in death. It is a beautiful sleep, a dreamless sleep, a sleep that is needed for you to move into another body, silently and peacefully. It is a surgical phenomenon; it is almost like anesthesia. Death is a friend, not a foe.

Once you understand death as a friend, and start living life without any fear that it is only a very small time span of seventy years – if your perspective opens to the eternity of your life – then everything will slow down; then there is no need to be speedy.

In everything, people are simply rushing. I have seen people taking their office bag, pushing things into it, kissing their wife, not seeing whether she is their wife or somebody else; and saying good-bye to their children. This is not the way of living! And where are you reaching with this speed?

I have heard about a young couple who had purchased a new car, and they were going full speed.

The wife was telling the husband again and again, "Where are we going?" Because women are still old-minded, "Where are we going?"

And the man said, "Stop bothering me, just enjoy the speed we are going with. The real question is not where we are going; the real question is with what great speed we are going?"

Speed has become more important than the destination, and speed has become more important because life is so short. You have to do so many things that unless you do everything with speed, you cannot manage. You cannot sit silently even for a few minutes – it seems a wastage. In those few minutes you could have earned a few bucks.

Just wasting time closing your eyes, and what is there inside you? If you really want to know, you can go to any hospital and see a skeleton. That is what is inside you. Why are you unnecessarily getting into trouble by looking in? Looking in, you will find a skeleton. And once you have seen your skeleton, life will become more difficult; kissing your wife, you know perfectly well what is happening – two skeletons. Somebody just needs to invent x-ray glasses, so people can put on x-ray glasses and see all around skeletons laughing. Most probably, he will not be alive to take his glasses off; so many skeletons laughing is enough to stop anybody's heartbeat.... "My God, this is the reality! And this is what all these mystics have been telling people, 'Look inwards' – avoid them!"

The West has no tradition of mysticism. It is extrovert: look outward, there is so much to see. But they are not aware that inside there is not only the skeleton; there is something more within the skeleton. That is your consciousness. By closing your eyes you will not come across the skeleton; you will come across your very life source.

The West needs a deep acquaintance with its own life source, then there will be no hurry. One will enjoy when life brings youth, one will enjoy when life brings old age and one will enjoy when life brings death. You simply know one thing – how to enjoy everything that you come across, how to transform it into a celebration.

I call the authentic religion the art of transforming everything into a celebration, into a song, into a dance.

An old man walked into a health clinic and told the doctor, "You have got to do something to lower my sex drive." The doctor took one look at the feeble old man and said, "Now, now sir, I have got the feeling that your sex drive is all in your head."

"That's what I mean sonny," the old man said. "I have got to lower it a little."

Even the old man is wanting to be a playboy. It shows one thing with certainty – that he has not lived his youth with totality. He has missed his youth, and he is still thinking about it. Now he cannot do anything about it, but his whole mind is continuously thinking about the days he had in youth which have not been lived; at that time he was in a hurry.

If he had lived his youth, he would be free in his old age of all repressions, sexuality; there would be no need for him to drop his sexual instinct. It disappears, it evaporates in living. One just has to live uninhibited, without any interference from your religions, from your priests and it disappears; otherwise, when you are young you are in church, and when you are old, you are reading the Playboy by hiding it in your *Holy Bible*. Every *Holy Bible* is used only for one purpose, hiding magazines like Playboy, so you are not caught by children – it is embarrassing.

I have heard of three men, old men. One is seventy, the other is eighty and the third is ninety. They are all old friends, retired, who used to go for a walk and sit on a bench in the park, and have all kinds of gossips.

One day the youngest of the three, the seventy year old man, looked a little sad. The second one, the eighty year old, asked, "What is the matter? You are looking very sad."

He said, "I am feeling very guilty. It will help me to unburden myself if I tell you. It is an incident. A beautiful lady was taking a bath. She was a guest in our house, and I was looking through the keyhole and my mother caught hold of me."

Both the old friends laughed; they said, "You are an idiot. Everybody does such things in childhood."

He said, "It is not a question of childhood; it happened today."

The second man said, "Then it is really serious. But I will tell you something which has been happening to me for three days, and I am keeping it like a stone, a rock on my heart. Continuously for three days my wife has refused to love me."

The first man said, "That is really very bad."

But the third, the oldest laughed and he said, "First you ask him what does he mean by love?"

So he asked, and the second old man said, "Nothing much. Don't make me feel more embarrassed. It is a simple process. I hold my wife's hand and press it three times, then she goes to sleep and I go to sleep. But for three days, whenever I try to hold her hand, she says, 'Not today, not today! Feel ashamed; you are old enough – not today!' so for three days I have not loved."

The third old man said, "This is nothing. What has been happening to me I must confess, because you are young and it will help you in your future. Last night, as the night was passing and the morning was coming closer, I started to make preparations to make love to my wife and she said to me, 'What are you trying to do you idiot?' I said, 'What am I trying to do? I am simply trying to make love to you,' and she said, 'This is the third time in the night; neither you sleep nor you allow me to sleep. Love, love, love.' So I think it seems I am losing my memory. Your problems are nothing; I have lost my memory."

If you listen to old people, you will be surprised; they are talking only of things which they should have lived, but the time has passed when it was possible to live them. At that time they were reading the Holy Bible and listening to the priest.

Those priests and those holy scriptures have corrupted people, because they have given them ideas against nature and they cannot allow them to live naturally.

If we need a new humanity, we will have to erase the whole past and start everything anew. And the first basic principle will be: allow everybody, help everybody, teach everybody to live according to his nature, not according to any ideals, and live totally and intensely without any fear. Then children will enjoy their childhood, the young people will enjoy their youth and the old people will have the grace that comes naturally, out of a whole life lived naturally.

Unless your old age is graceful and wise and full of light and joy, contentment, fulfillment, a blissfulness...in your very presence, unless flowers blossom and there is a fragrance of eternity, then it is certain that you have lived. If it is not happening that way, that means somewhere you have gone astray, somewhere you have listened to the priests, who are the corrupters, the criminals, somewhere you have gone against nature; and nature takes revenge. And its revenge is to destroy your old age and make it ugly – ugly to others and ugly in your own eyes. Otherwise old age has a beauty which even youth cannot have.

Youth has a maturity, but it is unwise. It has too much foolishness in it; it is amateurish. Old age has given the last touches to the paintings of his own life. And when one has given the last touches, one is ready to die joyously, dancingly. One is ready to welcome death.

CHAPTER 17

Gorbachev: A New Beginning

The man, Gorbachev, is,
perhaps for the first time
in the whole history of the Russian Revolution,
a man who has an insight into human values
and is trying his best to make the Soviet Union
a really communist democracy,
and open society.

Osho,

After six years of sannyas and a long, hard struggle with authorities and legal hindrances, I recently succeeded in leaving my home country – the Soviet Union. Sitting in darshan just a few meters from you, and seeing you, and hearing you talk for the first time in my life, I remembered all my sannyasin friends who are not able to travel to you, and my joy was mixed with deep sadness. Do you see the Soviet Union under Gorbachev becoming a more open society, so that your message of love and meditation will spread more easily there?

I can understand your sadness for those friends in the Soviet Union who cannot reach me. But the night in Soviet Union seems to be coming to an end. The man, Gorbachev, is, perhaps for the first time in the whole history of the Russian Revolution, a man who has an insight into human values and is trying his best to make the Soviet Union a really communist democracy, an open society.

The dictatorship of the proletariat is not a permanent part of Karl Marx' utopia. It is only for the interim period, while the society is becoming established in the new form and the old form is disappearing. Once the old form is gone, once the capitalist mind is no longer there, the necessity for dictatorship and a closed society automatically has to disappear. It is a long time since the revolution happened and enough time to allow the dictatorship.

Gorbachev is a new beginning. Perhaps he is not only bringing an open society in the Soviet Union; he will also be helping the outside world to become *really* open. It has only been a hypothesis up to now; it is not a reality.

If half the world is closed, the other half cannot remain open. It is as if half of you is dead, and the other half is expected to go on living. Life is an organic unity on many layers, in many dimensions. This beautiful planet of ours has a totality. The division between the

Soviet and the American blocks is ugly. And more particularly, any division between human beings – either in the name of religion or in the name of nationalities – is primitive and barbarous.

Man is one. His problem is one, his misery is one – his ecstasy is also going to be one.

In the whole field of politics, Gorbachev seems to be a category in himself. He cannot be categorized with other politicians. It is going to be very difficult for him to make the Soviet Union an open society. But the man seems to be courageous and intelligent, and it is a challenge to him to make his people live in freedom – freedom of thought, freedom of movement, freedom of expression.

I have been watching his steps. He is going slowly, but going steadily. The change *has* to come very slowly, because the whole bureaucracy has enjoyed dictatorial powers for more than half a century; and the Communist Party has enjoyed more power than any party in the whole history of man. To relax the lust for power is one of the most difficult things in the world.

But life is full of mysteries. In the first place, Karl Marx, the founder of communism, had not even dreamt that communism would happen in the Soviet Union. If he is awakened from his grave and told about the Russian Revolution he will be shocked because it is against all his calculations, against all his arguments. That's what I mean when I say life is full of mysteries. It never follows the logical, the mathematical way; it goes zigzag, like a river moving in the mountains towards the ocean. Life does not run like railway trains on settled rails – it is not predictable.

According to Karl Marx, communism was going to happen in America, and logically he was right. Where one part of humanity has become immensely rich and another part has become immensely poor, where the division between the poor and the rich is so big that it becomes, at a point, intolerable, it has to be changed, the society has to go through a revolution. America should have been the first to go through the revolution. But that is what logic predicts. Life has its own ways. It happened in a very backward country which was not even capitalist.

According to Karl Marx, communism can happen only when there is a very developed form of capitalism and a class struggle. Russia was still a pre-capitalist country, still living under feudalism, under the czars. There was no capitalist class, and there was no proletariat. Karl Marx could not have logically conceived that Russia would be the first communist country, the first to have the great revolution. But it happened like that: Russia was the first and China was the next – and Marx could not have thought either of Russia or of China.

Perhaps it is going to be again a mysterious phenomenon. People think America is a democracy – which is utterly false. And people think that in America there is freedom of expression, freedom of individuality, that what the constitution of America says is not only written in the constitution but is lived by the country, and that the government exists for the people, by the people, of the people. Nothing can be farther away from truth. America is the most hypocritical society today in the world, and the most dangerous to the human future.

Gorbachev's coming into power is a great hope, because the man does not seem to be a politician. He is a man in politics, but he is not a politician. His vision is for a better humanity – it is not confined to the Soviet Union alone. And he is slowly relaxing the dictatorial bureaucracy that has grown up like a monster in the past sixty years.

He is taking one of the most risky steps. If he succeeds...and I hope that he will succeed. For sixty years half of humanity has lived under such tremendous slavery that it can be expected that a second revolution will come. And a second revolution will be bigger than the first, greater than the first. The first revolution in the Soviet Union destroyed feudalism; the second revolution will destroy the dictatorship and the slavery of millions of people.

Gorbachev to me is almost a reincarnation of Lenin. In the world of politics, he is the only man I have any respect for.

It will not be a long time until the Soviet Union becomes an open society, and it will be possible for my sannyasins to come to me. It will be possible for them to be sannyasins openly.

I have dedicated my book on human rights to Gorbachev and Sakharov – I have never dedicated any of my books to anybody before – because I can see a ray of light in this man, and a courage to create a second revolution which will be bigger than the first. The sannyasins in the Soviet Union should help this second revolution to the utmost of their capacity. Gorbachev needs every support of all those who believe in freedom, who believe in individuality, and who respect differences in people; who are not of a fascist mind to impose themselves on others, but of a democratic spirit to help everybody to be himself.

Gorbachev has a task which not only can make the Soviet Union an open society, but will prove that all condemnation by the American politicians of the Soviet Union is utterly false and baseless. The Soviet Union becoming an open society will take away all the power that America has accumulated by creating fear in the world against it. If that fear disappears, the power of America will disappear with it. America does not want the Soviet Union to become an open society.

Now it has to be understood by every Soviet citizen, and every level of humanity, that it is absolutely urgent that the Soviet Union becomes open, available, so that all condemnations fall on their own, and America is proved to be cheating the whole humanity. This will be the real victory of the Soviet Union.

The question of a nuclear victory is simply not possible. And Gorbachev is the first man who has seen the fact that with the invention of nuclear weapons, the third world war has become an impossibility – because nobody can win, nobody can be victorious. If a third world war happens, everybody will be destroyed. There will not be somebody left even to write the history of what happened in the third world war.

It is again those mysterious things I talk about.... Gautam Buddha could not prevent people from fighting; Jesus could not prevent people from fighting; Leo Tolstoy, Prince Kropotkin, and all the people who have been against war, have not been able to prevent people from going to wars. What has prevented them is the invention of nuclear powers. Now war is simply impossible – unless humanity decides to commit suicide. And humanity is not in a position to decide for suicide. There is a tremendous longing in every heart to live, and to live joyously. A third world war is out of the question.

Gorbachev's greatness is in his insight that now America has to be defeated in a different way.

The Soviet Union becoming really democratic – a freedom-loving society – will be the defeat of America. It just has to penetrate into all people who have power in the Soviet Union that history has brought them to a point where they can win over America without any war. Just by bringing freedom to their own people they will take the mask off America – its so-called, pseudo, democracy. And Gorbachev is trying slowly to bring the people....

For this new kind of war, who is more free? Who is more independent? Who respects the individual? Who respects individuals' differences, their freedom of expression, their freedom of creativity? Now this is going to be the real war! And the Soviet Union can be victorious without fighting. Fighting is no longer possible.

For the first time a totally new kind of war has come into existence, and Gorbachev must be given the credit of seeing it. And he is not missing the opportunity – every moment he is moving towards an open society.

Give the message to my sannyasins in the Soviet Union: "Your day has come." Just as the first revolution had come unexpectedly to the Soviet Union, even more unexpectedly the second revolution is coming – it has already begun. They should rejoice and make every effort to help Gorbachev in making the Soviet Union the land of freedom, love, friendship, respect to human life. It is going to happen – you can take it from me, almost as a prediction.

Just a few days ago, I was seeing one of the most significant books to be published in this century, *Millennium*. It is a deep research into Nostradamus and his predictions. Eighty thousand copies were published – which is very rare – and they were sold within weeks. Now a second publication, a second edition, is happening in America, another is happening in England, and the book is being translated into many other languages – Dutch, German....

Nostradamus was a great mystic with an insight into the future. And you will be surprised to know that in his predictions, I am included. Describing the teacher of the last days of the twentieth century, he gives eight indications. Krishnamurti fulfills five, Maharishi Mahesh Yogi fulfills three, Da Free John fulfills four – and I was amazed that I fulfill all eight.

In this book *Millennium*, they have made a chart of the teacher about whom Nostradamus is predicting – that his people will wear red clothes, that he will come from the East, that he will be arrested, that his commune will be destroyed, that flying birds will be his symbol, that his name will mean moon.... Three hundred years ago that man was seeing something that fits perfectly with me – my name means "the moon." And in their chart they have declared me the teacher of the last part of the twentieth century.

I can see as clearly as Nostradamus:

I predict that Gorbachev is going to succeed in bringing the second and greater revolution to Russia, and his revolution in the Soviet Union is going to affect everything in the whole world.

I would like my sannyasins to meet him – they have to meet him to present my book that I have dedicated to him. Invite him to come to my people here whenever he needs a little encouragement and hope, whenever he needs a spiritual support, a nourishment. And tell him that his meetings with Ronald Reagan are not going to fulfill anything, but if he dances with my sannyasins he will gather a new spirit, a new joy to accept the great challenge that is his destiny.

And it will not be long before sannyasins from the Soviet Union will be allowed to come here, and my sannyasins from other countries will be entering into the Soviet Union.

I have gone around the world – except to the Soviet Union. It will be an immense help for Gorbachev to make the Soviet Union an open society if he invites me and my people.... Nobody else can destroy the people who are full of lust for power, and nobody else can revive the spirit of the people which has been repressed for sixty years.

If my people just go and sing and dance and move around in the Soviet Union, they will create an atmosphere in which Gorbachev can work more easily for the second great revolution. This is my message for my sannyasins, and for Gorbachev, and for Sakharov.

So when you go back, meet Sakharov and tell him from me that he should make arrangements for my sannyasins in the Soviet Union to meet with Gorbachev. He is the right person, in the right place, in the right moment.

Osho,

I am amazed. It is India, it is a hundred and five degrees in the shade, and you remain so cool, so calm, so quiet. What is it? Do you have something up your sleeve, or maybe under your hat?

A new flood is foretold, and nothing can be done to prevent it. In three days the waters will wipe out the world. The leader of Buddhism appears on television and pleads with everybody to become a Buddhist. That way they will at least find salvation in paradise.

The pope goes on television with a similar message: "It is still not too late to accept Jesus," he says.

Osho takes a different approach: "Look guys, we have three days to learn how to live under water."

Osho,

In my sixty-three years of life you are the first love relationship which has made me independent. How has this happened?

*L*ove brings freedom. And a love that does not bring freedom is not love. Love is not domination. How can you dominate someone you love? How can you make him dependent, and still be loving? But that's what goes on happening in the world in the name of love — something else — a lust to power, to dominate the other. Naturally independence cannot be allowed. Every effort is made that the other should be a carbon copy of you. You are afraid of the freedom of the other, because freedom is not controllable, and freedom is not predictable. So all so-called love tries in every way to destroy freedom — and the moment freedom is destroyed, love dies.

Love is very fragile, just like a rose flower. You have to allow it to dance in the rain, in the wind, in the sun.

Love is like a bird on the wing, having the whole sky as its freedom. You can catch hold of the bird, you can put it in a beautiful golden cage, and it seems it is the same bird that was flying in freedom and had the whole sky to itself. It only appears to be the same bird. It is not — you have killed it. You have cut its wings, you have taken away its sky. And the birds don't bother about your gold. However precious may be your cage, it is imprisonment.

And that's what we are doing with our love: we create golden cages. We are afraid because the sky is vast. The fear is that the bird may not return. To keep it under your control it has to be imprisoned. That's how love becomes marriage.

Love is a bird on the wing: marriage is a bird in a golden cage. And certainly the bird can never forgive you. You have destroyed all its beauty, all its joy, all its freedom. You have destroyed its spirit — it is just a dead replica. But you have made one thing certain, that it cannot escape you, that it will be always yours, that tomorrow also it will be yours, and the day after tomorrow....

Lovers are always afraid. The fear is because love comes like a breeze. You cannot produce it, it is not something to be manufactured — it comes. But anything that comes on its own, can go also on its own, that is a natural corollary.

Love comes, and flowers blossom in you, songs arise in your

heart, a desire to dance...but with a hidden fear. What will happen if this breeze that has come to you, cool and fragrant, leaves you tomorrow?...because you are not the limit of existence. And the breeze is only a guest – it will be with you as long as it feels to be, and it will go any moment.

This creates fear in people, and they become possessive. They start closing their doors and windows to keep the breeze in. But when your doors and windows are closed, it is not the same breeze. The coolness is lost, the fragrance is lost – soon it is disgusting. It needs freedom, and you have taken away the freedom; it is only a corpse.

In the name of love people are carrying each others' corpses, which they call marriage. And to carry corpses you have to go to a government registrar's office to make it a legal bond. Love cannot allow marriage. In an authentic world marriage will be impossible.

One should love, and love intensely and love totally, and not be worried about tomorrow. If existence has been so blissful today, trust that existence will be more beautiful and more blissful tomorrow. As your trust grows, existence becomes more and more generous towards you. More love will shower on you. More flowers of joy and ecstasy will rain over you.

In your sixty-three years' life whatever you have known in the name of love was not love. It may have been infatuation, it may have been biological attraction, it may have been a conspiracy of hormones against two individuals – but not love. You have known love for the first time...because this is the only criterion: your freedom grows deeper, your independence becomes more solid and integrated and crystallized. This is the only criterion that love has visited you, that love has been a guest in your heart.

And who cares about tomorrow? The people who care about tomorrow are the people who don't have today, who are miserable right now and try to hide it, try to ignore it in the hope, in the desire, in the dream for tomorrow. But tomorrow never comes, this is one of the difficulties. It is always today that comes. And you become accustomed to being miserable today, and hoping, desiring, dreaming for tomorrow. You have missed life. People have become so accustomed to tomorrows that they are not only thinking of tomorrows in this life, they are thinking of life after death.

People used to ask me, "What will happen after life? What will happen after death?" And I used to say to them, "Whatever is happening *before* death, the same will continue. Are you blissful today? – because tomorrow will be born out of today. Today is pregnant with your whole future."

Love intensely, joyously, totally, and you will never think of creating a bondage, a contract. You will never think of making the person dependent. You will never be so cruel – if you love – as to destroy the freedom of the other. You will help, you will make his sky bigger.

There is only one criterion of love: It gives freedom, and it gives unconditionally.

You have experienced love for the first time, but it is not too late – although you are sixty-three years old. Love transforms old age into youth. If you can go on loving to the very last breath, you will remain young. Love knows no old age. Love knows no death. If you can go on loving, your love will continue beyond death too. Love is the most precious experience in life.

People unnecessarily waste their time in empty words like *God* I was looking at the famous book, *Waiting For Godot*. In fact he wants to say *God* but has not the courage – it will offend many people – so he has created a word, *Godot*, which will remind you, you will understand. But I thought perhaps in some language *Godot* means *God*, and that language can only be the German.

One of my old sannyasins, Haridas, who is on the way – soon he will be here – I asked him, "What is the German word for God?"

He said, "For God? The German word is *Gott*!"

I said, "That is even more dangerous than Godot – Gott!"

Nobody has got it. But people are wasting their time....

Be more realistic, be more pragmatic. Don't betray the earth... and then you will see there is nothing more important than love, and love grows only in the atmosphere of freedom. That makes your complete religion.

Love, growing in freedom, is all that religion should mean. There is no other religion than love and freedom – and they are one phenomenon.

Freedom is empty without love – dry, desert-like.

Love is dead without freedom – a corpse.

Together they are all. Together they are more than you can imagine life to be. You have Gott it!…I love the word. It seems to be the best – *God* is far away, *Godot* is fictitious, but *Gott* is more earthly.

But it is possible only where love blossoms in the sky of freedom. And whenever it happens, at whatever age it happens, it brings youth to you, it brings spring to you. Millions of people are unfortunate – they live and die without knowing what love is, and without knowing the joy of giving freedom. And unless you are capable of giving freedom, you are not worthy of getting it either.

What has happened to you is a great blessing. You should pray that it happens to all.

CHAPTER 18

Existence is Taking Care

Existence is enough unto itself.
I want you to enquire into your relationship
with existence, and out of that enquiry
arises trust – not belief, not faith.
Trust has a beauty
because it is your experience.

Osho,

Please would you say something about the relationship between let-go and witnessing?

*L*et-go is the atmosphere in which witnessing flowers. They are almost two sides of the same experience – they are not different. One cannot allow let-go without witnessing, neither can one be a witness without being in a let-go.

Let-go simply means total relaxation: no tension, no thought, no desire – mind not moving, not going anywhere, just not functioning. Mind in silence allows the greatest experience of life, the arising of a new phenomenon – witnessing.

We are all living and we are all a little bit conscious too; otherwise life would be impossible. But our consciousness is very superficial, just skin-deep – or perhaps not even that deep.

Witnessing is as deep as you are, as existence is. It is the deepest point of life in existence where one simply watches what remains to watch: a tremendous silence, a great joy, a beautiful existence surrounding you, and a deep ecstasy – a song without words and a dance without movement. Witnessing is the ultimate experience of religion. Only those who arrive at it have really lived; others have been only vegetating.

Nancy and Ronald Reagan went out to eat in a high class restaurant, and after seating them at the best table, the waiter gave them the menus. He returned to take their orders, and Nancy gave hers first. "For the aperitif I will have a dry martini, and for the appetizer I will take the Hawaiian lobster salad," she said. "Then for the fish course I will have rainbow trout, and for the entrée I will take the steak."

"And what about the vegetable?" asked the waiter. And with only a few seconds hesitation, she replied, "Oh, he will have the same."

But it is true about most of the people in the world – they

are vegetables. They have not known anything that can make them claim to be more than vegetables. The whole effort of raising your consciousness is to make you transcend your vegetable existence. Let-go is to create the right soil, and witnessing, watching, being alert are the seeds. You have only to be the right soil for the right seed, and the lotuses are bound to grow in your being.

Osho,
What does the phrase "existence takes care" mean?

*W*e are part of existence, we are not separate. Even if we want to be separate, we cannot be. Our life is part of being together with existence. And the more you are together with existence, the more alive you are. That's why I insist continually to live totally, to live intensely, because the deeper your living is, the more you are in contact with existence. You are born of it; every moment you are renewed, rejuvenated, resurrected by each of your breaths, by each of your heartbeats – existence is taking care of you.

But we are not aware of our own being, we are not aware of our own breathing. Gautam Buddha gave to the world a tremendously simple, but immensely valuable, meditation – Vipassana. The word *vipassana* simply means watching your breath – the coming of the breath in, and the going of the breath out.

People used to ask Buddha," What will happen by this?" He was not a theoretician. He would say to them, "Just do it and see. Experiment and report to me what happens. Don't ask me."

Just as you start watching your breathing, you start seeing a great phenomenon – that through your breath, you are continuously connected with existence, uninterruptedly – there is no holiday. Whether you are awake or asleep, existence goes on pouring life into you, and taking out all that is dead.

Carbon dioxide is dead, and if it accumulates in you, you will be dead. Oxygen is life, and you need continuously that the carbon dioxide be replaced by fresh oxygen. Who is taking care? Certainly you are not taking care! If you were taking care, you would have been dead long ago; you would not have been here to ask the question. You would have forgotten sometimes to breathe, or sometimes the heart would forget to beat, sometimes the blood would forget to circulate inside you – anything could go wrong. There are a thousand and one things in you which could go wrong. But they are all functioning in deep harmony. Is this harmony dependent on you?

So when I say, "existence takes care," I am not talking philosophy. Philosophy is mostly nonsense. I am simply talking an actual fact. And if you become consciously aware of it, this creates a great trust in you. My saying to you, "existence takes care," is to trigger a consciousness that can bring the beauty of trusting in existence.

I don't ask you to believe in a hypothetical God, and I don't ask you to have faith in a messiah, in a savior; these are all childish desires to have some father figure who takes care of you. But they are all hypothetical.

There has not been any savior in the world.

Existence is enough unto itself.

I want you to inquire into your relationship with existence, and out of that inquiry, arises trust – not belief, not faith. Trust has a beauty because it is your experience. Trust will help you to relax because the whole existence is taking care – there is no need to be worried and to be concerned. There is no need to have any anxiety, no need of any anguish, no need of what the existentialists call *angst*.

Trust helps you to relax, it helps you to let go, and the let-go prepares the ground for witnessing to come in. They are related phenomena.

Three gray-haired mothers, Mrs. Fletcher, Mrs. Cornfield, and Mrs. Baum, were sitting in a Catskill hotel bragging about their children.

"My son is a doctor," said Mrs. Fletcher, "and he's an internist, a surgeon and a specialist. He makes so much money, he owns an apartment building on Park Avenue in New York."

"That's nice," said Mrs. Cornfield. "My son is a lawyer. He handles divorces, accidents, tax cases, insurance. He is so successful, he owns two apartment buildings on Fifth Avenue."

"Ladies," announced Mrs. Baum, "you should both be proud to have such successful sons. My boy, I have to tell you the truth, is a homosexual."

"That's a shame," said Mrs. Cornfield. "And what does he do for a living?"

"Nothing," said Mrs. Baum. "He has two friends: one is a doctor who owns an apartment building on Park Avenue, and the other is a lawyer who owns two apartment buildings."

Existence takes care.

Osho,

How can a blind and ignorant person be helped by a blind and ignorant therapist and his blind advice? Is it all just to make some firecrackers explode in the dark tunnel, to have a party and excitement together, to make the journey a bit "piff-paff-puff"? Can real help and guidance not just come from a master like you? If you like, please comment.

Your question is, *How can a blind and ignorant person be helped by a blind and ignorant therapist and his blind advice?* Do you mean to say that you cannot be helped by a doctor if you have a cancer and he has not? Are you going to look for a doctor who has a cancer? – only he can help you?

In life, you are being helped by many people who don't have

the experience but who have the expertise. The difference is great between experience and expertise – but the expert can also help.

A man was purchasing eggs, and he said to the shopkeeper, "These eggs are rotten."

The shopkeeper was very much shocked and angry, and he said, "Are you a hen? Have you ever laid an egg? What do you know about eggs? Neither are you an egg, nor are you a hen."

The man remained silent for a moment; he had never thought of this. He said, "That means to know that an egg is rotten, I have to be a hen – then life will become impossible. I will have to be so many things because life needs so many things."

So the first thing to remember is that a therapist is as blind and ignorant as you are – and perhaps that is a qualification, because he knows what blindness is, what ignorance is. He is as miserable as you are, he knows the taste of misery. The only difference between you and him is that he is also an expert of a certain art: therapy.

His knowledge about therapy may not have made him able to help himself, but his knowledge about therapy may be of some help to you. At least he has some expertise that you don't have. At least he can analyze your problem. He may not be able to give a solution, but there are problems in life which need only analysis – they don't need any other solution. Once you know why they are there, once you know their analytical basis, they disappear.

Do you think Sigmund Freud is psychologically different from you? But he has given the whole science of psychoanalysis which has helped many people, if not to become enlightened, at least to become aware that they are blind, that they are groping in darkness, that they need a master. This is not something small.

You are asking," Is it all just to make some firecrackers explode in the dark tunnel, to have a party and excitement together, to make the journey a bit 'piff-paff-puff'?"

Even if this much can be done by the therapist, it is a great service to have a beautiful party – in the Italian sense – in the dark tunnel, to explode a few firecrackers, and to make the journey a little joyous. You will not be going far, and you will not be going out of the tunnel because you cannot have the right direction – you may be going deeper into the tunnel. But the therapist at least puts you on the move. He greases your wheels.

Out of this movement, something is going to happen. He creates in you at least a longing. He may not be able to deliver the goods, but he creates a desire, a dream. And that is not a small thing, because there are millions of people who don't have dreams, who are so utterly content with their miserable lives that they don't think anything else is possible – this is all there is.

The therapist at least creates in you a new longing that there is something more; and you should be grateful to him. He may be searching himself – he *is* searching – and he has made you also infectious with the search.

You want real help and guidance, not just a longing, a desire. You want the flowers but you don't want the seeds. The therapist at least can sow the seeds, can prepare the ground. I have been using therapists to move you from your stagnant, dormant state into a pilgrimage for the unknown. Once that desire is awake, then a master can be of help. The therapists can do the spade work.

It is true that the real help and guidance can come only from a master. But do you need real help? Do you need real guidance? Do you deserve it? Even if a great master knocks on your doors, are you going to welcome him? Are you prepared for that?

To receive a master, even to acknowledge a master, needs a long preparation. The therapist can do that preparation, so that when you come across a real master…the therapist has given you the thirst; now the real master can quench it. Without the thirst, even the greatest master is of no help.

I understand that the blind cannot lead the blind, the ignorant cannot help you to move towards light, towards knowing, towards realization; but they can do something else which can be used as a device. Therapy has never been used by any master in the world as a device, but I find it to be immensely helpful: it helps those who participate in therapies to become thirsty for the real. The therapist cannot deliver the real, but he has made you thirsty for the real.

You should be grateful for that – it is not a small service that he has done for you.

And the therapy is a double-edged sword. On the one hand it helps the participant, and on the other hand it helps the therapist. The therapist is also in the same boat. He is also groping, he is also uncertain; he is also not in a state to say with a guarantee, "There is something like truth, or something like bliss, or something like ecstasy." But seeing so many people becoming thirsty, he also becomes more thirsty than he was ever before. If so many people can easily be made aware of a tremendous challenge for a pilgrimage towards the unknown...he himself also becomes a pilgrim. If he does not become a pilgrim, he has helped you but he has not been able to help himself.

He can become a false teacher – that is the danger of being a therapist. You can start thinking that you are a great teacher because you are making so many people thirsty for truth. And perhaps you may start delivering false goods to them too, because they don't know what is false and what is real; they cannot make any distinction.

There are many false therapists; they become false the moment they start becoming masters. They are not masters. They are as much a seeker as others; perhaps more articulate, more knowledgeable. If they remain therapists – knowing perfectly well that they know nothing much, only a certain expertise – they can help you, and they can help themselves, too; otherwise.... Kabir has a statement: "The blind people lead the blind, and they all fall into a well." There is nowhere else to go – they will find a well somewhere to fall in.

An Israeli visiting Paris goes to a brothel and insists on the services of a certain Michelle. He is told that Michelle is unavailable, but when he offers a thousand dollars, she is brought to him and they spend the night together.

The next night, the Israeli returns and repeats his generous offer, and again the third night. Finally, on the third night, Michelle asks why she has been singled out for this flattering attention.

"Well," says the man, "You see, I am from Israel."

"Why, so am I," says Michelle.

"Yes, I know," the Israeli replies. "It turns out that your grandmother lives in the same building as my parents, and when she heard I was going to Paris, she asked me to give you the three thousand dollars you had asked for."

A Jew is a Jew! – he cannot do anything else; a blind man is a blind man.

The therapist has to be very humble and very alert, and he has to make the people who come to him aware – "I am as far away from truth as you are, but I have a certain expertise which I can deliver to you. Perhaps that may help you to find the way. I am not the way but perhaps I can give you a candle which may help you."

It is not much, just a candle, but in a dark night of the soul even a candle is much – a treasure; it can help you to find the way.

The therapist has to become a bridge between the seeker and the master; he is not to become the master himself.

Osho,

In the video the other night, for the second time I heard you saying that no master has been betrayed by a woman. I don't understand that. What about Sheela and her gang? Didn't they betray you? So far as I'm concerned, in the moment, I can't imagine betraying you, but I can't say for sure that I would never do it. I don't know what I would do if I was in the position of Sheela. Saying all this, my heart hurts, but my mind keeps on going and doesn't understand. Please comment.

A master can be betrayed if he requires your faith. You cannot betray me, because I don't require your faith. You can be with me; you can choose to go away. Being with me is your free choice. Going away is also your freedom.

Nobody can betray me.

I don't give you the chance to betray.

I have removed the very basis, the very possibility.

Thousands of people have been with me, and walked with me as long as they could manage. And when it was impossible for them – and I am an impossible man, so it is not their fault – then they took off on a road separate from me. But I don't have any complaint, because I was never expecting them to hang around me forever and forever. In fact, I have to work on so many people that I want a few old people to take their own way, to create space for new people. My caravan is big enough.

The old masters were betrayed, but the fault was theirs because they asked for your total surrender. I don't ask anything from you. It is your choice to walk with me as long as you wish, and it is your choice to say good-bye at any time you want.

I am a bit of a strange master – a master who cannot be betrayed – because I am a master who does not ask you for any surrender, any commitment; who does not ask anything from you, but who gives you as much as he can and is grateful that you receive his love, is grateful that you receive his silence.

And it is absolutely your individual decision to remain my fellow traveler or to move in some other direction. And who knows, perhaps you may come back to the caravan again, or you may meet me somewhere ahead on some other crossroad; you will be welcome there.

I accept you when you are with me, I accept you when you leave me; I accept you if you never come back to me, I accept you if you want to come back to me. From my side, there is no question of any commitment; hence, when I said, "No master has been betrayed by a woman," you have not to include me in it. I am talking about the old masters; they all wanted absolute faith, total surrender. They wanted you to be almost in a spiritual slavery, and I think this very situation created in a few people's minds a desire to be free of them.

You cannot desire to be free of me; you are free. You cannot contemplate betraying me because that will be absurd. I have never asked your faith, so you cannot take it away. I have not taken anything from you, so you cannot disappoint me.

My statement was about the past masters.

I don't belong in their category.

I am the beginning of a new line, of a new category, where a master is a friend, where a master gives you freedom, where a master wants you to be on your own – the sooner the better. I would love that day, when all of you have betrayed me and I can sit silently, enjoying myself! I am enjoying myself right now too, but to enjoy in a crowd is one thing and to enjoy yourself in your bathroom is another.

So, if you are not sure…you don't want to betray me, but you are not sure. Who knows? – tomorrow, you may want to. So I want you to remember: even if you want to betray me, you cannot. I have made it impossible.

I am just a friend. We have met on the road; we are strangers. You liked me to walk with you, I liked you to walk with me, we enjoyed being together. But any moment you want to say, "Now it is time to depart," I will help you to depart without tears, joyously, because you are going to be independent – yourself.

You are not capable of hurting me. All those old masters were hurt, but they created the situation themselves. I don't expect anything from you, so how can you disappoint me? Whatever you do, I can bless it without knowing what it is.

"Mr. Baumgarten," said the doctor, "even though you are a very sick man, I think I will be able to pull you through."

"Doctor, if you do that, when I get well I will donate five thousand dollars for your new hospital."

Months later, the MD met his former patient. "How do you feel?" he asked.

"Wonderful, doctor, fine, never been better."

"I have been meaning to speak to you," said the doctor. "What about the money for the new hospital?"

"What are you talking about?" said Baumgarten.

"You said that if you got well, you would contribute five thousand dollars to the new hospital."

"I said that?" asked the patient. "That just shows how sick I was."

To expect anything from you is just not right; you are in such misery. Out of your misery you may surrender, out of your misery you may have faith, out of your misery you may believe – in any nonsense. I cannot exploit your misery which has been exploited all through the past.

I would like to help you to come out of your misery, and that will be my reward – if I can see you smiling and singing and dancing, it is more than enough.

CHAPTER 19

The Sunlit Peaks
of Sacredness

*If strong winds take you hither and thither,
don't resist;
they appear strong because of your resistance.
Relax, go with them.
Go with them, with totality.*

Osho,

I have just finished reading the book about Jesus and his journey to Kashmir after the crucifixion, and now I have a photographic picture in my mind of the man and his unquenchable thirst for truth. Hearing stories about you, or the Buddha before enlightenment, there was the same unquenchable thirst. But here I am with you feeling like a dry leaf, blowing in the wind – searching for truth, but being distracted by every gust of wind that takes me wherever it wishes to. Will being in your presence more and more help me to intensify my search, and enable me to use these gusts of wind to take me further on the path towards truth?

*T*here is a saying of Jesus: "Ask and it shall be given to you, seek and ye shall find, knock and the door shall be opened unto you." These are beautiful words, but only on a very superficial plane. They have poetry in them, and they have a certain truth also; but unfortunately I have to disagree with them.

If I were to write them again, I would say, "Ask not, and it shall be given to you," because asking is desiring, asking is demanding, asking is impatience. Asking is not trust, is not love. Love never asks, but it is given all. It never asks, but it is always understood.

"Seek not; otherwise you will miss it," because every search leads you away from yourself; every path leads you away from yourself. "Seek ye not; just be, and you have found it," because it is something within you. It is not something far away, it has not to be found; it is the finder himself. It has not to be sought, it is the seeker himself. The moment you are silent, neither asking nor seeking, you have it, you *are* it.

"Knock not, because every knock makes you a beggar," because all knocking is on the doors of others. And it is not a question of finding it in somebody else's house; it is there within you. There are no doors for you to knock on. You have just to be utterly centered, and the doors are always open. This is what Lao Tzu would say, and this is what Chuang Tzu would say. I know if Jesus had been born in the East, he would have said the same thing. It is the Western atmosphere, where all search is for the object and nobody cares about the seeker.

There are great scientists of tremendous intelligence who discover many things in their lives, but go on missing themselves. The reason is that they are always searching for something; but one's own being is already there – you have just to be in a relaxed state of consciousness, in a let-go.

I am reminded of one of the most important women who has walked on the earth, Rabiya al-Adabiya. She is truly a rebel, and without being a rebel nobody can be religious. Rebellion is the very foundation of being religious. The orthodox can never be religious, the traditional can never be religious.

She was going to the market, just to fetch some vegetables, and she saw a great Sufi, well known all over the country, Junnaid. He was sitting outside the mosque praying loudly and looking at the sky, crying, "When are you going to hear me? Why don't you open the doors? I have been waiting so long, do you hear me or not? I'm tired of knocking on your doors."

Rabiya stood behind him, heard all this and hit his head. He looked back – because it is very sacrilegious to disturb someone who is in prayer – and there stood that strange woman, Rabiya. And she said, "Junnaid, are you going to mature or not? Are you absolutely blind? – because the doors are open. The doors are always open, twenty-four hours, day and night. What kind of nonsense is this, that you go on asking God 'Open the doors'? Even God cannot do anything – how can he open doors which are always open? Just look silently; the doors are not outside. Close your eyes and see. And remember, the next time I hear you say all this nonsense I'm going to hit you really hard! By your prayer you are avoiding yourself."

It was a sudden enlightening experience. Junnaid closed his eyes, looked within…the doors *are* open. What you are seeking is hidden within you, and if you go on seeking it you will go on missing it.

Don't make the search for truth a serious phenomenon. Take it easy, and remember "easy is right." If strong winds take you hither and thither, don't resist; they appear strong because of your resistance. Relax, go with them. Go with them, with totality.

Lao Tzu became enlightened sitting under a tree, seeing an old dead leaf falling from the tree, slowly. Winds were taking it this way and that way, and it had no resistance. It was totally willing to go anywhere – because the truth that you are seeking is everywhere. All that is needed is a relaxed consciousness to see it.

Those winds are not against you, they are not distracting you. Your resistance is the problem. You have made your search very serious. Be a little more playful. Dance with the wind; allow the wind to take you to the north, to the south, to the east, to the west, without any resistance.

In your resistance exists your ego. "What is ego?" people ask. It is your resistance to existence. "And what is egolessness?" It is your relaxed state of being, a let-go. Wherever the winds take you, go with totality – willingly, joyously, dancing, singing.

It is not that you will find the truth where the winds are taking you. You will find the truth in your non-resistance; you will find the truth in your let-go, in your playfulness, in your non-seriousness, in your laughter.

Sick people have dominated humanity for too long – psychologically sick, spiritually sick – and they have made everybody serious. My whole approach is that of playfulness, non-seriousness, taking it easy.

Relaxation is prayer.

Non-resistance is egolessness.

And in egolessness all is found.

The serious are tense, the serious are worried. The serious are always concerned whether they are on the right path…and there are no milestones.

All paths are imaginary.

Existence is just like the sky, there are no paths. The birds fly, but they don't leave any footprints; the sky remains pathless. So is your consciousness a far more clean and far more clear space, where there are no footprints, no paths.

You cannot go astray. To go astray you need a path. And finding the truth is not the goal, finding the truth cannot be made an ambition. Finding the truth is finding yourself. And you can find yourself only in a relaxed state. Who can distract you from yourself? The wind may take you to the north, or to the south, but it cannot distract you from yourself; wherever you are you *are*.

If you start being playful in life, you have learned the greatest prayer; you have learned the pathless path.

Most major cities have a dial-a-prayer number for anyone requiring religious reassurance in the form of a brief, pre-recorded sermon. Now there is talk of establishing a similar number for atheists: when you dial it, no one answers.

And I think that will be far closer to reality than a pre-recorded sermon. If you can listen to the silence – no one is answering, you are left alone – it can become a meditation.

There is no goal. You are not to go somewhere, and there is not some object to be found. You have just to relax into such a deep state that you can settle within yourself. In that very settling you have come home.

Osho,

The other day, when out of the silence of your namaste came the unexpected gift of your dance. My heart burst open, and suddenly I was like a child, innocent and utterly in awe of the mystery of your presence. Would you please say something about how it is that the slightest gesture made by you affects us so deeply?

*L*ove is the greatest alchemy in the world. It transforms small things into great, into precious experiences. Just a bird singing, received in silence and love, is more valuable than God speaking to Moses, because that is a fiction – and not a very nice one, either.

When Moses reached the mountain on Sinai to meet God, he saw a miracle; he saw a green bush, lush green, and yet surrounded by flames. As he came closer, a voice from the bush shouted at him, "Moses, take your shoes off! You are on holy ground" – not a very nice beginning to a conversation. Moses must have been a very obedient person; otherwise he would have asked, "Can you tell me where is the land which is not holy? Should I carry my shoes on my head?"

The whole existence is holy.

But the poor fellow was so amazed by a voice without any person around, and the bush on fire, and yet green, lush green....

God gave him ten commandments, ten pieces of stone, and on each piece one commandment was written: "Thou shall not commit adultery"...not a great meeting – in a way insulting and humiliating. And poor Moses carried all those ten stones; they must have been heavy.

But, in the whole thing, the only significant part is the green bush in the flames of fire. As far as I am concerned, I take only that part to be important in the whole encounter. Jews have not bothered much about the bush and the fire; they are much more concerned with the ten commandments and God's declaration of the Holy Land.

If you enter into yourself you will find this very experience: flames of life and the green bush with flowers of ecstasy, of blissfulness, existing together. Those flames represent the revolution, and that green bush represents the coolness and the calmness....

You may have come across calm and cool people, but they are not revolutionaries; they are dull, unintelligent, almost idiots. You may have come across revolutionaries who are fiery, but they don't have the calmness and the quietness and the peace which can make their revolution meaningful. Otherwise, the same fire that cooks your food can burn your house too.

To me, the meeting of Moses with God is simply a myth. Real religion, authentic religion, is concerned with your love, with your trust, with your joy. And when you see through the eyes of love, a small flower becomes so mysterious, the faraway song of a cuckoo becomes far more holy than any scripture.

You love me; that's why my smallest gesture makes an immense impact on you. It is not the gesture, it is your love. There may be somebody else sitting by your side to whom the gesture means nothing, just a movement of the hand. If his heart is not full of love, then just the movement of the hand is meaningless; if his heart is full of love, the hand, its grace, can be indicative of greater mysteries and secrets of life.

This is one of the mysteries of life, that life is how you see it. It depends on your eyes. If you have the eyes of a poet the same trees are greener, livelier; they have a message, they whisper things into the ears of the poet. But if you are not a poet you pass by the same trees without even noticing them. All depends on you.

Your whole life experience goes on growing with your growing consciousness. As your consciousness becomes more and more juicy, life becomes more and more divine. Because you love me, my words have a meaning to you which they will not have without your loving heart. Your love contributes ninety percent, at least, to the meaning of my words or my gestures.

The day you are capable of contributing one hundred percent, then my gesture becomes your gesture, then my word becomes your word, then my heartbeat becomes your heartbeat. That state I call the state of the devotee: a merger, a melting of two souls into one.

But, unfortunately, in the name of love such pseudo things exist in the world that they have contaminated the greatest word we have. People "love" their cars, people "love" their houses. They don't understand that love is a sacred experience, it is not mundane. The moment you pull it down to the world of mundane reality you are being terribly destructive. You have to raise the mundane reality to the level of love, the sunlit peaks of sacredness.

But people are doing just the opposite – and suffering unnecessarily. Life is not meant to be a suffering; it is meant to be a blissfulness. But one has to learn the art.

Brickman and Horowitz were relaxing on the beach in Puerto Rico. "You know," said Brickman, "this Racquel Welch – what does everyone see in her? Take away her hair, her lips, her eyes and her figure, and what have you got?"

Horowitz said, "My wife."

These are our love relationships. Rather than adding to things, beautifying existence, we are living in such negativity that we take away. Take away the lips of a beautiful woman, take away her hair, take away her eyes, and what is left? And of course, if this is your approach to looking at things, your life is going to be a hell – worse than hell.

Love contributes tremendously, beautifies things. Where it was prose, love makes it a poetry; where it was just an ordinary flower, love makes it extraordinary. Love has the magic of transforming the whole world around you into a sacred existence.

I call the man materialistic who does not know the art of love; I don't call a man materialistic who does not believe in God. And I don't call a man religious who believes in God. I call a man religious who goes on growing in his love, in his trust, and goes on spreading his ecstasy all around existence.

People are so stupid that they are trying to demystify everything. The whole effort of science is to demystify existence, to know everything. So, of course, the way to know Racquel Welch is to dissect her on the table of the scientist. Take her hair apart, her eyes apart…and then see what is left. There is no beauty, there is no soul, there is no life; science has demystified a beautiful woman.

Religion mystifies existence. It makes the meaningless songs of birds as meaningful as great poetry, as great music. It makes ordinary trees as significant as great paintings.

It is up to you where you want to live, in hell or in heaven, because wherever you want to live you will have to create it. It is not something ready-made, so that you purchase a ticket and catch a train. It is something to be created.

Love can create paradise herenow.

My whole teaching is love more, to the point when you yourself become just a source of love, and nothing else.

"Hey man," one hippie said to another, "turn on the radio."

"Okay," the second hippie answered. And then leaning over very close to the radio he whispered, "I love you." He is turning on the radio."

We have destroyed beautiful words so ignorantly, and by destroying them we have destroyed ourselves – because what are we except our attitudes?

You could see in my movements a beauty, a grace, a significance because your heart is full of love. I want to remind you that the beauty is not in the gestures, the beauty is in the eyes that see it. I want you to be responsible for the hell or heaven in which you live. And once you understand the responsibility, I don't think anybody is going to live in hell.

Osho,

How can I tell the difference between one part of the mind observing another part of the mind, and the watcher? Can the watcher watch itself? One time I thought I had got it and then that same day I heard you say in a discourse, "If you think you've got the watcher, you've missed." Since then I try watching feelings in the body, thoughts, and emotions. Mostly, I'm just caught in them. But, once in a while, rarely, I feel tremendously relaxed and nothing stays – it just keeps moving. Is there anything to do?

*D*eva Waduda, one has to start watching the body – walking, sitting, going to bed, eating. One should start from the most solid, because it is easier, and then one should move to subtler experiences. One should start watching thoughts, and when one becomes an expert in watching thoughts, then one should start watching feelings. After you feel that you can watch your feelings, then you should start watching your moods, which are even more subtle than your feelings, and more vague.

The miracle of watching is that as you are watching the body, your watcher is becoming stronger; as you are watching the thoughts, your watcher is becoming stronger; as you are watching the feelings, the watcher is becoming even more strong. When you are watching your moods the watcher is so strong that it can remain itself – watching itself – just as a candle in the dark night not only lights everything around it, it also lights itself.

To find the watcher in its purity is the greatest achievement in spirituality, because the watcher in you is your very soul; the watcher in you is your immortality. But never for a single moment think, "I have got it," because that is the moment when you miss.

Watching is an eternal process; you always go on becoming deeper and deeper, but you never come to the end where you can say, "I have got it." In fact, the deeper you go, the more you become aware that you have entered into a process which is eternal – without any beginning and without any end.

But people are watching only others; they never bother to watch themselves. Everybody is watching – that is the most superficial watching – what the other person is doing, what the other person is wearing, how he looks…. Everybody is watching; watching is not something new to be introduced in your life. It has only to be deepened, taken away from others, and arrowed towards your own inner feelings, thoughts, moods – and finally, the watcher itself.

A Jew is sitting in a train opposite a priest. "Tell me, your worship," the Jew asks, "why do you wear your collar back to front?"

"Because I am a father," answers the priest.

"I am also a father, and I don't wear my collar like that," says the Jew. "Oh," says the priest, "but I am a father to thousands."

"Then maybe," replies the Jew, "it is your trousers you should wear back to front."

People are very watchful about everybody else.

Two Polacks went out for a walk; suddenly it began to rain. "Quick," said one man, "open your umbrella."

"It won't help," said his friend, "my umbrella is full of holes."

"Then why did you bring it in the first place?"

"I did not think it would rain."

You can laugh very easily about the ridiculous acts of other people, but have you ever laughed about yourself? Have you ever caught yourself doing something ridiculous? No, you keep yourself completely unwatched; your whole watching is about others, and that is not of any help.

Use this energy of watchfulness for a transformation of your being. It can bring you so much bliss and so much benediction that you cannot even dream about it. A simple process, but once you start using it on yourself it becomes a meditation.

One can make meditations out of anything.

Anything that leads you to yourself is meditation. And it is immensely significant to find your own meditation, because in the very finding you will find great joy. And because it is your own finding – not some ritual imposed upon you – you will love to go deeper into it. The deeper you go into it, the happier you will feel – peaceful, more silent, more together, more dignified, more graceful.

You all know watching, so there is no question of learning it. It is just a question of changing the object of watching. Bring them closer.

Watch your body, and you will be surprised. I can move my hand without watching, and I can move my hand with watching. You will not see the difference, but I can feel the difference. When I move it with watchfulness, there is a grace and beauty in it, a peacefulness, and a silence. You can walk, watching each step; it will give you all the benefit that walking can give you as an exercise, plus it will give you the benefit of a great simple meditation.

The temple in Bodhgaya where Gautam Buddha became enlightened has been made in memory of two things...one is a Bodhi tree under which he used to sit. Just by the side of the tree there are small stones for a slow walk. He was meditating, sitting, and when he would feel that sitting had been too much – a little exercise was needed for the body – he would walk on those stones. That was his walking meditation.

When I was in Bodhgaya, having a meditation camp there, I went to the temple. I saw Buddhist lamas from Tibet, from Japan, from China. They were all paying their respect to the tree, and I saw not a single one paying his respect to those stones on which Buddha had walked miles and miles. I told them, "This is not right. You should not forget those stones. They have been touched by Gautam Buddha's feet millions of times. But I know why you are not paying any attention to them, because you have forgotten completely that Buddha was emphasizing that you should watch every act of your body: walking, sitting, lying down."

You should not let a single moment go by unconsciously. Watchfulness will sharpen your consciousness. This is the essential religion – all else is simply talk. But Waduda, you ask me, "Is there something more?" No, if you can do only watchfulness, nothing else is needed.

My effort here is to make religion as simple as possible. All the religions have done just the opposite: they have made things very complex – so complex that people have never tried them. For example, in the Buddhist scriptures there are thirty-three thousand principles to be followed by a Buddhist monk; even to remember them is impossible. Just the very number thirty-three thousand is enough to freak you out: "I am finished! My whole life will be disturbed and destroyed."

I teach you: just find a single principle that suits you, that feels in tune with you, and that is enough.

CHAPTER 20

The Second Russian Revolution

Love is a contagious disease which has no cure.
The world is loveless so much
because very few people are there
to spread the disease.

Osho,

A few months before his death Edgar Cayce, in one of his trance "sleep talks" said, "Through Russia comes the hope of the world. Not in respect to what is sometimes termed communism or bolshevism, no; but freedom, freedom! That each man will live for his fellow man. The principle has been born there. It will take years for it to be crystallized. Yet out of Russia comes again the hope of the world." Could you please comment?

Edgar Cayce was one of the strangest human beings, a category in himself.... There have been utterly conscious people having clear visions of the world – like Nostradamus; but Cayce was not anything special when he was conscious. Only when he was in a sort of unconsciousness, a trance-like sleep, would he start saying things of tremendous importance, many of which have come true.

Many of these are bound to happen, sooner or later, for the simple reason that whatever he has seen in his trance state is absolutely transparent, clear, without ifs and buts – it is absolute. And because it was not coming in his conscious state, his ego was not involved. It was coming out of his innocence; and anything that comes out of innocence has a validity, has an authority of its own.

There are thousands and thousands of pages of notes collected by his disciples from when he was speaking in his trances; almost a whole library exists containing his predictions. When he used to come to consciousness, out of the trance, he himself was not aware what he had said – as if it was not said by him but by an unknown source, by an unknown energy, as if existence itself had spoken itself through him. He had been only a vehicle, and a very correct vehicle, because his ego was not in the way, his mind was not in the way. He was simply transmitting whatever was coming from the very roots of life. There have not been many people like him. There have been a few people, but none has the height and the depth, and immensity of Edgar Cayce.

In one of his trance-sleeps he said, "Through Russia comes the hope of the world." Once it had already come: the Russian Revolution in 1917 was the end of an old world and the beginning of a new. It proclaimed many truths about man – that property should not be individual, that property is of the commune. The founders of the revolution, particularly Lenin, wanted marriage to be dissolved; because marriage came into existence with private property, it should go out of existence when private property is being dissolved.

It is a historical fact that because of private property, man became interested in marriage, in monogamy; otherwise, by nature, he is polygamous. But to protect his property, so that even after his death it should remain in the hands of his own sons, man decided in favor of monogamy – which was not natural to him. Hence, on the one hand marriage came into existence, and on the other hand, prostitution. They both are by-products of private property.

Property should belong to all – just as the air belongs to all, and the water belongs to all, and the sun belongs to all. Private property creates immense problems. On one hand, people go on becoming richer; on the other hand, people go on becoming poorer. And the poor man is the producer: he toils in the field, he works in the orchards – and he remains hungry. He weaves the clothes – and he remains naked. He makes the beautiful mansions and palaces – and he has no house, not even a hut to hide his head in.

This exploitation was condemned by the Russian Revolution, and against this exploitation a new age of a classless society was declared, where everybody would have the equal opportunity to grow. A great hope had arisen with the Russian Revolution, but it died. The revolution fell into wrong hands. Instead of bringing a new age and a new humanity, it repeated the old game under new names. The only change was of labels: where in the past there were the rich and the poor, now there were the bureaucrats and the people. But the distinction was the same, and the exploitation was the same.

For sixty years Russia has lived in a new kind of slavery. Nobody else in the world has known that kind of slavery. The whole country has become a concentration camp. Beautiful words sometimes prove very dangerous: instead of bringing equality to man it has taken away all freedom, even the freedom of expression. It has made the whole society a society of slaves.

For a moment in 1917 a great hope arose around the world, particularly in those who were intelligent enough to see the immense possibility that was opening up – but the bud never became a flower. But you cannot keep millions of people in a concentration camp forever. There is a limit to tolerance – and that limit has come. There is great restlessness for a new revolution in the Russian youth. And Gorbachev simply represents the tremendous longing for freedom, for equality, for the dignity of being human beings, for self-respect. He has given another chance to the intelligent people of the world, for a new hope again.

Where Lenin left off, Gorbachev has to begin.

The sixty years in between have been a long nightmare – but that which is gone is gone, that which is past, is past. And the Soviet youth, with the courage and insight of Gorbachev, is looking, not backwards to the sixty ugly years of inhumane dictatorship, but to a new future of an open society, in the authentic sense.

Perhaps Edgar Cayce is going to be true again in his prediction: *Through Russia comes the hope of the world. Not in respect to what is sometimes termed communism or bolshevism, no; but freedom, freedom! That each man will live for his fellow man. The principle has been born there, it will take years for it to be crystallized.* Those years have passed. The principle is now crystallized.

Yet out of Russia comes again the hope of the world – the second great revolution. Russia seems to be a land of destiny – not only for its own people, but for the whole world. It was the first to revolt against capitalism; it is going to be again the first to revolt against dictatorial communism. The future is of a democratic communism, a communism rooted in the freedom of man.

Equality is valuable, but it is not more valuable than freedom. Freedom cannot be sacrificed for it. Freedom cannot be sacrificed for anything else. It is the most precious treasure of your being. There are all signs that the Soviet Union is going to fulfill the great hope, the great dream. Millions of people have been hoping for it, dreaming for it – it has been the utopia for centuries. Gorbachev is in a position to make it a reality. A tremendously great responsibility has fallen on his shoulders. And as I can see, he seems to be strong enough, intelligent enough to fulfill the expectations.

Only one thing I would like my Russian sannyasins to convey to Gorbachev from me: if the dimension of meditation also opens for him, he cannot allow the opportunity to be distorted.

Joseph Stalin destroyed the whole revolution for a single reason, and the reason was materialism. He believed that man is nothing but matter. According to Karl Marx, consciousness is only a by-product of matter, and as you die matter disperses; nothing is left as consciousness – there is no soul. Because of this wrong idea he could manage to kill at least one million Russians in the name of revolution without any trouble; otherwise even to kill one man would destroy your whole life's sleep. It would haunt you – you would never be able to forgive yourself. But to kill one million people without any concern was possible under the umbrella of materialism.

I would like Gorbachev not only to introduce freedom to the Soviet Union and its people, but also some spiritual dimension so that it is clear that they are not just matter. Matter cannot have any dignity – matter can be used, but cannot be respected. Matter can be destroyed, but you need not feel that you have committed a crime, or a sin.

Unless the Soviet Union and its people not only desire freedom, but also desire a search for the soul…because what will you do with freedom? Freedom for what? There are two kinds of freedom: freedom from and freedom for. Freedom from is not much of a freedom. The real freedom is the second freedom – freedom for spiritual growth, freedom for inner search, freedom for knowing the secrets and the mysteries of life.

If Gorbachev can introduce the Soviet Union to Gautam Buddha, to Mahavira, to Zarathustra, to Lao Tzu…why be so confined to Karl Marx? Why be so poor? Why not make the whole sky yours? – all the stars and the whole beauty of the night, yours. Why remain confined? If he can open the doors for the spiritual search, then, certainly, he can fulfill the prophecy of Edgar Cayce that Russia is the hope for all of mankind.

And I think him a man intelligent enough to understand that materialism is as confining as Christianity, as confining as Hinduism. I am making my people available to all dimensions because the whole past is your heritage. Why remain so poor, clinging to one small tradition? Why not allow the whole sky to be yours? Why not open your wings?

Communism missed the first revolution because it was not revolutionary enough. It was a reaction against Christianity; and whenever you react to something, you start behaving in the same way. In America they are becoming more and more a closed society because of fundamentalist Christianity. You will be surprised to know that in America thousands of books have been removed from the libraries – in this twentieth century, just now in this year – because they do not conform with the fundamentalist Christian attitudes, with the fanatic and fascist Christian mind.

Even in American education Charles Darwin's theory of evolution cannot be taught; it has been prohibited, because it goes against Christianity. Christianity believes in creation. Perhaps you have never thought that the idea of creation and the idea of evolution are diametrically opposite. God created the world; now there is no question of any evolution. You cannot improve upon God.

Charles Darwin and his theory of evolution is against Christianity. In no other country is it banned. But some American states have banned it; now it is a crime to teach it. And all books – and there are thousands of books written on the theory of evolution – have been removed from the libraries of colleges, universities and national libraries.

A strange polarity. The Soviet Union has been up to now a closed society, and America at least pretended to be an open society. Now the Soviet Union is making every effort to become an open society, and America is becoming more and more closed.

I would like to add a few words to Edgar Cayce's prediction: If the Soviet Union is the hope for mankind, then the United States of America is the greatest danger for mankind. It is preparing for human death. And if the Soviet Union becomes not only politically open but also philosophically open – not confined to the out-of-date ideas of Karl Marx, but open to all kinds of theories, philosophies, religions; experiences of Zen, and Sufism, and Hassidism, of Tao and Yoga – it can certainly prove the savior of humanity.

Osho,

I have often heard you speak of aloneness and loneliness as being opposed; of aloneness being a state in which one is so full – fulfilled; of loneliness being a state in which one is missing the other, feeling very empty. Reading Ryokan's poetry, I feel some loneliness, yet the man is known as an enlightened Zen monk.

"Standing alone beneath the solitary pine,
quickly the time passes.
Overhead the endless sky.
Who can I call to join me on the path?"

In the hankering for a true companion, in the need to share that richness, I wonder if in the heart of aloneness, there is a kind of loneliness. Please explain if aloneness and loneliness are interrelated.

*L*oneliness is loneliness, and aloneness is aloneness – and the two never meet anywhere. They cannot by their very nature. Aloneness is so full, so abundantly full of yourself there is no space for anybody else. And loneliness is so empty, so dark, so miserable that it is nothing but a constant hunger for someone to fill it...if not to fill it, at least to help you to forget it.

You are quoting from Ryokan's poetry. I don't think Ryokan is yet enlightened. He was certainly a Zen monk, and a great poet, but he fell short of being a mystic. He reached very close, but even to reach very close is not to be enlightened.

I have also loved Ryokan's poetry. But beware of poets, because they appear so close to the mystics. Sometimes their words are more juicy than the words of the mystics, because the poet is the artist of words; the mystic is an expert of silence.

Ryokan was a Zen monk; hence something of the mystic echoes in his poetry. But that is because he lived in an atmosphere in communion with the mystics. But he himself was not a mystic.

These are his lines, and you can see immediately what I mean:

Standing alone beneath a solitary pine,
Quickly the time passes.
Overhead the endless sky.
Who can I call to join me on the path?

He is still in need of a companion, and he is still searching. He is still talking of "the path," and the enlightened man knows there is no path. All paths are wrong, without exception, because every path leads you away from yourself. And to come to yourself you don't need any path: you have to be just awake and you are there.

It is almost like you are asleep in your room and dreaming that you are far away in London, in New York, in San Francisco. Do you think that if suddenly you are awakened you will find yourself in San Francisco? You were there, but that was only a dream. Awake, suddenly you find you are in your miserable room, and you have not even gone out of the door. You may be angry with the person who has awakened you, but he has brought you back to the reality. And there was no need of booking a ticket, because you had never gone out; you were only dreaming.

You are only dreaming what you are. If you wake up, suddenly you will find all that you used to think your personality, your body, your mind, your knowledge, your feelings, your love – they were all dreams. You are only a witness. But you cannot dream about the witness; that is an impossibility.

The witness remains a witness, never becomes a dream. Your aloneness is your witness, is your being. And it is so full, there is no need of any companion. And what is the need of a path? Where are you going? You have arrived.

Ryokan was a beautiful poet, and perhaps a very disciplined monk, but he was not a mystic and certainly not an enlightened man.

Let this be an opportunity to remind you again: beware of poets. They are like false coins, although they look exactly like authentic coins. But the false is false, and there is no way to make it real. Ryokan has still to wake up and see there is no solitary pine tree standing alone, there is no need of a companion, and there is no path.

One is, and has always been, at home.

To realize this at-homeness is aloneness.

Going around in your dreams you will always find yourself lonely. Loneliness is a misunderstanding. Aloneness is an awakening.

Osho,

The other night I heard you speak of betrayal, and how it is impossible to disappoint you. My eyes filled with tears. Your eyes were so luminous, shining with enough love to fill this universe. I realized that I have been trying not to disappoint the people I love all my life, and my tears were of gratitude for your love, a love that cannot be touched or tarnished whatever happens. Your look had a burning intensity, yet a wholly impersonal quality too. What kind of love is this?

Two little children were playing with their dog by the sea when the dog was carried out to sea by a big wave. A passing rabbi dived in, saved the dog and revived it by artificial respiration.

The children asked, "Hey, rabbi, are you a vet?"

"Am I wet?" replied the rabbi. "I am absolutely soaked!"

I am talking about a love in which you are not only wet, but absolutely soaked.

And there is no need to make any effort for it. Just being here, slowly, slowly, you will find your hardness melting. It cannot resist the temptation, because love is such a joy, such a bliss, that once you have seen a man of love you can never be the same again.

Seeing the man of love, you have seen your own future. And things will start happening. The hardness which prevents you from being loving, melts; the heart which you have completely forgotten is suddenly remembered. The mind which has become your permanent residence is no more your residence, but only a workshop – useful as far as work is concerned and utterly harmful as far as love is concerned. Your heart becomes your home, and your life starts radiating without any effort on your part.

Love is a contagious disease which has no cure. The world is loveless so much because very few people are there to spread the disease.

I have heard that the doctor of Mulla Nasruddin knocked on his door. He was very angry, and he said, "I have waited for one month, and you have not paid me and I cured your child of smallpox!"

Nasruddin said, "Listen. I have been patient enough; otherwise, the reality is that you owe much money to me."

The doctor said, "What? I owe money to you?"

Nasruddin said, "Yes. Who do you think spread the disease to the whole school? My child! And from all that you have earned during this whole month, I have a percentage. I was being a gentleman and not asking for it, but you are being such a nasty fellow, so miserly, and you have some nerve, too."

Love has disappeared from the world for the simple reason that there are not enough lovesick people to spread it, not enough love-soaked people to spread it. It is something which is not taught, which is caught.

Just don't be worried about it. Being here you are going to be soaked. My whole presence, my silence, my words are nothing but to push you into the ocean so that you can be soaked.

Osho,

I love to watch you retreat so gracefully backwards out of the hall until you are safely inside. I wonder how you avoid the door and the wall. But tell me, beloved one, are you afraid to turn your back on us?

I will have to tell you a story. Mulla Nasruddin was invited to a conference where many wise people were gathered. He had his own disciples. He collected all the disciples and rode on his donkey.

But the disciples said, "What are you doing?" – because he was riding on the donkey in the wrong way, not facing where the donkey was going. He was facing the disciples who were following him.

They said, "Mulla, we know that to go with you anywhere is to get into trouble. Now the whole city will laugh and we will feel embarrassed because we are your disciples."

He said, "Don't be worried about the city. I will see to those idiots."

"But," they said, "at least to us you should explain the great principle."

He said, "The great principle is simple. If I ride on the donkey in the usual way, my back will be towards you. That is insulting you. I cannot do that. I respect you as much as you respect me. If I tell you to walk ahead of me, then your back will be towards me. That will be even worse – the disciples insulting the master.

"I could not sleep the whole night until I discovered this great principle: I can ride on my donkey *facing* you; neither I am being disrespectful to you nor are you being disrespectful to me. And as far as the donkey is concerned, he is accustomed to me; he knows that I am a little crazy. He will giggle a little. As far as the city people are concerned, let them laugh. You need not feel embarrassed – you are disciples of a great master."

They said, "The principle seems to be great, but still we are feeling very much afraid."

And it happened just the way the disciples were thinking. People came out of the shops, crowds gathered. People started asking, "What is the matter?"

The disciples said, "It is a very complicated thing. Its name is the Great Principle. If you want to understand you will have to come to the school where our great master teaches us."

They said, "It is a strange principle: sitting the wrong way on a poor donkey. But, if he says it is a great principle, it must be" – because they have known him, and every time he has proven himself right. He has his own way. They said, "We are going to come tomorrow to the school to understand the Great Principle."

And when the Great Principle was explained to them, they all looked at each other. Of course, it was right, because Mulla Nasruddin said to them: Unless a master respects his disciples, he should not expect any respect from them.

It is the Great Principle.

FULL CIRCLE

FULL CIRCLE publishes books on inspirational subjects, religion, philosophy, and natural health. The objective is to help make an attitudinal shift towards a more peaceful, loving, non-combative, non-threatening, compassionate and healing world.

FULL CIRCLE continues its commitment towards creating a peaceful and harmonious world and towards rekindling the joyous, divine nature of the human spirit.

Our fine books are available at all leading bookstores across the country.

FULL CIRCLE *PUBLISHING*

Editorial Office

J-40, Jorbagh Lane, New Delhi-110003
Tel: 24620063, 24621011 • Fax: 24645795
E-mail: fullcircle@vsnl.com • website: www.atfullcircle.com

Bookstores

5B, Khan Market, New Delhi-110003
Tel: 24655641/2/3

N-8, Greater Kailash Part I Market, New Delhi-110048
Tel: 29245641/3/4

Number 8, Nizamuddin East Market, New Delhi-110013
Tel: 41826124, 41826125

Join the

WORLD
WISDOM BOOK CLUB

GET THE BEST OF WORLD LITERATURE
IN THE COMFORT OF YOUR HOME AT
FABULOUS DISCOUNTS!

Benefits of the Book Club

Wherever in the world you are, you can receive the best of books at your doorstep.

- Receive FABULOUS DISCOUNTS by mail or at the **FULL CIRCLE** Bookstores in Delhi.
- Receive Exclusive Invitations to attend events being organized by **FULL CIRCLE**.
- Receive a FREE copy of the club newsletter — The World Wisdom Review — every month.
- Get UP TO 25% OFF.

Join Now!

It's simple. Just fill in the coupon overleaf and mail it to us at the address below:

FULL CIRCLE
J-40, Jorbagh Lane, New Delhi-110003
Tel: 24620063, 24621011 • Fax: 24645795

Yes, I would like to be a member of the

World Wisdom Book Club

Name ☐ Mr ☐ Mrs ☐ Ms...

Mailing Address...

....

....

City................................. Pin.....................................

Phone............................... Fax....................................

E-mail..

Profession............................ D.O.B...............................

Areas of Interest..

....

Mail this form to:
The World Wisdom Book Club
J-40, Jorbagh Lane, New Delhi-110003
Tel: 24620063, 24621011 • Fax: 24645795

MEDITATION: THE ONLY WAY